NEW FRONTIERS IN THEOLOGY

Discussions among Continental and American Theologians

VOLUME II
THE NEW HERMENEUTIC

NEW FRONTIERS IN THEOLOGY

Discussions among Continental and American Theologians

Volume II

The New Hermeneutic

Edited by

James M. Robinson · John B. Cobb, Jr.

Southern California School of Theology at Claremont

HARPER & ROW, PUBLISHERS

New York, Evanston, and London

Grateful acknowledgment is made to Fortress Press for permission to reprint "Word of God and Hermeneutic" from *Word and Faith* by Gerhard Ebeling, translated by James W. Leitch.

FIRST EDITION

C-O

LIBRARY OF CONGRESS CATALOG CARD NUMBER: 64–14380

CONTENTS

NEW FRONTIERS IN THEOLOGY

I. THE LATER HEIDEGGER AND THEOLOGY

Contributors:

Heinrich Ott
Arnold B. Come
Carl Michalson
Schubert M. Ogden

II. THE NEW HERMENEUTIC

Contributors:

Gerhard Ebeling
Ernst Fuchs
John Dillenberger
Robert W. Funk
Amos N. Wilder

III. THEOLOGY AS HISTORY (*in preparation*)

Contributors:

Wolfhart Pannenberg
William Hamilton
Kendrick Grobel
Martin J. Buss

Foreword to the Series

Continental, and especially German, theology has played a leading role in the creative theological thinking of modern times. American theology has shown a characteristic openness to hearing, adapting, and assimilating the significant movements of European theology.

As long as this relationship was characterized by a considerable time lag in the translation and introduction in America of theological trends from the Continent, the American role was of necessity often that of receiving the results of a largely terminated discussion, so that the ensuing American discussion could hardly affect the ongoing discussion abroad. In recent years the greatly increased number of personal contacts among Continental and American theologians, and the steady flow of translations, indicate the possibility of a more direct interaction.

This series of "discussions among Continental and American theologians" is intended to provide a means for such a theological interaction. Rather than translating the finished systems of mature scholars, it proposes to identify future trends at the germinal stage of programmatic essays, and by means of critical discussion to share constructively in their development. Accordingly, each volume will present in translation such a programmatic essay—in the present volume, two such essays—introduced by Professor Robinson with an analysis of the situation in which it emerged and in terms of which it has its significance. This will be followed by constructive and critical contributions to the issue by American theologians of promise. Finally, reappraisals of the issue in the light of these American contributions will be presented both by Professor Cobb and by the author of the essay under analysis.

Editors' Preface

The decisions with regard to translational policy discussed in the Preface to Volume I of this Series apply to Volume II as well. That is to say, the equation of *existenziell* and *existenzial* with "existential" and "existentialist" respectively, of *das Sein* and *das Seiende* with "being" and "beings" respectively, and of *geschichtlich* and *historisch* with "historic" and "historical" respectively, has been carried through to the extent that these terms occur. For the present volume one further decision as to translational policy is of sufficient prominence that its background should be sketched.

The German term *Hermeneutik*, like the terms *Logik, Ethik, Ästhetik,* and *Dogmatik,* is singular in number. Indeed Heidegger has come to the defense of this use of the singular in the case of logic, ethics, and aesthetics by construing them as Greek adjectives modifying the unexpressed noun *epistēmē,* knowledge (*Nietzsche,* I, 1961, 92). Ebeling has applied this argument to the term dogmatics, which derives from the singular adjective in Protestant orthodoxy's term *theologia dogmatica* (*Theologie und Verkündigung,* 1962, pp. 105–109). Plato refers (Politicus 260D) to (*hē*) *hermēneutikē* (*technē*), so that in the instance under consideration the singular would seem to have philological priority. With regard to general English usage, the singular -ic (formerly written -ik, -ike, or -ick) was employed in the Middle Ages in dependence upon the French -ique, as in arithmetic, logic, magic, music, and rhetoric. But in the fifteenth century the plural used for the name of a treatise (Greek *-ika,* Latin *-ica,* French *-iques*) led to the English ending -ics, and in the second half of the sixteenth century this plural form was applied to the subject matter of treatises as well, such as economics and mathematics. The fact that in Latin the feminine singular and the neuter plural endings are both *-ica* made such a transition

easier. The plural form has been customary since the seventeenth
century in the names of sciences, such as acoustics, conics, dynamics, ethics, linguistics, metaphysics, optics, physics, and statics,
which are however construed as singular. More recently, under
German and French influence, the singular form has gained
ground in English usage, as in the case of the terms dialectic,
dogmatic, ethic, metaphysic, static. Sometimes when both forms
are available the singular form refers more to the philosophy of
the matter, the plural form more to its science, as in the case of
aesthetic and aesthetics. In their first drafts the contributors to
this volume betrayed the emergence of the singular form "hermeneutic" alongside of the plural "hermeneutics" to an extent
not yet fully acknowledged by the dictionaries, although the Oxford English Dictionary listed both forms at the opening of this
century. It was in the light of these considerations that it seemed
most appropriate to translate the term *Hermeneutik,* which has
gained a new prominence and connotation in German, into the
English language discussion as the new "hermeneutic." "Hermeneutics" is used only in the introductory essay, in instances
when its association with traditional hermeneutics serves to distinguish this from the new hermeneutic. With regard to the adjective, both -ic and -ical are in current usage without distinction
of meaning. Since there is a general tendency to prefer -ical for
an adjective based upon a noun ending in the singular form -ic,
the translation "hermeneutical" has been adopted.

The translation of Gerhard Ebeling's essay was made by James
W. Leitch as a part of his translation of *Wort und Glaube* (published in English as *Word and Faith*), a comprehensive collection of Ebeling's essays. It is used here with the permission of
the SCM Press and the Fortress Press. A translation of that essay
prepared by Robert W. Funk for the Drew Consultation on Hermeneutic, out of which the present volume grew, was consulted
in the final revision of the translation prior to publication in
Word and Faith. The translation of the Latin quotations and the
references to English translations in the notes were provided by
Professors Karlfried Fröhlich and Robert W. Funk of Drew Uni-

versity. Translation of the Latin was checked and completed by
Professor Jane Dempsey of Claremont. Only minor editorial ad-
justments in terms of American usage and the editorial policies
of the present Series have been made by the editors.

Professor Fuchs's essay was written especially for this volume,
although it has also been published in German (*ZThK,* LVIII,
1961, 198–226). The translation is by James M. Robinson. It
includes a few minor alterations from the German original proposed by the author.

Scripture quotations throughout are from the Revised Standard Version unless marked otherwise.

Dean Stanley R. Hopper convened a Consultation on Hermeneutic under the auspices of the Graduate School of Drew University, which happily made it possible for all contributors, including Professors Fuchs and Ebeling, to engage in extended
conversation. The Consultation was efficiently chaired by Professor Carl Michalson and was enriched by the participation of
members of the theological faculty of Drew University and other
guest faculty, especially members of the New Testament Col-
loquium.

The essays of Professors Fuchs and Ebeling were presented and
discussed at the Convocation in substantially the form in which
they appear in this volume. The American contributors—Robinson, Dillenberger, Funk, and Wilder—also presented papers.
These have been extensively revised as a result of the discussion
at Drew and of subsequent research and reflection. The editors
wish to express their appreciation to Dean Hopper and the Graduate School of Drew University for making possible a memorable
occasion.

Without the support of President Ernest C. Colwell of the
Southern California School of Theology no volume in this Series
would be possible. To him we would express our continued and
renewed gratitude. One of the important forms which his assist-
ance has taken has been the provision by the school of student
assistants. Duane Priebe has carried a heavy burden of responsibility for editing the materials in this volume for consistency and

clarity and has given constructive criticisms at important points. Ernst Eberhard Fincke, James Goss, and Jack Sanders have also made valuable contributions. The school has also made available the indispensable help of a capable typist. To Mrs. Robert Hagelbarger also we would express sincere thanks.

PART I. The Issue

1. Hermeneutic Since Barth

JAMES M. ROBINSON

Southern California School of Theology

I. HERMENEIA

The English term hermeneutic only partially corresponds to the "equivalent" Greek noun *hermēneia*. The meaning of the Greek term was determined by the Greek verb *hermēneuein,* corresponding to the Latin verb *interpretari,* to "interpret."

Hermēneia meant "interpretation" so broadly that it could be applied to whatever activity was involved in bringing the unclear to clarity. Indeed it is this broad scope of clarification, rather than any one specific kind of clarification, that seems to be basic to *hermēneia.* It is in this way that one is to understand the constant application of *hermēneia* to the messages of the gods, in that they are by their very nature mysterious, obscure, and in need of clarification. The *hermēneia* of the will of the gods doubtless shared in this broad, numinous sensitivity even when the *hermēneia* in question has become specific and concrete.

An instance of this general sensitivity to the numinous quality of theological *hermēneia* is the spiritual gift *"hermēneia* of tongues." This gift, listed in 1 Cor. 12:10 alongside of speaking in tongues, is not simply to be identified with the capacity for rational translation. For the speaking in tongues did not (*pace* Luke) involve foreign languages, but rather ecstatic, divine ("angelic" 1 Cor. 13:1) utterance, calling for interpretation, such as

I

is required for various kinds of obscure divine communication. The interpretation itself has revelatory character, and consequently ranks as itself a charismatic gift. Thus, in 1 Cor. 14:26, although *hermēneia* is again paired with speaking in a tongue, one could perhaps best translate it "illumination," rather than simply "translation." For the gift has some independent significance in communicating divine will, which makes it suited to stand in this verse alongside of "psalm," "teaching," and "revelation," as well as alongside of "tongue" as its translation.[1]

Speech

Hermēneia is already involved in the activity of a herald or spokesman for the gods, whose function it is to proclaim clearly the will of the gods. This meaning of *hermēneia* as proclamation is implicit in the name of the divine herald Hermes, who invented language as a medium of interpretation. The people of Lystra call Barnabas, Zeus, but Paul, Hermes, "because he was the chief speaker" (Acts 14:12). Since Moses is told that Aaron "shall speak for you" (Exod. 4:16), Philo can refer to Aaron as Moses' "spokesman" (*hermēneus*).[2] But the inspired prophet himself is designated with the same term, as God's "spokesman."[3] Similarly Plato refers to the poets as "nothing but spokesmen (*hermēnēs*) of the gods," and to rhapsodists, whose function it was to recite Homeric poems, as "spokesmen for spokesmen" (*hermēneōn hermēnēs*).[4] In this case interpretation takes the form of a continuing recurrence of language, from the poet's utterance to the rhapsodist's recital. Here language is itself interpretation,[5] not just the object of interpretation. Hence *hermēneia* can mean "linguistic formulation" or "expression," and it can

[1] In Sirach 47:17 countries are amazed at Solomon "for songs and proverbs and parables and for illuminations (*hermēneiai*)." Cf. further 1 Cor. 12:30; 14:5, 13, 27, 28.

[2] *That the Worse is Wont to Attack the Better*, 39.

[3] Cf. the passages from Philo collected by Johannes Behm, in Gerhard Kittel, ed., *Theologisches Wörterbuch zum Neuen Testament*, II (Stuttgart: W. Kohlhammer Verlag, 1935), 661.

[4] Plato, Ion, 534 E, 535 A.

[5] The term interpretation retains a somewhat analogous significance in the arts, where a musician or actor's "interpretation" refers to his rendition or performance of the work of art, rather than to a commentary on the work of art.

be used to designate a work on logical formulation or artistic elocution,[6] the discipline we today call "speech."

If this understanding of language as itself interpretation has been hardly sensed in traditional hermeneutics, it has become central in the new hermeneutic, and is indeed one of its distinguishing characteristics. Gerhard Ebeling begins his encyclopedia article on hermeneutic with the statement: "The etymological origin of *hermēneuein* and its derivatives is contested, but it points in the direction of roots with the meaning 'speak,' 'say' (connected with the Latin *verbum* or *sermo*)."[7] If this etymology is admittedly uncertain, and yet serves to open the presentation, it is because it symbolizes the scope of the new hermeneutic. This

[6] Georg Heinrici in Albert Hauck, ed., *Realencyklopädie für protestantische Theologie und Kirche* (abbreviated *PRE*), VII (Leipzig: J. C. Hinrichs, 1899), 719, and Gerhard Ebeling in Kurt Galling, ed., *Die Religion in Geschichte und Gegenwart* (abbreviated *RGG*), 3rd ed., III (Tübingen: J. C. B. Mohr, 1959), 243, cite for the former Aristotle's *Peri hermēneia* and for the latter (Pseudo-) Demetrius of Phaleron's use of the same title.

[7] *RGG*, 3rd ed., III (1959), 243. Indeed the Latin *verbum* is derived from a root *wer* or *wre* meaning to "say." This has as its Greek cognate a form originally using a Greek letter digamma subsequently dropped from the Greek alphabet and replaced by the rough breathing transliterated in English with "h." Consequently, the Latin stem *verb-* and the Greek stem *herm-* could be cognates of each other and of the German *Wort* and English "word." One Greek term for "word," *rhēma*, is also involved in this group of cognates. The Latin *sermo* may be related to the verb *sero*, meaning to arrange in a row, or thread, whose Greek cognate form was originally *serjo*. Since such an initial *s* tended to be replaced by the rough breathing (transliterated in English with "h"), this Greek root survived as *her-* (e.g., *herma*, which means "earring"). Thus the Latin stem *serm-* could also be related to the Greek stem *herm-* involved in *hermēneuein*. But *hermēneuein* can hardly be derived both from the root beginning with *digamma* meaning "to say" and from the root beginning with *sigma* meaning "to arrange in a row," in spite of the fact that both roots came to be written with the rough breathing and thus to converge with each other and with the Greek stem of *hermēneuein* (and perhaps each to produce a distinct verb of identical spelling, *eirein*). Furthermore, *sermo* is more probably derived from a root *swer* meaning to speak and cognate to the German *schwören*, English "swear." Cf. Menge-Güthling, *Enzyklopädisches Wörterbuch der lateinischen und deutschen Sprache*, Part I (Latin-German), written "with regard to etymology" by Hermann Menge (Berlin-Schöneberg: Langenscheidt KG Verlagsbuchhandlung, 8th ed., 1954), p. 792, s.v. *verbum*, and p. 692, s.v. *sermo*; Emile Boisacq, *Dictionnaire étymologique de la langue grecque étudiée dans ses rapports avec les autres langues indo-européennes* (Heidelberg: Carl Winter Universitätsverlag, 4th ed., 1950), pp. 282 f., s.v. *hermēneus*, etc., and pp. 229 f., s.v. *eiro*.

embraces the whole theological enterprise as a movement of language, from the word of God attested in Scripture to the preached sermon in which God speaks anew, and is not confined to a subdivision within Biblical studies treating of the theory of exegesis.

The "interpretation" involved in *hermēneia* could also take the specific form of "translation" out of a foreign tongue.[8] This meaning of *hermēneia* was not carried over into traditional hermeneutics. But it is distinctive of the new hermeneutic that it does understand its task as translating meaning from one culture to the other, from one situation to the other. The deeper implication involved in translating from one language to another, namely, the constitutive role attributed to man's historicness in appraising the hermeneutical task, is a significant aspect of the contemporary renewal of the hermeneutical question.

Translation

This deeper implication involved in translation can be brought to attention within English usage by recalling a meaning of the term "translation" that has passed out of common usage and is largely confined to ecclesiastical concepts derived from the past. One can speak of "translating" a bishop from one see to another, just as one used to speak of a saint's "translation" to heaven. This usage of the term "translate" to refer to a movement from one place to the other has largely been replaced by other terms, such as the term "transfer," derived from the same Latin verb. In German one can still speak of "trans-lating" a person or thing across a river in a ferry, whether or not the river be Jordan. And the Greek verb *hermēneuein* betrays much the same sensitivity in its proclivity for the use of the prefixes *dia-* and *meta-*, equivalent to the Latin prefix *trans-*, when meaning "to translate." Indeed Plato made the same analogy without benefit of the play on words, when he referred to "translating and ferrying (*hermēneuon kai diaporthmeuon*) to gods what comes from men and to men what comes from gods."[9] The new hermeneutic has to do with this slippery business of "translating" meaning.

[8] John 9:7: "Siloam, which is translated (*hermēneuetai*) 'Sent.' " Cf. similarly Matt. 1:23; Mark 5:41, 15:22, 34; John 1:38, 41, 42; Acts 4:36, 9:36, 13:8; Heb. 7:2.

[9] Sym. 202 E. Kornelis Heiko Miskotte, *Zur biblischen Hermeneutik* (*The-*

Another specific form of *hermēneia* was that of a commentary, *Commentary*
where no foreign language was involved but where the obscurity
of an utterance or text called for some clarification. In Luke
24:27 the resurrected Lord "interpreted (*diermēneusen*) to them
in all the Scriptures the things concerning himself."[10] Thus in
Greek usage one meaning of *hermēneia* is synonymous with *exēgēsis*, a synonymity carried over into their Latin translations, *in-
terpretatio* and *expositio* respectively,[11] and thus into the English
synonyms interpretation and exposition. Hence our modern distinction between hermeneutics as the theory and exegesis as the
practice of the art of interpretation cannot be attributed to antiquity. In the introduction to his *"Exēgēsis* of the Lord's Sayings" Papias speaks of what is to follow as "interpretations" (*hermēneiai*).[12] Hence *hermēneia* became a patristic name for "commentary," in which meaning it is only now being revived.[13] One

ologische Studien, Zollikon: Evangelischer Verlag, No. 55, 1959), p. 4, arrives at a similar understanding of hermeneutic as translation without recourse to the play on words.

[10] The numinous nature of such revelatory interpretation is reflected in the
parallel statements "he opened to us the Scriptures" (vs. 32) and "he opened
their minds to understand the Scriptures" (vs. 45); the role of such interpretation as itself proclamation is reflected in the parallel statement "beginning
with this Scripture he told him the good news of Jesus" (Acts 8:35).

[11] E.g., the Latin translation of Photius' *Bibliotheca* by Andr. Schott, S.J.
of 1605 (printed 1653) follows consistently this translational policy for the
instances of *hermēneia* listed in n. 13 below, with the exception of the anonymous *Hermēneia* on the Octateuch, where *hermēneia* is translated *expositio.*
Cf. J.-B. Migne, *Patrologiae cursus completus, Series graeca* (Paris: Garnier
Frères), CIII (1900).

[12] Cited by Eusebius, *Ecclesiastical History,* III, 39, 3. *The Gospel According to Thomas,* edited and translated by A. Guillaumont, H.-Ch. Puech, G.
Quispel, W. Till, and Yassah 'Abd al Masih (New York and Evanston:
Harper & Row, 1959), has as its first introductory saying "Whoever finds the
hermēneia of these words will not taste death" (p. 3). Thus *hermēneia* seems
early to have been the standard term for an interpretation of the sayings
of Jesus.

[13] A ninth-century library catalogued by Photius, Patriarch of Constanti-
nople, listed a *Hermēneia* on Daniel by Hippolytus of Rome (who also wrote
a *Hermēneia* on Ruth), one on Genesis by Theodore of Mopsuestia, head of
the Antiochene school of exegesis, another on Daniel by the Antiochene Theodoret of Cyrus, and an anonymous *Hermēneia* on the Octateuch (as well as
Theodoret's *Exēgēsis* on the Octateuch). Cf. J.-B. Migne, *op. cit.,* CIII
(1900), Codices 202, 38, 203, 36, 204. An international critical commentary
series now being planned has been entitled *Hermeneia; A Critical and Historical Commentary on the Bible.*

significant aspect of the new hermeneutic is its return to this
close association of hermeneutic with the *practice* of the art of
interpretation, so that "hermeneutic" can become coterminous
with Christian theology as the statement of the meaning of Scripture for our day.

The Greek noun *hermēneia* thus embraced the whole broad
scope of "interpretation," from "speech" that brings the obscure
into the clarity of linguistic expression, to "translation" from an
obscure, foreign language into the clarity of one's own language,
and to "commentary" that explicates the meaning of obscure language by means of clearer language. The profound implication
that these three functions belong together as interrelated aspects
of a single hermeneutic was lost in traditional hermeneutics,
which was the theory of but one aspect of *hermēneia,* exegesis.
This narrowing of the concept may suggest that some of the dimensions of the hermeneutical task had been lost from sight.
Thus the rather explicit return to the breadth of *hermēneia* on
the part of the new hermeneutic is to be seen not as etymological
pedantry, but rather as a new grasp of the proportions and nature
of the hermeneutical task.[14]

It is an initial indication of the approach of the new hermeneutic that its understanding of the hermeneutical task has been
here worked out in seeking to translate the meaning of the term
hermēneia into our language. Involved has been the assumption
characteristic of the new hermeneutic that the language pointing
to the subject matter is not simply in need of interpretation, but
is already itself an initial interpretation of that subject matter.
This is not meant as an invitation to seek that subject matter in
intuitive immediacy apart from the language interpreting it.
Quite to the contrary, it is intended to indicate the positive and
indispensable role of language in understanding. Rather than the
language being a secondary, distorting objectification of meaning
that must be removed to free the meaning behind the language,
the language of the text is regarded positively as an interpretative

[14] Ebeling, "Hermeneutik," *RGG,* 3rd ed., III, 243: "Therein emerges the
complexity of the hermeneutical problem, to which not merely one of these
meanings, but rather their structural relatedness, points."

proclamation of that meaning and hence as our indispensable access to it. Similarly the understanding of this meaning is not held in speechless profundity, but rather within our language. For only when the subject matter has been translated into our language, in spite of the historicness and finiteness of that language, has it been interpreted into our historic and finite world of understanding and hence been really understood. The insistence upon the unbroken linguisticality of understanding is an insistence upon the thoroughgoing historicness of the process of understanding. Thus one may say that the new hermeneutic, guided by the basic recognition of the historicness of man and of his understanding, has elevated language and translation, the more historic dimensions of interpretation, into positions of principle significance in the understanding of hermeneutic.

To listen to the Greek term *hermēneia* as an interpretation of the subject matter of hermeneutic—and to listen to it means to translate it into our language as "interpretation" in the three senses of "speech," "translation," and "commentary"—is not to stay on the outside of hermeneutical reflection, merely within linguistic objectifications behind which some neglected realm of immediacy is assumed to lie. Rather it is to understand hermeneutic as best man in his historic finiteness can understand, i.e., within the hermeneutical structures of his own existence, of which his linguisticality is primary.

II. HERMENEUTICS

Hermēneia, interpretation, is constantly being carried on without calling attention to itself, as people seek to understand one another and make themselves understood. Only when such normal communication breaks down due to some serious impediment to understanding (such as a foreign language) is attention drawn to the understanding process itself in such a way as to call forth reflection upon the *theory* of interpretation.

The factors that have usually combined to produce the main efforts at theorizing about interpretation in Western civilization have been two. First, theorizing has emerged in the process of interpreting bodies of literature whose authority is in one way or the other binding and whose meaning is therefore crucial. Second, theorizing has been especially required when these classical or canonical literatures are to assert their authority in a situation to which they no longer directly speak, and into which their meaning must be translated if they are to be heard at all. This necessity for translating authoritative literature has been the *agens* in the history of hermeneutical theory.

In antiquity it was, on the one hand, classical Greek literature, binding aesthetically, morally, and religiously, whose authority was put in question by enlightenment and was vindicated, e.g., in the allegorical method of the Stoics. On the other hand, it was the Old Testament whose canonical authority for Jew and Christian was to be vindicated—in spite of the replacement of theocracy and temple by synagogue and church—by its translation into Rabbinic casuistry, Qumranian and primitive Christian eschatological exegesis, and Philo and Origen's allegory. When the Renaissance and the Reformation coupled a revival of the authority of the classics and the Bible with a sense of the newness of the times, the hermeneutical question again became a focus of attention. The necessity to interpret the *corpus juris* so as to reach a legal decision in cases to which that body of law does not directly speak has, alongside Homer and the Bible, provided the third main subject matter for hermeneutical reflection over the years. Thus the history of hermeneutical theory[15] has in each case been determined by a very practical dimension, the necessity of man to act in the present, and yet to act correctly in terms of

[15] The detailed history is presented in most standard treatments. Cf., e.g., E. C. Blackman, *Biblical Interpretation* (Philadelphia: The Westminster Press, 1957); James D. Wood, *The Interpretation of the Bible; A Historical Introduction* (London: Gerald Duckworth and Co. Ltd., 1958); Gerhard Ebeling, "Hermeneutik," *RGG,* 3rd ed., III (1959), 245–258; Kendrick Grobel, "Interpretation," *The Interpreter's Dictionary of the Bible* (abbreviated *IDB*), edited by George A. Buttrick, II (New York and Nashville: Abingdon Press, 1962), 719–723. Cf. further B. Smalley, *The Study of the Bible in the Middle Ages* (Oxford: Blackwell, 1941; 2nd ed., 1952); Robert M. Grant, *The Bible in the Church* (New York: The Macmillan Company, 1948); "History of the Interpretation of the Bible," by Robert M. Grant, Samuel Terrien, and John T. McNeill, *The Interpreter's Bible* (abbreviated *IB*), edited by George A. Buttrick, I (New York and Nashville: Abingdon Press, 1952), 106–141.

traditional norms. For hermeneutic itself is rooted in man's historicness, namely, the call placed upon him to encounter the history of the past in such a way as not to deny his own existential future and present responsibility.

The Greek term *hermēneia* had long since disappeared from the Latinized vocabulary of scholarship when the theory of interpretation emerged as a science as a result of the Renaissance and Reformation.[16] The vogue to return to the original Greek during the pseudo-classicism of the seventeenth century is responsible for coining—alongside the already existing Latin expression *ars interpretandi*—the Greek-sounding term *hermeneutica*,[17] from which the English term "hermeneutics" is derived.[18]

The precedent for the neologism (but not its plural form) is provided by Plato's allusion to (*hē*) *hermēneutikē* (*technē*), "(the) hermeneutical (art)," which, in distinction from the critical arts that judge between true and false, belongs to those arts that merely give commands, and this not in one's own name, but, like the prophet and the herald, under another's authority. It is one of the arts that do not impart wisdom since they "only know what is said, but have not learned whether it is true."[19]

---

[16] Cf. Wilhelm Dilthey, "Die Entstehung der Hermeneutik," *Gesammelte Schriften*, V (Leipzig and Berlin: B. G. Teubner, 1924), 323 ff. Classical philology developed rules known as *ars critica*, "but the final constituting of hermeneutic is to be attributed to Biblical interpretation" (p. 324). "The definitive founding of a scholarly hermeneutic" is attributed first to Schleiermacher (p. 327).

[17] Ernst von Dobschütz, *Vom Auslegen des Neuen Testaments* (Göttingen: Vandenhoeck und Ruprecht, 1927), p. 5, n. 2. The first work to use this in a title was J. C. Dannhauer, *Hermeneutica Sacra, sive methodus exponendarum Sacrarum Literarum* (Strasbourg, 1654).

[18] The Oxford English Dictionary (*A New English Dictionary on Historical Principles*) V (Oxford: Clarendon Press, 1901), 243, lists as the first instance of the term the following formulation from the 2nd ed. of Waterland's *Eucharist* of 1737: "Taking such liberties with sacred Writ, as are by no means allowable upon any known rules of just and sober hermeneuticks." Although *hermeneutica* was construed as feminine singular, the frequency of neuter plural names for sciences with the same ending -*ica* made it almost inevitable that the plural form "hermeneutics" would prevail in English. Up until the present (when the singular form is gaining ground) the plural form has been so prevalent that it can function in the present essay to designate the discipline as it was understood up until the emergence of the new hermeneutic.

[19] The Statesman 260 D; the Pseudo-Platonic Epinomis 975 C.

An analogy to this distinction is to be found in more recent times in that between hermeneutics and criticism, a distinction quite characteristic in the period of traditional hermeneutics,[20] but, significantly enough, put in question by the new hermeneutic.[21] Conversely, hermeneutics did not build upon *hermēneia* in its rich suggestiveness of the interpretive interrelatedness of language, translation, and exegesis, but rather limited itself to but one dimension of interpretation, exegesis. Even here the original synonymity of *hermēneia* with exegesis was replaced by a distinction, in terms of theory and practice, into hermeneutics and exegesis.[22]

[20] E.g., J. A. Ernesti distinguishes the "hermeneutical" from the "critical" use of Biblical allusions in the church fathers, "one pertaining to understanding, the other to judging as to the integrity of the words." *Institutio interpretis Novi Testamenti* (Havniae: Ex Officina Hallageriana, 1761; cited from 4th ed., 1776), p. 130. Schleiermacher taught in sequence hermeneutics and criticism, so that the two were published posthumously in one volume by Friedrick Lücke under the title *Hermeneutik und Kritik mit besonderer Beziehung auf das Neue Testament,* in the *Sämmtliche Werke,* I, 7 (Berlin: G. Reimer, 1838). The "General Introduction" began as follows: "Hermeneutics and criticism, both philological disciplines, both arts, belong together, since the execution of each presupposes the other. The former is in general the art of understanding correctly the speech of another, especially when it is written down. The latter is the art of judging correctly the authenticity of the writings and passages, and of establishing on the basis of adequate attestation and data." This passage is cited by Martin Heidegger, *Unterwegs zur Sprache* (Pfullingen: Neske Verlag, 1959), p. 97. Heinz Kimmerle omits the material on criticism from his edition, "for the development of Schleiermacher's thoughts on hermeneutics shows that hermeneutics is an independent theme in the context of his thought." Friedrich D. E. Schleiermacher, *Hermeneutik,* newly edited from the manuscripts and introduced by Heinz Kimmerle, in the *Abhandlungen der Heidelberger Akademie der Wissenschaften, Philosophisch-historische Klasse,* Jg. 1959, 2. Ahb. (Heidelberg: Karl Winter Universitätsverlag, 1959), p. 13. For the association of hermeneutics and criticism Schleiermacher is dependent upon Friedrich Ast, *Grundlinien der Grammatik, Hermeneutik und Kritik* (Landshut, 1808).

[21] Ebeling, "Hermeneutik," *RGG,* 3rd ed., III (1959), 243. Cf. also the criticism of Emilio Betti's distinction between cognitive, normative and reproductive functions of interpretation in Hans-Georg Gadamer, *Wahrheit und Methode; Grundzüge einer philosophischen Hermeneutik* (Tübingen: J. C. B. Mohr, 1960), pp. 293 f.

[22] "Exegetical theology or *exēgesis* and the verb *exēgeisthai* can be regarded as synonymous with *hermēneuein* and *hermeneutica,* and are indeed used in such a significance, so that *theologia hermeneutica* and *exegetica* are one and the same. More fittingly, however, these two expressions are distinguished from each other, so that a new subdivision into *exegesis theoretica* and *practica* can be avoided. Thus hermeneutics actually embraces the theory of the rules of the interpretation of Holy Scripture, while *exēgesis* or exegetical theology refers to the real execution or application of these rules in individual

It is this narrowing inherent in the term hermeneutics, set off on the one side from criticism and on the other from exegesis, that gave the discipline in recent times a specialized, technical connotation partly responsible for its neglect in theological education. Even Schleiermacher, who first posed the broad hermeneutical problem as to how understanding takes place at all, separated hermeneutics proper from linguistic and historical study of the text on the one hand and from the modern formulation and application of the text's meaning on the other.[23] With the increasing complexity of theological scholarship, hermeneutics became such a narrow subdivision within a subdivision[24] as to be often omitted as a discipline altogether.[25]

---

cases on real passages and books of Holy Scripture." *D. Siegmund Jacob Baumgartens ausführlicher Vortrag der Biblischen Hermeneutic (sic!)*, edited by M. Joachim Christoph Bertram (Halle: Johann Justinus Gebauer, 1769), pp. 5 f.

[23] Cf. Heinz Kimmerle, "Hermeneutische Theorie oder ontologische Hermeneutik," *ZThK*, LIX (1962), 115.

[24] Cf., e.g., Georg Heinrici's designation of the place of hermeneutics in theological scholarship: "It is not directed to the history of Israel and primitive Christianity in general, but rather to the specific products of the religious spirit that are united into a canon of Old and New Testament, i.e., to the sources and documents collected in the Bible. In that it teaches one to establish and apply the principles and methods for their fitting interpretation, it presupposes all the information that the research disciplines of Biblical scholarship provide, as this information is collected in Biblical linguistics, introduction, archaeology, and the history of Biblical times. Similarly it requires prior work in criticism with regard to the transmission of the text of its materials. Their hermeneutical treatment can lead to reliable results only if the question as to the reliability or the corruption of the text is set clear and, to the extent the sources permit, rectified. On the other hand, hermeneutics must have done its work and have presented its results in the exposition of Scripture if the descriptive disciplines of Biblical scholarship, the history of Israel and of the gospel, the history of apostolic times and especially of Biblical theology, are not to become a playground for the dilettante with his curious and arbitrary hypotheses or with his dogmatic prejudice." *PRE*, 3rd ed., VII (1899), 723.

[25] One may compare with Heinrici's classification of the subdivisions of New Testament scholarship that presented a generation later by A. Meyer, "Bibelwissenschaft," *RGG*, 2nd ed., I (1927), 1085: "I. Research into the *language*, Koine Greek . . . II. The establishment of the *text* and its history. III. The history of the New Testament *canon*. IV. The history of New Testament *times* . . . V. *Interpretation* of New Testament writings. VI. *Introduction* to the New Testament. . . . The objective is a *history of primitive Christian literature* . . . VII. *Historical* presentation, a) '*Life of Jesus*' . . . ; b) *Paul;* c) *the apostolic period* . . . ; d) *the sub-apostolic period* . . . ; 3) *the history of primitive Christianity* as a whole. VIII. *Biblical theology.*

Yet when one considers what was normally treated in the discipline called hermeneutics, one immediately observes that it is not these contents themselves that have ceased to be the subject of scholarly discussion. For example, hermeneutics normally began with a discussion of the language of the text.[26] In the case of the New Testament this had to do with the problem that the vocabulary and grammar are not those of classical Greek, but rather those of Hellenistic Greek with more or less Semitic influence. He who has familiarized himself with "Bauer-Arndt-Gingrich"[27] and "Blass-Debrunner-Funk,"[28] with some awareness of what is involved, such as is provided by Walter Bauer's "Introduction to the Lexicon of the Greek New Testament"[29] and E. C. Colwell's article on "The Greek Language,"[30] has as accurate a knowledge of this division of hermeneutics as was provided for an earlier day by the textbooks on hermeneutics. Hermeneutics as a discipline became irrelevant in spite of the continuing relevance of such philological lore. For it failed to go beyond what such specialized philological resources can be expected to provide and investigate the relation of language itself to the process of interpretation.

A second major segment of hermeneutics had to do with the

... The objective is a *history of the religion of primitive Christianity*. ..." Here hermeneutics has ceased to be a subdivision within the discipline of New Testament scholarship. Perhaps the fact that the term interpretation tends to embrace both hermeneutics and exegesis is partly responsible for its greater popularity in recent times, as this instance would tend to indicate.

[26] Cf., e.g., *PRE*, 3rd ed., VII, 724 f., Part 2a, "Linguistic Explanation"; Frederik Torm, *Hermeneutik des Neuen Testaments,* Ch. 2, "New Testament Greek," pp. 39–96.

[27] *A Greek-English Lexicon of the New Testament and Other Early Christian Literature,* by Walter Bauer, translated and adapted from the 4th German edition by William F. Arndt and W. Wilbur Gingrich (Chicago: The University of Chicago Press, 1957). A revised edition incorporating the additions in the 5th (and last) German edition is being prepared by Professor Gingrich.

[28] *A Greek Grammar of the New Testament and Other Early Christian Literature,* by F. Blass and A. Debrunner, translated and revised from the 9th–10th German edition by Robert W. Funk (Chicago: The University of Chicago Press, 1961).

[29] *Op. cit.,* pp. ix–xxv.

[30] *IDB,* II (1962), 479–487.

historical setting of the Biblical literature, in terms of which its 2.
original meaning is to be understood.[31] Its advice ranged from
the necessity of such historical analogy if one is to avoid modern-
izing, to the danger of drawing parallels where the similarity is
very superficial. Here too the debate and refinement of method
has continued without benefit of the discipline of hermeneutics.
One need merely consider the immense literature about gnosticism in its relation to primitive Christianity, or that concerning
Qumran and the New Testament, from Hermann Gunkel's prediction of the discovery of such a sect, made while emphasizing
the hermeneutical relevance of such comparative religious parallels,[32] to Samuel Sandmel's most recent warning against "parallelomania."[33] Yet such research has often worked in terms of a
rather superficial grasp of the hermeneutical task, as when "understanding" is taken to mean simply explaining where ideas or
influences come from, rather than penetrating into the meaning
of the text. The unique position held by Hans Jonas' work within
the study of gnosticism[34] stands hermeneutically in judgment
upon such research that, though philologically more exacting,
never moved beyond explaining, i.e., never really entered in upon
the task of understanding the deeper meaning of the text.

Krister Stendahl has pointed out that the purely descriptive
approach of the *religionsgeschichtliche Schule* "does not necessarily imply the disintegration of the Biblical material into unrelated bits of antiquated information." Indeed "the result of
descriptive Biblical theology has raised the hermeneutical problem in a somewhat new form," in that it forces upon us the recognition of systematic theology's task to translate the Biblical

[31] Cf. e.g., *PRE*, 3rd ed., VII, 726 f., P. 2b, "Historical Explanation,"
Torm, *Hermeneutik des Neuen Testaments*, Ch. 6, "Special Problems of
Understanding (The Relations of the Text to Its Contemporary Back-
ground)," pp. 170–207.

[32] *Zum religionsgeschichtlichen Verständnis des Neuen Testaments* (Göttingen: Vandenhoeck und Ruprecht, 1903). An English translation appeared
the same year in the *Monist* (Chicago: Open Court Publishing Co.), No. 3,
pp. 398 ff.

[33] "Parallelomania," *Journal of Biblical Literature*, LXXXI (1962), 1–13.

[34] *Gnosis und spätantiker Geist* (Göttingen: Vandenhoeck und Ruprecht),
I (1934), II, 1 (1954); *The Gnostic Religion* (Boston: Beacon Press, 1958).

message into modern categories.[35] Yet it is this profound hermeneutical significance of the purely descriptive achievement of the
religionsgeschichtliche Schule that was first recognized as such by
the new hermeneutic.

Another major subdivision within hermeneutics has been vari-
ously characterized as "psychological" or "technical" (terms used
by Schleiermacher), or "generic" (Boeckh), or "stylistic" (Heinrici). Here the text is to be classified in terms of the rhetorical or
other stylistic figures it employs and the literary category to which
it belongs. The significance of the individual text, i.e., what the
author was at, can be sensed from the style he is using. Here is
where the deeper task of interpretation emerges within traditional
hermeneutics.[36] And yet this relation of form to meaning came
into its own after traditional hermeneutics had faded away, when
form criticism emerged in all its theological relevance for what
the text is trying to say.[37] Traditional hermeneutics had tended to
use the literary categories as a foil for determining the originality,
individuality, and thus personality of the author, his personal
"style."[38] The scope as a whole that is to be brought into a
fruitful interaction (a hermeneutical circle) with the specific text
was the "author's personality."[39] Schleiermacher's term "psycho-

[35] Cf. the article "Contemporary Biblical Theology," *IDB,* I (1962), 418–
432, esp. 425 and 427.

[36] Heinrici, *PRE,* 3rd ed., VII, 728, cites Luther's focus upon the *scopus*
of the text, and declares (p. 729): "Here the hermeneut has reached his
goal."

[37] Apart from Old Testament *Gattungsgeschichte,* whose classic instances
are Hermann Gunkel's *Die Sagen der Genesis* (Göttingen: Vandenhoeck und
Ruprecht, 1901) and his *Einleitung in die Psalmen,* I (Göttingen: Vandenhoeck und Ruprecht, 1928), one should cite as classic primarily Martin
Dibelius' *From Tradition to Gospel* (New York: Charles Scribner's Sons,
1935, German 1st ed., 1919), Rudolf Bultmann's *History of the Synoptic
Tradition* (New York and Evanston: Harper & Row, 1963; German 1st ed.,
1921), and Karl Ludwig Schmidt's "Die Stellung der Evangelien in der
allgemeinen Literaturgeschichte," in the *Festschrift* for Gunkel, *Eucharis-
tērion,* edited by Hans Schmidt, II (Göttingen: Vandenhoeck und Ruprecht,
1923), 50–134, where the theological issue is posed with an acuteness un-
equaled since the outsider Franz Oberbeck published "Uber die Anfänge der
patristischen Literatur" forty years earlier (*Historische Zeitschrift,* XLVIII,
1882, 417–472, reprinted apart in 1954 in Darmstadt by the Wissenschaftliche Buchgesellschaft).

[38] *PRE,* 3rd ed., VII, 724.

[39] This is the concept dominating Torm's *Hermeneutik des Neuen Testaments.*

logical" did indeed characterize the net outcome.[40] Consequently, the subject matter of the text itself tended to be lost from view as the goal of interpretation. It is here that Barth's criticism found its point of departure.

It was often in connection with the special rhetorical figures and literary forms of Biblical literature that one came to treat the problems of allegory, typology, prophecy, and, in general, the Christian interpretation of the Old Testament. This part of hermeneutics had in a sense been replaced by the debate about the critical historical method, so that the decline of hermeneutics was in this regard in direct proportion to the rise of critical scholarship. Liberalism and conservatism tended to divide criticism and hermeneutics between them. This may in part explain the fact that hermeneutics as a discipline has survived in conservative circles even down to the present.[41] And yet the creative work on

[40] It may be indicative that Heinrici's criticism of this term was that it was too broad, in that "historical explanation" also provides a psychological interpretation. *PRE*, 3rd ed., VII, 724. Willi Lütgert, "Bibelerklärung des NT," *RGG*, 2nd ed., I (1927), 1016, also associates "psychological" explanation with "historical" explanation. This broadening of the "psychological" is partly a missing of the deeper point and justification for the designation of formal analysis as "psychological." Whereas traditional rhetoric has regarded composition as a mechanical applying of rules adorned with literary figures, Schleiermacher traced literary form back to the author's individuality, his form or "style," so that the literary form reflects the author's personal scope. This could lead to psychologizing, but it could also lead to Heidegger's hearing of "world" in language, and to the Heideggerian literary criticism of Emil Staiger, *Die Zeit als Einbildungskraft des Dichters* (Zürich: Atlantis Verlag, 1939; 2nd ed., 1953).

[41] Without a doubt Milton S. Terry's *Biblical Hermeneutics; A Treatise on the Interpretation of the Old and New Testaments* has been the American textbook in the field. First published in the *Library of Biblical and Theological Literature,* edited by George R. Crooks and John F. Hurst (New York: Eaton and Mains), in 1883, it was republished in a revised edition in 1890 and in a further revision in 1911, only to be republished in 1952 (Grand Rapids: Zondervan Publishing House) for use as a textbook today. Indicative of the persistence of hermeneutics in conservative circles are the following: David Robert Dungans, *Hermeneutics. A Textbook,* 1888, which has been republished since (Cincinnati: The Standard Publishing Co., n.d.) ; Sylvester Burnham, *The Elements of Biblical Hermeneutics* (Hamilton, N.Y.: The Republic Press, 1916); George H. Schodde, *Outlines of Biblical Hermeneutics. A Handbook for Students of the Word* (Columbus: Lutheran Book Concern, 1917); J. Edwin Hartill, *Biblical Hermeneutics* (Grand Rapids: Zondervan Publishing Company, 1947, reprint 1960); Rollin Thomas Chafer, *The Science of Biblical Hermeneutics. An Outline Study of Its Laws* (Dallas: Bibliotheca Sacra, n.d., 1939). More recently the term hermeneutics has been

the problem of the Christian interpretation of the Old Testament
has gone on quite apart from the conservative discipline of hermeneutics.[42]

Of particular interest is the apologetic role that the study of
the "forms or kinds of speech" and "literary modes" used in the
Bible play in Roman Catholic hermeneutics. "By this knowledge
and exact appreciation of the modes of speaking and writing in
use among the ancients can be solved many difficulties, which are
raised against the veracity and historical value of the Divine
Scriptures, and no less efficaciously does this study contribute to
a fuller and more luminous understanding of the mind of the
Sacred Writer."[43] Thus form criticism has provided a hermeneu-

---

relegated to the subtitle, in favor of the more popular term interpretation:
Louis Berkhof, *Principles of Biblical Interpretation (Sacred Hermeneutics)*
(Grand Rapids: Baker Book House, 1950; 2nd ed., 1952); Bernard Ramm,
*Protestant Biblical Interpretation. A Textbook of Hermeneutics for Conserva-
tive Protestants* (Boston: W. A. Wilde Co., 1950; "complete revised edition,"
1956).

[42] For the period since World War II cf. the programmatic double issue
of *Evangelische Theologie*, XII (1952), Heft 1/2, leading to the *Biblischer
Kommentar; Altes Testament*, edited by Martin Noth (Neukirchen Kreis
Moers: Neukirchener Verlag, 1955 ff.). Most of these essays have appeared
in English in *Interpretation*, XV (1961): Martin Noth, "The 'Re-presenta-
tion' of the Old Testament in Proclamation," pp. 50–60; Gerhard von Rad,
"Typological Interpretation of the Old Testament," pp. 174–192; Walther
Zimmerli, "Promise and Fulfillment," pp. 310–338; Hans Walter Wolf, "The
Hermeneutics of the Old Testament," pp. 439–472. Cf. also *Vergegenwärti-
gung. Aufsätze zur Auslegung des Alten Testaments* (Berlin: Evangelische
Verlagsanstalt, 1955); and the discussion following upon the programmatic
essay by Wolfhart Pannenberg, "Heilsgeschehen und Geschichte," *Kerygma
und Dogma*, V (1959), 218–237, 259–288, English translation of the Old
Testament part in *Essays on Old Testament Hermeneutics*, edited by J. L.
Mays (Richmond: John Knox Press, 1964). The symposium edited by Pannenberg, including contributions by him, R. Rendtorff, U. Wilckens, and
T. Rendtorff, *Offenbarung als Geschichte, Beiheft* 1 of *Kerygma und Dogma*
(Göttingen: Vandenhoeck und Ruprecht, 1961; 2nd augmented ed., 1963),
led to a discussion in a double issue of *Evangelische Theologie*, XXII (1962),
1/2. Vol. 3 of *New Frontiers in Theology*, entitled *Theology as History*, will
be devoted to a discussion of this position. Most of these and other essays
from the decade 1950–1960 are included in the volume edited by Klaus
Westermann, *Probleme alttestamentlicher Hermeneutik*, Vol. 11 in the *Theologische Bücherei* (Munich: Christian Kaiser Verlag, 1960).

[43] The Papal Encyclical *Divino Afflante Spiritu* of Sept. 30, 1943, ¶ 39.
(Published in pamphlet form by the National Catholic Welfare Conference,
Washington, D.C. English translation provided by the Vatican.) Cf. also the
section *De generibus litterariis in S. Scriptura* in the encyclical of Oct. 20,
1943, *De Sacrorum Bibliorum studiis*, quoted in Denzinger and Umberg (edi-

tical principle for the acceptance of critical positions that would otherwise have been dogmatically inadmissible.

If one can then hardly say that the subject matter traditionally handled in hermeneutics had dropped out of scholarly discussion with the disappearance of the discipline, one *can* say that the disappearance of hermeneutics is in any case indicative of a disintegration of the principle discussion of the hermeneutical problem within critical scholarship at the opening of the century. Part of the shock caused by Barth's *Romans* is due to this vacuum into which it exploded.

Symptomatic of this situation is the following remark made at about that time: "In the period from 1720–1820 almost every year a hermeneutics appeared; now, since J. Chr. K. von Hofmann's *Biblische Hermeneutik,* which appeared posthumously in 1880, nothing worth mentioning has appeared."[44] Georg Heinrici had written the article on "Biblical hermeneutics" called for by an encyclopedia in 1899,[45] but in a supplementary volume in 1913[46] he could only comment: "The scholarship of the present collects and catalogues facts with especial interest; it rejoices in statistical investigations and concerns itself with making use of

---

tors), *Enchiridion symbolorum definitionum et declarationum de rebus fidei et morum* (Freiburg im Breisgau: Herder, 26th ed., 1947), § 2294. An instance of the application of this hermeneutical principle is provided, e.g., by Myles M. Bourke, "The Literary Genus of Matthew 1–2," *The Catholic Biblical Quarterly,* XXII (1960), 160–175. This article, while distancing itself at the beginning from Renan's argument that, being a haggadic commentary, Matt. 1–2 does not have "the slightest historical basis," concludes with a position whose most striking difference from Renan consists in that such a position has become ecclesiastically acceptable: "Admittedly, the gospel presents Jesus' ministry, death and resurrection as events which really happened. But that the author of such a work might have introduced it by a midrash of deep theological insight, in which Jesus appears as the true Israel and the new Moses (thus containing the theme of the entire gospel), and in which the historical element is very slight, seems to be a thoroughly probable hypothesis."

[44] Ernst von Dobschütz, *Vom Auslegen des Neuen Testaments,* 1927, p. 6, n. 2. He concedes that there has been some activity on the part of Roman Catholic scholarship, and mentions Eduard König's *Hermeneutik des Alten Testaments* of 1916, which however treats only the Old Testament. It is indicative of the waning of the term "hermeneutics" that von Hofmann's work has been published in English under the title *Interpreting the Bible,* translated by Christian Preus (Minneapolis: Augsburg Publishing House, 1959).

[45] *PRE,* 3rd ed., VII, 718–750.

[46] *PRE,* 3rd ed., XXIII, 642.

insights of natural science even for one's world view. The drive toward a fundamental grounding of the problems, the interest in philosophical speculation, in methodological investigations, has been repressed. The basic tone determining wide circles of scholars is provided by the empiricists of England and America." It is perhaps not surprising that the next treatment of hermeneutics also derives from the exigencies of an encyclopedia. Ernst von Dobschütz supplied the article on "Interpretation" in Hasting's *Encyclopaedia of Religion and Ethics*[47] and used the fruits of his research for his rectoral address at Halle in 1922,[48] which began as follows: "The interpretation of the New Testament has made astounding achievements precisely in the last decades. It is all the more striking how little time it has found for reflection as to its nature, goals and paths. Yet without this the best practice threatens to sink back to a technician's skill, and dilettantism and lust for originality crop up on all sides. What one calls hermeneutics, once the discipline carried on most actively, then criminally neglected for two generations, must be awakened to new life."[49]

Since the theological faculty of the University of Copenhagen in the 1920's still required New Testament hermeneutics in the curriculum and on comprehensive examinations, their Professor of New Testament, Frederik Torm, published in Danish in 1928 a textbook on hermeneutics,[50] without pretense of doing more than temporarily filling a practical pedagogical need. But its use-

[47] VII, 390–395 (New York: Charles Scribner's Sons, 1920). Von Dobschütz, *Vom Auslegen des Neuen Testaments,* p. 6, n. 2, dates the encyclopedia article in 1914.

[48] "Vom Auslegen insonderheit des Neuen Testaments," published as number 18 in the series *Hallesche Universtätsreden* (Halle: Max Niemeyer Verlag). Von Dobschütz' book *Vom Auslegen des Neuen Testaments* of 1927 includes the rectoral address and two others of 1926, one entitled "Ein neuer Weg zum Verständnis des Neuen Testaments, die formgeschichtliche Methode," the other "Die Pneumatische Exegese, Wissenschaft und Praxis."

[49] *Vom Auslegen des Neuen Testaments,* p. 5. Cf. his statement in Hasting's *Encyclopaedia of Religion and Ethics,* VII, 392: Exegetical theology has "striven to the utmost to gain a grammatical and historical comprehension of Scripture. Nevertheless, it has failed to provide its ever-expanding industry with a proper rationale in a theoretic discussion of the hermeneutical problem. This failure is now beginning to bring its retribution, inasmuch as an art that does not reflect upon its own essential function readily degenerates into a mechanical routine."

[50] *Nytestamentlig Hermeneutik* (Copenhagen: G.E.C. Gads Forlag).

fulness in view of the vacuum to which von Dobschütz had called attention was recognized,[51] and a German translation appeared in 1930.[52] Yet this work does not alter the situation, but rather documents the hermeneutical sterility of the traditional approach. It marks the end of an epoch, rather than a new beginning. One must close the chapter on hermeneutics with a comment by Schleiermacher: "As long as hermeneutics is still treated as an aggregate of individual observations of a general and special nature, no matter how fine and commendable they may be, it does not yet deserve the name of an art."[53]

III. UNDERSTANDING

At the turn of the century a distinction was emerging in philosophical discussion of the Dilthey type between "explaining" (*Erklärung*) and "understanding" (*Verstehen*). "Over against the explaining of occurrences of nature there emerged, as a fundamentally different way of human knowing, historic 'understanding.' "[54] "We explain nature, we understand the life of the soul."[55]

One may trace in the opening third of the century the gradual shift in hermeneutical discussion from the one to the other term. Heinrici's presentation of 1899 uses the rubrics: A. Linguistic Explanation; B. Historical Explanation; C. Stylistic Explanation.[56] Hermann Gunkel does not seem to sense any distinctive implica-

[51] Cf. the review by Exling Eidem in the *Theologische Literaturzeitung* (abbreviated *ThLZ*), LIV (1929), 104–105.
[52] *Hermeneutik des Neuen Testaments* (Göttingen: Vandenhoeck und Ruprecht).
[53] *Kurze Darstellung des theologischen Studiums zum Behuf einleitender Vorlesungen* (Berlin: G. Reimer, 2nd ed., 1830), ¶ 133, pp. 59 f.
[54] Wilhelm Windelband and Heinz Heimsoeth, *Lehrbuch der Geschichte der Philosophie* (Tübingen: J. C. B. Mohr, 14th ed., 1950), p. 589.
[55] Cf. Wilhelm Dilthey, *Gesammelte Schriften*, V (Leipzig and Berlin: B. G. Teubner, 1924), 144. Max Weber's incompleted work, posthumously published under the title *Wirtschaft und Gesellschaft* (Tübingen: J. C. B. Mohr, 1956), was intended by Weber to be an "outline of understanding-psychology." "Max Weber calls this sociology 'understanding,' since its object is the intended meaning of social activity." Hans-Georg Gadamer, "Hermeneutik und Historismus," *Philosophische Rundschau* (abbreviated *PhR*), IX (1962), 245.
[56] *PRE*, 3rd ed., VII (1899), 724–729.

tion in his title "On the History-of-Religions Understanding of the New Testament" (1903), but rather speaks of the *religions-geschichtliche Schule* "with broad vision bringing Western and Eastern material together into an explanation," and thus "explaining not a little in the New Testament."[57] Indeed he identifies the two terms when he opposes those who prefer merely "exact reproduction" to those who seek "explanation," i.e., "historical classification," which then is called "genuinely living, historical understanding."[58] A generation later in 1927 the second edition of the standard German encyclopedia *Die Religion in Geschichte und Gegenwart*[59] still treated hermeneutics under the title "Explanation of the Bible." Yet by the time the last volume appeared in 1931 an article on "understanding" by Joachim Wach was included.[60] Indeed it was Wach's three-volume work on "Understanding"[61] that marked the clear shift to the preference for "understanding."[62] Thus the term understanding in its distinction from "explanation" characterized the first move toward the new hermeneutic.

It was Wilhelm Dilthey who relativized traditional hermeneutics in terms of the deeper role of understanding. He had detected in the history of hermeneutics an inner logic, in that thought had penetrated deeper and deeper into the problem until it had finally arrived at "the analysis of understanding" as "the sure point of departure for working out the [hermeneutical] rules."[63] If the sum of such rules is hermeneutics, then the analysis of under-

[57] *Zum religionsgeschichtlichen Verständnis des Neuen Testaments,* 3rd unaltered ed., 1930, pp. 4 f.
[58] *Ibid.,* p. 6.
[59] I (1927), 1011–1018, by Baumgärtel (O.T.) and Lütgert (N.T.).
[60] V, 1570–1573.
[61] *Das Verstehen. Grundzüge einer Geschichte der hermeneutischen Theorie im 19. Jahrhundert* (Tübingen: J. C. B. Mohr), I (1926), II (1929), III (1933).
[62] Cf., e.g., Erich Fascher's title *Vom Verstehen des Neuen Testaments; Ein Beitrag zur Grundlegung einer zeitgemässen Hermeneutik* (Giessen: Adolf Töpelmann, 1930), esp. pp. 100 ff., where the distinction is derived primarily from H. Gomperz, *Über Sinn und Sinngebilde, Verstehen und Erklären* (Tübingen: J. C. B. Mohr, 1929), and Rudolf Bultmann's collected essays entitled *Glauben und Verstehen* (Tübingen: J. C. B. Mohr), I (1933), II (1952), III (1960).
[63] "Die Entstehung der Hermeneutik," *Gesammelte Schriften,* V (1924), 320. He attributes this decisive step to Schleiermacher, pp. 327 ff.

standing is a discipline prior to, more fundamental than, herme-neutics. It is in this sense that Erich Fascher defined his treatise "On Understanding the New Testament" as "a contribution to laying the foundation for a modern hermeneutic." "We do not wish to do what is done in text books on hermeneutics, simply to develop the skills of interpreting on the basis of exegetical prac-tice. Nor do we wish to do what happens in the discussion today, namely describe the qualities the exegete must have. Rather we turn to the question prior to all hermeneutics and exegesis: How then is understanding possible, what means are there for under-standing? This is not the same as hermeneutics. Rather its parts are here put in an epistemological light."[64] Thus one can say that the new hermeneutic began to emerge in a recognition of the superficiality of hermeneutics, and hence in an intentional distinction of its deeper concern for understanding from that of hermeneutics. It is not surprising that the dominant term in the first movement toward the new hermeneutic has been "under-standing."

When Dilthey focused the hermeneutical task upon literature, he did so with the justification "that in language alone does what is inside man find its complete, exhaustive and objectively intel-ligible expression. Hence the art of understanding has its center in the interpretation of the remains of human existence contained in writing."[65] Here language is evaluated only as the objectifica-tion through which one must penetrate to the understanding of the existence expressing itself in the text. In somewhat the same way Heidegger in his analysis of understanding regards under-standing as a basic existential whose articulation in interpretation may (but does not necessarily) lead to "expression" as but a "de-rivative mode."[66] It is this secondary role of linguistic "expres-

Note impor-tance of a depth of under-standing which stands at the heart of the new Hermeneu-tic.

[64] *Vom Verstehen des Neuen Testaments; Ein Beitrag zur Grundlegung einer zeitgemässen Hermeneutik,* p. 12.

[65] "Die Entstehung der Hermeneutik," *Gesammelte Schriften,* V (1924), 319. The word translated "existence" is *Dasein,* which was later to become the technical term in Heidegger used in Bultmannian hermeneutic.

[66] *Sein und Zeit* (Tübingen: Max Niemeyer Verlag, 9th Ed., 1960), pp. 153 ff. English translation entitled *Being and Time,* by John Macquarrie and Edward Robinson (New York and Evanston: Harper & Row, 1962), pp. 195 ff. Their translation of *Aussage,* "assertion," has been here replaced by "ex-

sion" in the Heidegger of *Being and Time* that provided the context for relating language to understanding in the Bultmannian
school during the past generation.

Into the void left by the collapse of hermeneutics exploded
Karl Barth's *Romans.*[67] This book is not hermeneutics, a theory
about interpretation, but rather *hermēneia:* a commentary, in
which the subject matter of Paul's language is radically translated
and proclaimed anew in the language of our day. It is this *fait
accompli* that has called forth the hermeneutical reflection of our
times.

Only the beginnings of this reflection were provided by Barth
himself. With a few swift strokes of the brush he sketched its direction in the Preface to the first edition of *Romans,* written in
1918: "The critical historical method of Biblical research has its
validity. It points to the preparation for understanding that is
never superfluous. But if I had to choose between it and the old
doctrine of inspiration, I would decidedly lay hold of the latter.
It has the greater, deeper, more important validity, for it points
to the actual work of understanding, without which all preparation is useless. I am happy not to have to choose between the two.
But my whole attention was directed to looking *through* the historical to the spirit of the Bible, which is the eternal Spirit. What
once was serious is still serious today, and what today is serious,
and not just accidental and peripheral, stands in direct relation
to what was once serious. Our questions, if we understand ourselves aright, are the questions of Paul, and Paul's answers, if
their light illumines us, must be our answers. . . . The under-

---

pression," so as to retain the implication heard in the German word that
something inward is being "spoken out." The following section on discourse
and language (pp. 203 ff.) defines discourse as being as basic an existential
as is understanding, and thus points toward the post-Bultmannian development.

[67] *Der Römerbrief* (Bern: G. A. Bäschlin, 1919; reprint 1963, Zürich:
EVZ Verlag) ; the 2nd ed. of 1922 was thoroughly rewritten and has been
reprinted substantially unaltered. Citation is from the German original, the
8th reprinting of the 2nd ed. (Zollikon-Zürich: Evangelischer Verlag, 1947).
There is also an English translation by Edwyn C. Hoskyns (London: Oxford
University Press, 1933). Hans-Georg Gadamer, "Hermeneutik und Historismus," *PhR,* IX (1962), 246, declares Barth's Romans to have been a
"hermeneutical manifesto."

standing of history is a continuous, increasingly open and urgent discussion between the wisdom of yesterday and the wisdom of tomorrow, which are one and the same."[68]

Here the view of the relation of subject to object basic to the critical historical method, to the effect that the subjective element is to be eliminated so as to attain the highest possible objectivity, has been relativized by the basic recognition of the hermeneutical relevance of the subject. This basic insight is what Hans Jonas has called the "metaphysical *a priori*" of the history of ideas.[69]

The question with regard to the subject is not simply whether he can eliminate his subjectivity as a source of prejudice, but whether he "understands himself aright," i.e., whether he is grappling with what is "serious," or, as we might say today, whether he is asking the right questions, whether his concern is with the ultimate. If that be the case, his subjectivity provides an access to the subject matter of the text that is indispensable as a heuristic medium of interpretation, if it is really that subject matter, serious both then and now, that he is seeking to understand. One's subjectivity does not simply introduce distortions; it insures that the phenomena with which the text was grappling— if it is a serious text—are not overlooked or distorted into curiosities. It is this relevance of "Bultmannian" hermeneutic for the understanding of the past in its own right (in distinction from any modern appropriation of the message of the past) that is often overlooked.[70] Hans Jonas' *Gnosis und spätantiker Geist* (and its more popular English form *The Gnostic Religion*), more unambiguous even than Barth's *Romans,* demonstrated this *ad oculos.*

Thus the flow of the traditional relation between subject and object, in which the subject interrogates the object, and, if he masters it, obtains from it his answer, has been significantly reversed. For it is now the object—which should henceforth be

[68] P. v of the 1st ed. and of the 8th reprinting of the 2nd German ed.

[69] *Augustin und das paulinische Freiheitsproblem. Ein philosophischer Beitrag zur Genesis der christlich-abendländischen Freiheitsidee, FRLANT* 44, new series 27, edited by Rudolf Bultmann (Göttingen: Vandenhoeck und Ruprecht, 1930), p. 6.

[70] This is the case with Krister Stendahl's penetrating discussion of "Contemporary Biblical Theology," *IDB,* I (1962), 418–432.

called the subject matter—that puts the subject in question. This
is true not simply at the formal level, in inquiring as to whether
he understands himself aright, i.e., is serious, but also at the
material level, in inquiring as to whether the text's answers il-
lumine him.

The first at the formal level is a more ontological, philosophical query, as to whether he is asking the right questions, irrespective of the way he is answering them. Bultmann's recourse to
Heidegger's existentialist analysis was an attempt to meet this
question. For Bultmann's objective was to penetrate beneath a
superficial theology of moralism to one that came to grips with
the problem of man's very being. " 'God's will is the requirement
of the good.' . . . This is not a genuinely religious concept of
God, but rather, as is always characteristic of naïve thinking, the
binding power of the good appears under the mythical conception of a God who demands and punishes, pardons and rewards.
This faith does not become religion simply in that special psychic
conditions—being shaken up or inspired—accompany it, but only
when it gains a new content. That is to say, when the person
who bows to the requirement of the good experiences thereby an
inner history in which he lays hold of a reality that is not that of
the ethical ideal, but rather a reality of life from which he feels
himself growing, to which he feels himself quite subjected, and
by which he feels himself carried; when the person who stands in
obedience to the good feels that he thereby experiences a fate
through which he is transformed; when experiences that lead him
through depths and heights, experiences that in religious language are called sin and grace, lead him—not to fulfilling the
ethical requirements, but rather to fulfilling his being. In religion
it is not a matter of doing, but rather of being, not of the intention directed to the goal of the good but rather of the experience
of passing away in the presence of God's reality and of being endowed by divine grace, of transformation, new creation to a being whose deed is not the fulfillment of a requirement but rather
the portrayal of his being."[71] It was Heidegger who provided

[71] "Ethische und mystische Religion im Urchristentum," *Christliche Welt*
(abbreviated *ChrW*), XXXIV (1920), 741. This quotation reveals clearly

Bultmann with structures ("existentials") for talking more adequately about man's being, his "existence." With this aid it would become possible to determine whether a "mythical conception" contains "religion" or not.

The second query at the material level is more ontic, theological, as to whether the interpreter decides to understand his being the way the text understands existence. This question as to how man understands his being, his very existence, is the "existential" question that theology helps preaching to pose.

Something of what is involved hermeneutically begins to emerge in Barth's debate with Adolf von Harnack in 1923.[72] To Harnack it is obvious that theology's task is to "establish the content of the gospel," i.e., "to get intellectual control of the object."[73] Barth replies that "the 'scholarliness' of theology consists in being bound to the recollection that its object was *first subject* and must again and again become subject."[74] What is emerging here is the recognition that God is not a phenomenon at the disposal of scientific investigation as are phenomena of the world. Barth hurls the category of revelation into opposition to that of scholarship as known in that day. All this seemed to Harnack no better than a pious platitude, to which he could only reply that scholarship's sole task is "the pure knowledge of its object."[75]

Yet it is precisely here that Barth was in fact moving decisively beyond Harnack, even though it would take a generation for his advance to be recognized fully and elevated to a new understanding of hermeneutic. For Barth first sensed the odd incongruity between the results of the rigid application of "method" in contemporary scholarship and the dimension of truth in which we actually live—an incongruity that has been raised to a basic issue

the positive influence of Wilhelm Herrmann in Bultmann's rejection of "religious moralism" in favor of "ethical religion." Cf. the summary of Herrmann's position in this regard in my introductory essay "For Theology and the Church" in Vol. I of the *Journal for Theology and the Church* (Tübingen: J. C. B. Mohr, 1964).

[72] "Ein Briefwechsel mit Adolf von Harnack," in Karl Barth, *Theologische Fragen und Antworten: Gesammelte Vorträge,* III (Zollikon: Evangelischer Verlag, 1957), 7–31.

[73] *Ibid.,* pp. 8, 14.

[74] *Ibid.,* p. 10.

[75] *Ibid.,* p. 31.

of philosophical hermeneutic only within the last few years. Barth states the issue as follows: "I think I am acquainted with 'thinking persons' in earlier and later centuries who as theologians went in ways completely different from those considered normal since the eighteenth century, and whose 'scholarliness' cannot be denied (if 'scholarship' means 'doing justice to the subject matter'!). When one appeals to the theology of Paul or Luther, you seem to be able to explain it only as a proud attempt at imitation. On my side of the 'chasm' separating us the situation looks this way: The material superiority of these and other earlier theologians, no matter how poorly they fit today's club standards, forces itself upon us so irresistibly that . . . we cannot regard ourselves as relieved of the duty to take their basic approach more seriously into consideration in terms of its possible validity than has been the case of late, in spite of all Pauline research and enthusiasm for Luther. This has nothing to do with repristination. Of course it is my private opinion that practicing the repristination of a classic theological train of thought regarded as 'theology' in the medieval period or during Protestant scholasticism would probably be more instructive than the chaotic business of our faculties today, for whom the concept of an authoritative *object* has become foreign and uncomfortable over against the pervasive normativeness of *method*. But I think I also know that the *same thing* cannot and should not return, and that we have to think *in* our time *for* our time. And my objective is not to remove from theological research the critical historical method of studying the Bible and history that has developed in the last centuries. Rather my objective is to identify the relevant place for it and the sharpening of the issue for theological research that it has effected."[76]

This is precisely the point of departure for the philosopher Hans-Georg Gadamer's *magnum opus* on "Truth and Method," whose critical analysis of wide segments of contemporary interpretation is represented by the following quotation: "What gives dignity to scholarly opinion is giving proofs, methodical verifi-

[76] *Ibid.,* pp. 19 f.

cation (and not doing justice to the subject matter in and of it-self). In the eyes of the Enlightenment lack of proofs does not leave room for other kinds of certainty, but rather implies that the opinion has no basis in the subject matter itself, i.e., is 'un-founded.' "[77] It is the task of the present introductory essay to trace this development from Barth's intuitive insights to the explicitly hermeneutical formulations of Gadamer.

At the time Barth wrote his *Romans* the incomprehension expressed in Harnack's response was all that could be expected. For here not only two generations, but two worlds, meet—or, more precisely, fail to meet, but rather bypass each other. Perhaps Barth senses this when he refuses to be determined by "the protest of the spirit of modern times (which must perhaps first learn to understand itself!)."[78]

In retrospect we can to some extent understand what Harnack did not, since the spirit of modern times is gradually becoming audible for what it really is. Perhaps Martin Heidegger has analyzed it in the way most relevant to the point at issue in his book *Der Satz vom Grund*.[79] Here he draws attention to the fact that the principle of sufficient cause, namely, that nothing is without a cause, was first clearly formulated in the Cartesian period and, consequently, was immediately identified with the idea that everything must give account of itself, state its cause, to the investigating subject to which it is answerable. Thus nature ceases to be for itself, but *is* only as that which gives account of itself to us, that which we put before us for our investigation, that which we objectify. The objective world, since it is defined by a science that understands reality as answerable to the inquiring subject, is a world seen from this viewpoint of the investigating subject, and hence is actually subjective, the subject's world view. This Cartesian subjectivism of the objectified world is responsible for the subject-object schema that gained ascendancy in the natural sciences and was then carried over to the humanities. This objec-

[77] *Wahrheit und Methode. Grundzüge einer philosophischen Hermeneutik*, 1960, p. 255.
[78] *Theologische Fragen und Antworten*, p. 19.
[79] Pfullingen: Neske Verlag, 1957; 2nd ed., 1958.

tifying approach is all Harnack could conceive of science as being, so that theology as a science necessarily consisted in gaining intellectual mastery over its object of inquiry.

Only if we can relativize and to this extent transcend this Cartesian mentality can we even conceive of a scholarly relation to reality that would not consist in our pinning objects down, but that would instead consist in beings calling up their being to us, so that the scholar's role would be to answer responsibly with his own words this tolling of the being of beings as it comes to him. Yet this emerging insight into the nature of the Cartesian epoch, which is itself potentially the transcending of that epoch, is of quite recent date, at least in the form here under consideration, so that we must return to what was the immediate outcome of Barth's *Romans*. It suffices at this stage to call attention to the clearly audible way in which the supposed objectivity of Harnack's critical historical method reveals what Heidegger was subsequently to identify as the subjectivism of the Cartesian epoch, whereas Barth was gropingly speaking in terms of a post-Cartesian world.

It is not surprising that the New Testament scholars of Harnack's generation did not understand what had happened in Barth's *Romans*. Their reviews associated Barth's failures in mastering critical historical detail with his achievement in letting the subject matter of the text put us in question, to conclude that his commentary is merely practical and edifying, i.e., of no further interest to scholarship.[80] The failure of such reviews to see what was going on was the direct result of the hermeneutical vacuum at that time, as was further documented by the dismal debate about "pneumatic exegesis" in the mid-twenties. Although set in motion by Karl Girgensohn's *Die Inspiration der heiligen Schrift*,[81] it took on proportions explainable only in terms of the hermeneutical embarrassment scholarly circles sensed in trying to

[80] Cf. the reviews by such leading New Testament scholars as Adolf Jülicher, "Ein moderner Paulus-Ausleger," *ChrW*, XXXIV (1920), 453–457, 466–469; *ThLZ*, XLVII (1922), 537–542; and Hans Windisch, *ThLZ*, XLV (1920), 200 f. Jülicher's first review was answered by Friedrich Gogarten, "Vom Heiligen Egoismus des Christen," *ChrW*, XXXIV (1920), 546–550, who introduces Kierkegaard's "subjectivity" into the debate.

[81] Dresden: C. L. Ungelenk, 1925; 2nd ed., 1926.

cope with Barth's *Romans*.[82] It is significant that it was Rudolf
Bultmann who called pneumatic exegesis terminologically "re-
pulsive" and materially "senseless," and said the sooner the discussion was terminated the better[83]—for it was Bultmann who
had something better to say. He had recognized the theological
validity of Barth's *fait accompli*—at least in its second edition—
and thereupon devoted himself to working out a hermeneutic in
terms of which such an outcome could be defended by purifying
and clarifying the method and thus making it available to scholarship as a whole.

The basic weakness of the first edition Bultmann identified as
residing in the incompleteness of Barth's translation of the subject matter of Pauline theology into our modern world, in that
Barth retained myth and dogma. "The artificiality of a Catholi-
cizing repristination of the ancient cult, as well as the orthodox
transfiguration of Pauline myth and ecclesiastical dogma, are
condemned from the outset. This applies also to the fanatical renewal of the Pauline myth in Barthian polish. As much as I wel-
come the religious criticism of culture in Barth's *Romans*, I cannot see, in what he presents positively, anything other than an
arbitrary adaptation of the Pauline myth of Christ. The judg-

---

[82] E.g., Ph. Bachmann, "Der Römerbrief verdeutscht und vergegenwär-
tigt," *Neue Kirchliche Zeitschrift*, XXXII (1921), 518, referred to Barth's
"pneumatic-prophetic exegesis." For the debate on pneumatic exegesis cf.
O. Procksch, "Über pneumatische Exegese," in Girgensohn's periodical *Christentum und Wissenschaft*, I (1925), 145 ff.; Johannes Behm, *Pneumatische
Exegese?* (Schwerin: Fr. Bahn, 1926); the lectures of 1926 by Heinrich
Frick, *Wissenschaftliches und pneumatisches Verständnis der Bibel* (*Samm-
lung gemeinverständlicher Vorträge und Schriften aus dem Gebiet der The-
ologie und Religionsgeschichte*, 124 [Tübingen: J. C. B. Mohr, 1927]), and
by Ernst von Dobschütz, "Die Pneumatische Exegese: Wissenschaft und
Praxis," *Vom Auslegen des Neuen Testaments*, pp. 49–64; R. Seeberg, "Zur
Frage nach dem Sinn und Recht einer pneumatischen Schriftauslegung,"
Zeitschrift für systematische Theologie, III (1926), 3–59; E. Seeberg, "Zum
Problem der pneumatischen Exegese," *Beiträge zur Religionsgeschichte und
Archäologie Palästinas, Festschrift* for Sellin (Leipzig: A. Deichert, 1927),
pp. 127–137; W. Macholz, "Pneumatische Exegese," *Pastoralblätter*, LXX
(1927), 705–724; Fr. Traub, "Wort Gottes und pneumatische Schriftauslegung," *Zeitschrift für Theologie und Kirche* (abbreviated *ZThK*), new series
VIII (1927), 83–111; Fr. Torm, *Hermeneutik des Neuen Testaments*, 1930,
pp. 17 ff.; Erich Fascher, *Vom Verstehen des Neuen Testaments*, 1930, pp.
25–30.

[83] *Glauben und Verstehen*, I, 127 f.

ment that Barth passes upon 'liberal theology' strikes Barth himself to the same extent."[84]

The second edition seemed to Bultmann to have overcome this
major limitation to an extent that made it possible to systematize
its position in terms of a philosophy of religion, or what Barth
would call a normative statement of the nature of faith. "Although in the original form of a commentary, it falls in line with
works such as Schleiermacher's *Speeches on Religion* and Otto's
Idea of the Holy, with modern attempts to work out a religious
a priori, and finally with Romans itself, whose radical antithesis
between works and faith is really attempting to do the same
thing. No matter how different these may be in details, all of
them are attempts to express in language the awareness of the
distinctiveness and absoluteness of religion."[85]

Yet even here Bultmann criticized Barth's unwillingness to concede that Paul himself at times gave inadequate expression to this
normative subject matter. "The 'measuring by the subject matter'
of 'all words and groups of words' contained in the source to be
explained, rightly insisted upon by Barth in the Preface, cannot
take place without criticism, if it is meant seriously. . . . It is
the consistent implementation of the principle, recognized as correct, that the text is to be understood from the subject matter. In
terms of the subject matter one must then in fact *measure* to
what extent in all words and statements of the text the subject
matter has really achieved adequate expression. For what else
could 'measuring' mean? . . . The subject matter is greater than
the interpreting word. . . . When in exegeting Romans I identify tensions and contradictions, heights and depths, when I exert
myself to show where Paul is dependent upon Jewish theology
or upon common Christianity, Hellenistic enlightenment, or Hellenistic sacramentalism, I am not merely carrying on historical

---

[84] "Ethische und mystische Religion im Urchristentum," *ChrW,* XXXIV
(1920), 740.

[85] "Karl Barths 'Römerbrief' in zweiter Auflage," *ChrW,* XXXVI (1922),
320–323, 330–334, 358–361, 369–373, esp. 320. It is because of this that
Jülicher opened his negative review of the 2nd ed. with a slap at an un-
named "well-wishing reviewer," his junior colleague at Marburg, Rudolf Bultmann. *ThLZ,* XLVII (1922), 538.

philological criticism (at least if I do not conceive mechanically my task as exegete). Rather I do it to show where and how the subject matter comes to expression, in order that I may lay hold of the subject matter itself, which is greater even than Paul. And I am of the opinion that such criticism can only aid the clarity of the subject matter. For the more strongly I sense that with *this* subject matter it is a question of uttering the unutterable (and Barth knows this quite well), the more clearly I also sense and as exegete point out the relativity of the word. And it is a matter not only of the relativity of the word, but also of the fact that no man—not even Paul—can always speak only from the subject matter. Other spirits also come to expression through him than the Spirit of Christ. Hence criticism can never be radical enough."[86] Here Bultmann is calling for what became known as *Sachkritik,* criticism in terms of the subject matter, "content-criticism."

Barth's reply to this criticism actually bypasses the point, for he treats it only as a recognition of the inadequacy of language, which he is willing enough to concede.[87] What he was not willing to face squarely is the question as to whether in given places the point Paul makes—not just the language he uses—is inadequate to the subject matter basic to Paul himself. Hence Bultmann presses the issue again in his discussion of Barth's commentary on 1 Corinthians.[88] Yet here again *Sachkritik* is at times formulated

[86] *ChrW,* XXXVI (1922), 372 f. Cf. already Jülicher, *ChrW,* XXXIV (1920), 466, 468, and the arguments of Friedrich Traub, "Wort Gottes und pneumatische Schriftauslegung," *ZThK, n.F.,* VIII (1927), 88 ff., and Erich Fascher, *Vom Verstehen des Neuen Testaments,* 1930, pp. 36–40.

[87] "What is expressed in words in Romans are simply the 'others,' the Jewish, common Christian, Hellenistic, and other 'spirits' he [sc. Bultmann] cites. Or on what place can one lay one's finger with the claim that precisely *there* the *pneuma Christou* comes to expression in words? Or, put the other way around: Is the Spirit of Christ, e.g., a spirit that can be conceived of as competing *along side of other* spirits? . . . Everything is *litera,* voice of the 'other' spirits. Whether and to what extent everything can also be understood in connection with the 'subject matter,' as voice of the *spiritus* (*Christi*), that is the question with which the *litera* must be studied." Preface to the 3rd ed., p. xix of the 8th reprinting of the 2nd ed.

[88] *Die Auferstehung der Toten: Eine akademische Vorlesung über 1. Kor. 15* (Munich: Christian Kaiser Verlag, 1924). English translation by H. J. Stenning, *The Resurrection of the Dead* (New York: Fleming H. Revell Co., 1933). Cf. Bultmann's review article, *Glauben und Verstehen* I, 38–64.

by Bultmann as a criticism of the language employed, just as his original criticism of the first edition of the *Romans* was directed at the use of myth and dogma, as if these were by their very nature a language unsuited to faith. And indeed the problems of inadequately making the point and of inadequate language are interrelated, in that objectifying language inappropriate to the subject matter can lead away from that subject matter by focusing attention on the inconsistent element in the language as if it were precisely that foreign ingredient that is intended. Thus the concern for language emerges in the hermeneutical discussion primarily in the context of *Sachkritik,* where language is envisaged as an objectification inappropriate to the subject matter, a source of distortion rather than an aid in understanding.[89]

This defective aspect of language is most prominent in the case of mythological language. For here the objectification can easily be meant literally, so that the language itself speaks and drowns out the understanding of existence coming to expression in it. "It seems to me just as certain that in 1 Cor. 15 Paul is talking of such history of final things (*Schlussgeschichte*) as that in truth he cannot and does not wish to speak of such a history. That is to say, one cannot get by in 1 Cor. 15 without thoroughgoing *Sachkritik* (not only occasionally, as Barth does in verse 29 in spite of himself). For however little Paul proclaims such a thing as a 'Weltanschauung,' there still is for him, as for any one else, the necessity to say what he says in the terminology of his *Weltanschauung.* And it is not permissible simply to regard the ideological (in this case mythological) elements as 'parable' or to eliminate them by twisting their meaning. What Barth concedes for later Christian eschatologists—that they construct of the Biblical material a history of final things (*Schlussgeschichte*) that is in truth not at all historic in an ultimate sense (*endgeschichtlich*)—is true for Paul too, who derives his material from

[89] " 'God remains always subject in the relationship that is created by this witness. He does not transform himself into the object, man's possession, man's being in the right, man's having the last word' (*Die Auferstehung der Toten,* p. 4)—correct! But in our talking, to the extent we must undertake it (e.g., in affirming the 'from God' of 1 Cor.), God is object." *Glauben und Verstehen,* I, 41. Cf. also the allusions to "uttering the unutterable" and "the relativity of the word," *ChrW,* XXXVI (1922), 373, cited above.

Jewish or Jewish-gnostic apocalypticism."[90] Thus the language comes to say nothing about the subject matter, human existence, and ceases to be relevant, "serious." "In that the myth is narrated, nothing is said about my existence, about the reality in which alone I could hear God. For how should I know about all the things the myth is talking about (archons, the camouflage of the divine being, the deception of the demons, etc.)?"[91]

Thus one can detect two kinds of *Sachkritik* intertwined in Bultmann's position, one in which the subject matter coming to expression in the language is criticized as inconsistent with the subject matter dominant in the text, and the other in which the use of mythological language as such is criticized as an objectification, in which worldly categories are simply elongated to express what actually is wholly unworldly. Such objectified language is even prone to have its own say at the objectified level and thus to spin itself out without any existential meaning behind it.

It is interesting that even after the emergence of the program of demythologizing the inadequacy of mythological language can continue to be treated in the context of *Sachkritik*. "But from the fact that theological statements are by nature the explication of believing comprehension it also follows that *these statements may be only relatively appropriate, some more so, others less so*. The possibility exists that in some of them the believing comprehension may not be clearly developed, that it may be hindered— bound perhaps by a pre-faith understanding of God, the world, and man and by a corresponding terminology—and consequently may speak of God's dealing and of the relation between God and man in juristic terms, for instance. Or it may speak of God's relation to the world in mythological or cosmological terms which are inappropriate to faith's understanding of God's transcendence. Or the consequence may be that it expresses God's transcendence in the terminology of mysticism or of idealistic thinking. From this possibility arises the task—even in the case of the New Testament writings—of *content-criticism* (*Sachkritik*) such as Luther, for example, exercised toward the Épistle of James

---

[90] *Glauben und Verstehen,* I, 52.
[91] *Ibid.,* I, 43.

and the Revelation of John."[92] Here the basic inadequacy of objectifying mythological language to its own nonobjective subject matter is cited in the midst of a list of situations calling for *Sachkritik*.

It is this second ingredient originally included within *Sachkritik,* the criticism of the dangerous inadequacy of mythological and dogmatic language, that has now been largely lifted out of the broader context of *Sachkritik* and developed into the hermeneutic distinctive of Bultmannianism: demythologization, or, put positively, existentialist interpretation. The obscuring of the interrelation between *Sachkritik* and demythologizing is doubtless due in part to the apologetic necessity to distinguish liberalism's "elimination" of the incredible from demythologizing as a "decoding" of the myth's meaning. Yet demythologizing does "eliminate" the inadequate mythical conceptualization for the sake of stating more adequately the myth's meaning, and, if the objectifying conceptualization has been spun out into speculative *theologoumena* without existential meaning, such meaningless arabesques are to be "eliminated."

It is the contribution of Hans Jonas, the student of Heidegger and Bultmann, to have opened the way to this development. Bultmann wrote a revealing Preface to Volume I of *Gnosis und spätantiker Geist,* which is omitted from the published bibliographies of Bultmann's works and hence is easily bypassed, in which the indebtedness to Jonas is explicit. "I would like to say that I, who for years have devoted a large part of my work to the study of gnosticism, have learned from none of the previous studies in this area—and one knows that there are very excellent ones—so much toward a real grasp of gnosticism as a phenomenon in the history of ideas as from this work. Indeed it was here that the significance of this phenomenon was first made clear to me in its full dimension. . . . The method of the author, of laying hold of the real meaning of a historical phenomenon by means of the principle of the analysis of existence, seems to me to have proven brilliantly its fruitfulness. I am certain that this

[92] *Theology of the New Testament,* translated by Kendrick Grobel (New York: Charles Scribner's Sons), II (1955), 238.

work will fructify research in the history of ideas in many regards, and not least also the interpretation of the New Testament."[93]

Jonas' analysis of the dogmatic controversy between Augustine and Pelagius was directed to "analyzing which things this struggle is basically concerned with, and how these basic phenomena get along in this struggle, in the grip of the concepts and formulae needed in argument; what becomes of the phenomena in the expressedness of a given rational structure; what of their own subject matter was misunderstood and covered over by the debaters themselves and missed in the 'logical' exposition; finally, how the truth does not reside in a position, but rather is to be reconstructed out of it in a distinctive hermeneutical correction."[94]

Thus Jonas brought to focus a recognition that had been emerging already among historians of the *religionsgeschichtliche Schule,* to the effect that myths bear meaning that lies behind the uncongenial language, from which that meaning must be freed by a procedure of reconstruction. In the same year in which Bultmann was publishing this work of his pupil Jonas in a monograph series of which he was editor, he republished in the same series an older work by Hermann Gunkel in which that insight is clearly enunciated: "It will frequently be shown in what follows that New Testament material is reminiscent of *myths* and the *mythical.* But a word of warning is in place lest without further ado one connect with these words the negative connotation of the pagan, the wildly fantastic, the confused. The mythical emerges everywhere that a naïve spirit regards the divine in a living way

[handwritten: Explanation of what is meant by "myth" and "mythical."]

[93] *Gnosis und spätantiker Geist,* I, vii. In his original essay on demythologizing, "Neues Testament und Mythologie," *Kerygma und Mythos; Ein theologisches Gespräch, Theologische Forschung* 1 (Hamburg: Reich und Heidrich Evangelischer Verlag, 1948), Bultmann (p. 25) refers the reader seeking to understand "the critical interpretation of myth" to "the important explanations about the hermeneutical structure of dogma in Hans Jonas, *Augustin und das paulinische Freiheitsproblem,* pp. 66–76"; and, as a model of demythologizing, he refers (p. 28) to Jonas' *Gnosis und spätantiker Geist* I. Here as elsewhere the English translation by Reginald H. Fuller, *Kerygma and Myth: A Theological Debate* (London: S.P.C.K., 1953; Torchbook ed., New York and Evanston: Harper & Row, 1961, pp. 12, 16), has been so free as to omit completely part of the text.

[94] *Augustin und das paulinische Freiheitsproblem,* 1930, p. 6.

and paints it to himself in his fantasy. Hence in itself the myth-ical is in no sense a perversion, but rather a necessary phase of religious thought. Even the *most precious treasures of religion* can conceal themselves in mythical form. Hence we should guard against throwing away the mythical unexamined, before we have carefully released its precious kernel from the foreign husk."[95]

For Jonas it is not simply the problem of myth, but rather the problem of language as such, or, more precisely, a problem in-herent in the human spirit, whose nature it is to symbolize[96] meaning in objective formulae that lead away from the very meaning they intend to convey. And it is precisely in this context, in describing the turn away from the language back to that meaning, that the term demythologizing is first attested, in de-scribing the consciousness that seeks the path back from the sym-bolic language to the existential meaning it was intended to con-vey. "All this derives from an unavoidable fundamental structure of the spirit as such. That it interprets itself in objective formulae and symbols, that it is 'symbolistic,' is the innermost nature of the spirit—and at the same time most dangerous! In order to come to itself, it necessarily takes this detour via the symbol, in whose enticing jungle of problems it tends to lose itself, far from the origin preserved symbolically in it, taking the substitute as ulti-mate. Only in a long procedure of working back, after an ex-hausting completion of that detour, is a demythologized (*ent-mythologisiert*) consciousness able terminologically to approach directly the orignal phenomena hidden in this camouflage (cf. the long path of the dogma of original sin up to Kierkegaard!)."[97]

[95] Hermann Gunkel, *Zum religionsgeschichtlichen Verständnis des Neuen Testaments,* 3rd ed., 1930, pp. 14 f. This booklet is Heft 1 of the series originally edited by Bousset and Gunkel entitled *Forschungen zur Religion und Literatur des Alten und Neuen Testaments.* It first appeared in 1903 (and the same year in English in the *Monist,* Chicago: Open Court Publish-ing Co., No. 3, pp. 398 ff.). When the 3rd ed. appeared Bultmann was editor of the series, and its republication coincided with the publication the same year of Hans Jonas' work *Augustin und das paulinische Freiheitsproblem* as Heft 44 of the same series.

[96] The understanding of language is in the context of Ernst Cassirer's *Philosophie der symbolischen Formen* (Oxford: Bruno Cassirer, 2nd ed., 1923; reprinted 1956 by the Wissenschaftliche Buchgesellschaft, Darmstadt).

[97] *Augustin und das paulinische Freiheitsproblem,* 1930, p. 67. The history of the term demythologizing may be traced further in Hans Jonas' *Gnosis*

Thus Bultmann's program of demythologizing is embedded in a specific view of language as the objectification of understanding, an objectification that is itself contrary to the understanding seeking expression in it:

"The real intention of myth is not to provide an objective world view. Rather in it is expressed the way man understands himself in his world. Myth is not intended to be interpreted cosmologically, but rather anthropologically, or, better still, existentialistically. Myth speaks of the power or powers that man thinks he experiences as ground and limit of his world, of his own action, and of what happens to him. To be sure it speaks of these powers in such a way that it incorporates them conceptually into the sphere of the known world, of its things and forces, and into the sphere of human life, of its emotions, motives, and possibilities. For example, it speaks of a world egg or world tree, to provide a picture of the basis and origin of the world. Or it speaks of battles of the gods, from which the conditions and principles of the known world emerged. It speaks of the unworldly in a worldly way, of the gods in a human way.

Bultmann on the meaning of "myth" [handwritten marginalia]

---

und spätantiker Geist, II, 1, which, though published only in 1954, had already been printed in 1934 in its relevant parts and hence was known to Bultmann, editor of the series, if not to the public at large. Here Jonas says (pp. 3 f.): "In the metaphysical emanation and deprivation schema we find gnostic myth in depersonalized (*entpersonalisiert*), logicized form, i.e., in a sense indeed demythed (*entmythisiert*), and yet, because of its nature as hypostasized, still mythical. We will run across these mythological, philosophical mediating forms in the *metaphysics* of Origen and Plotinus. But we first turn to an anthropological, ethical sphere of concepts, in which we would not in principle expect such mythographic analogies, and in which we too are primarily concerned with something else: to show how the assumed existential basic principle, the 'gnostic' principle, if it really is capable of separation from the mythological world of symbol and of treatment as a more general *arche,* is here in a quite distinctive way drawn back out of the outward mythical objectification and transposed into inner concepts of *Dasein* and into ethical practice, i.e., it appears as it were 'resubjectivized'—just as on the other hand also in this sphere the mythical element is not really overcome. Rather even in 'immanence' (i.e., even without mythological transcendence) the concepts of *Dasein,* with regard to their ontological structure, remain in a very broad sense 'mythical'—because of their pervasive origin in a basic *objectification.*" One may see here a groping toward the concept and term *Entmythologisierung,* especially in the aspect of the steps toward demythologizing taken within the sources themselves, to which Bultmann calls attention in *Kerygma und Mythos* I, 24, 31 ff. (*Kerygma and Myth,* Torchbook ed., pp. 12, 20 ff.).

"In myth there is expressed the faith that the known and controllable world in which man lives does not have its ground and goal in itself. Rather its ground and its limit lie outside the known and controllable. This known and controllable sphere is constantly interpenetrated and threatened by the weird powers that are its ground and limit. And, along with this, myth expresses the knowledge that man is not master of himself, that he is not only dependent within the known world, but that before all he is dependent on the powers ruling beyond the known, and that in this dependency he can become free from just these very known powers.

"Hence in the myth itself there is contained the motive for criticizing itself, i.e., for criticizing its objectifying conceptualizations, to the extent that its own intention of speaking of a power beyond to which the world and man are subjected is restricted and obscured by the objectifying nature of its statements."[98]

The characteristic flow of Bultmannian hermeneutic is thus away from language—of which mythological language serves as model—back to the understanding prior to, and more authentic than, the language. It is at this point that Ebeling seeks to supplement Bultmann's hermeneutic with a more positive correlation of language and hermeneutic.[99]

The emergence of the term understanding was not—any more than that of *hermēneia* and *hermeneutics* before it—an irrelevant terminological fluctuation. Rather, like them, it stated the par-

---

[98] Cf. *Kerygma und Mythos*, p. 23; *Kerygma and Myth*, Torchbook ed., pp. 10 f. Translation is from the German original. A complete survey of the demythologizing debate has been provided by Günther Bornkamm, "Die Theologie Rudolf Bultmanns in der neueren Diskussion. Zum Problem der Entmythologisierung und Hermeneutik," *ThR*, n.F., XXIX (1963), 33–141 (the full bibliography pp. 33–46 is by Egon Brandenburger). The omission here of such an analysis should not imply that the demythologizing issue is past (which would in fact suggest it might well be bypassed), but rather that it was the vanguard of a movement that has emerged in the new hermeneutic. "In fact in Rudolf Bultmann's own view the issue and concept of demythologizing is relatively speaking confined to the surface of the matter. It is not new, and calling attention to it is really a *testimonium paupertatis*. For it has necessarily been always taking place in various ways, although usually without adequate hermeneutical reflection. According to Rudolf Bultmann it has its real theological meaning only within the context of comprehensive hermeneutical reflection" (*ibid.*, p. 125).

[99] Cf. below, p. 84.

ticular hearing of the subject matter characteristic of its day. Its implication of getting behind the words to the existence objectifying itself in them calls to attention both the depth and the limitation characteristic of this first step toward a new hermeneutic.[100] The reintroduction of the term *Hermeneutik* in our day presumably calls up a different scope, which, while not "hermeneutics," is not simply "understanding" either;[101] it is this scope that the following pages seek to make audible in the term hermeneutic.

IV. HERMENEUTIC

It is a central recognition of the new hermeneutic that language itself says what is invisibly taking place in the life of a culture. An instance of this would be the sudden re-emergence of the term *Hermeneutik* within post-Bultmannian German theology. If the last textbook in hermeneutics, the German translation of Torm's *Nytestamentlig Hermeneutik,* had appeared in 1930, it was indicative of something when in 1954 another New Testament scholar, Ernst Fuchs, published a volume entitled *Hermeneutik.*[102] Then in 1959 the term suddenly appeared on all sides. The third edition of the standard German theological encyclopedia, *Die Religion in Geschichte und Gegenwart,* published an article on *Hermeneutik* by Gerhard Ebeling,[103] an entry missing from the first two editions. In the same year Ernst Fuchs published a volume of collected essays under the title *Zum hermeneu-*

[handwritten margin note: The Sudden growth of Hermaneutic]

---

[100] Hans-Georg Gadamer, "Verstehen," *RGG,* 3rd ed., VI (1962), 1381 f., distinguishes between understanding the subject matter coming to expression in language and understanding the psychic, inner element in an expression. When he then refers the reader for the former to the article on "Hermeneutik" and treats only the latter in his article on "Understanding," he has by implication carried through a systematic distinction confirming the historical distinction made in the present paper.

[101] Indicative of the fact that "understanding" has not continued to be a reliable hallmark of the *avant garde* discussion is Martin Magnusson, *Der Begriff "Verstehen" in exegetischem Zusammenhang unter besonderer Berücksichtigung der paulinischen Schriften,* I. *Allgemeine Probleme des exegetischen Verständnisses* (Lund: CWK Gleerup, *Studia theologica lundensia* 8, 1954).

[102] *Hermeneutik* (Bad Cannstatt: R. Müllerschön, 1954; 2nd ed., 1958 with *Ergänzungsheft*).

[103] *RGG,* 3rd ed., II (1959), 242–262.

tischen Problem in der Theologie; Die existentiale Interpreta-tion.[104] In 1962 the University of Zürich created an *Institut für Hermeneutik* under the directorship of Gerhard Ebeling, and in 1963 a similar institute was founded at the University of Marburg directed by Ernst Fuchs. Together with their close friend Man-fred Mezger, Professor of Homiletics at Mainz, they have also founded a monograph series entitled *Hermeneutische Untersuch-ungen zur Theologie.*[105]

These developments were counterbalanced by a new promi-nence of the term from the other side of Continental theology. The Dutch theologian Kornelis Heiko Miskotte published in 1959, in the series *Theologische Studien* edited by Karl Barth, four radio speeches on *Biblische Hermeneutik.*[106] Then a pupil of Her-mann Diem in Tübingen, Lothar Steiger, wrote in 1960 a dis-sertation *Die Hermeneutik als dogmatisches Problem.*[107] This was followed in 1961 by a volume from the Professor of Practical Theology at the University of Erlangen, Kurt Frör, entitled *Bib-lische Hermeneutik.*[108] Yet in spite of such works retaining more continuity with traditional hermeneutics, the term *Hermeneutik* has clearly received a new overtone oriented to the position of Fuchs and Ebeling. As such it has come to serve as a label for their position, and has been countered by a call to return to the more customary practice of the historian's trade. Thus Oscar Cullmann calls for objectivity in the sense of an exegesis without presuppositions:

"I myself am a theologian. But I present my lectures in Paris

[104] Tübingen: J. C. B. Mohr, 1959.
[105] Vol. I (1962) is Gerhard Ebeling's essays entitled *Theologie und Ver-kündigung; Ein Gespräch mit Rudolf Bultmann;* Vol. II (1962) is Eberhard Jüngel's dissertation *Paulus und Jesus; Eine Untersuchung zur Präzisierung der Frage nach dem Ursprung der Christologie.* The series is published in Tübingen by J. C. B. Mohr.
[106] *Zur biblischen Hermeneutik, Theologische Studien,* 55 (Zollikon: Evan-gelischer Verlag, 1959). The radio speeches were given in 1957.
[107] *Die Hermeneutik als dogmatisches Problem; Eine Auseinandersetzung mit dem tranzendentalen Ansatz des theologischen Verstehens* (Gerd Mohn: Gütersloher Verlagshaus, 1961).
[108] *Biblische Hermeneutik; Zur Schriftauslegung in Predigt und Unter-richt* (Munich: Chr. Kaiser Verlag, 1961). Cf. Eduard Schweizer's review in the *Neue Zürcher Zeitung,* July 17, 1963 (III, Abendausgabe, Nr. 2810, pp. 1–2).

at the Ecole des Hautes-Etudes and at the Sorbonne—where I hold a strictly neutral 'comparative religions' chair for the New Testament branch of science under the secular designation 'Histoire des origines du Christianisme'—no differently than in Basel, where I belong to the Theological Faculty. This is possible for me since I regard the non-violation of the limits imposed on the New Testament scholar in studying New Testament texts as precisely a *theological* duty applicable to all, not only to the scholars: first, before all evaluation, all judging, perhaps even prior to all 'being addressed' in my 'understanding of existence,' prior to all believing, simply to be obedient to what the men of the new covenant want to communicate to me as revelation, even if it is quite foreign to me. I am aware that I thereby stand in contradiction to a 'hermeneutical' trend widely prevalent today. Whether listening with understanding is possible at all without faith and whether it cannot precisely in this way lead to faith, is to be worked out in my next book frequently anticipated here."[109]

[109] "Retrospect upon the Effect of the Book in Post-War Theology," written in the summer of 1962 in the place of a new Preface to the 3rd ed. of *Christus und die Zeit* (Zürich: EVZ-Verlag, 1962), pp. 25 f. One may compare the argument of S. Maclean Gilmour, in his article "Jesus Christ" in the revised edition of Hastings' *Dictionary of the Bible,* edited by F. C. Grant and H. H. Rowley (New York: Charles Scribner's Sons, 1963), p. 494, that "a careful distinction must be drawn between the functions of 'historical' and of 'theological' exegesis." The former involves "the rigid exclusion of the interpreter's personal, apologetic, or polemical interests," whereas the latter runs the danger that "occasionally the theologian reinterprets and recasts his source material so as to force it into the service of the theological or philosophical position he represents." The assumption that the historian can hold off his historicness until he is ready to shift consciously into the category of theologian is naïve, and avoids rather than meeting the thrust of Bultmann's question, "Is Exegesis without Presuppositions Possible?" (*Existence and Faith, Shorter Writings of Rudolf Bultmann,* translated by Schubert M. Ogden [New York: Meridian Books, Inc., 1960], 289–296.) The discussion of hermeneutic has come to the center of the Bultmannian movement precisely because these scholars know they must face this issue squarely. Cf. my review article of Gilmour's essay in the *Andover Newton Quarterly,* n.s. III (1963), 37–39. Cf. also Krister Stendahl's comment in his essay on "Contemporary Biblical Theology," *IB,* I, 421: "It is not quite clear how Cullmann understands the relation between such a descriptive Biblical theology in its first- and second-century terms and its translation into our present age; his hermeneutical discussions have nothing of the radical penetration of Bultmann's . . . Cullmann (and Stauffer) have not clarified their answer to why or how they consider the NT as meaningful

The extent to which such a statement does not meet the Bultmannian position can be seen by comparing it with the following methodological statement by Bultmann himself. "The theological investigator obviously cannot presuppose his own faith as an epistemological instrument and make use of it as a presupposition for methodical work. What he can and should do is keep himself ready, open, free. Or, better, keep himself questioning—or knowing the questionability of—all human self-understanding, in the knowledge that existential understanding of one's self (in distinction from existentialist interpretation of man's being) is real only in the act of existing and not in the isolated reflection of thought."[110]

Somewhat sharper is the reservation about the new hermeneutic expressed by Ernst Käsemann from within the Bultmannian school itself (if that term has not already become an anachronism). "Not everyone can do everything, and in the present high tide of 'interpretation' some must devote themselves to administering the estate left by the historians, if for no other reason than to disturb the interpreters. . . . This state of affairs awakens the suspicion that *sub rosa* historiography and interpretation are exchanging the roles appropriate to them, in that interpretation no longer serves historiography in need of clarification, but rather turns it into a quarry for its buildings arbitrarily erected for contemporaries in need of a roof. Ultimate hermeneutical problems emerge here, as already the discussion between Ebeling, Fuchs, and myself proves. It seems to be, e.g., a quite inappropriate category taken over invalidly from traditional natural science into the realm of history, when one speaks of the occurrences of the past as objectively at hand and under our control. That can be asserted just as well and just as poorly about things in the present. The mistakes of historians and interpreters and the misunderstanding of the neighbor belong very much together, are not in

*Ernst
Käsemann*

for the present age. Because of this lack of clarification, their works are read by many—perhaps most—readers as being on the same level of present meaning as Bultmann's or Barth's highly 'translated' interpretations; and there are indications that they do not mind such a use of their works."

[110] *Theology of the New Testament,* translated by Kendrick Grobel, II, 241.

the least merely the result of stupidity, and indeed prove that one is victim of a short circuit when one makes what is foreign in a contemporary or past history into something objective in the sense of being subject to our control. I regard the confusion of understanding and decision as no less dangerous. The assumed compulsion of having always to take a stand, rather than first hearing for once and waiting for what is given or taken by that which is foreign, is usually the death of understanding, the strangling of the real question, the missing of the chance to grow by learning. How many of our students still perceive that understanding is always a process of one's own growth, and hence requires time and leisure even to the extent of self-forgetfulness; that only unripe fruit is shaken from the tree of knowledge by him who does not himself ripen in the handwork of the historian's trade? The cardinal virtue of the historian and the beginning of all meaningful hermeneutic is for me the practise of hearing, which begins simply by letting what is historically foreign maintain its validity and does not regard rape as the basic form of *engagement*."[111] Thus the German theological debate of the sixties has become to a large extent a debate about *Hermeneutik*.[112]

The fate of the term *Hermeneutik* in our century—where "fate" means *fatum,* "what is spoken"—can be illustrated by the case of Martin Heidegger. He was first introduced to hermeneutics as a student at the Roman Catholic Theological Faculty of the University of Freiburg in Breisgau.[113] He took the term

[111] "Zum Thema der urchristlichen Apokalyptik," *ZThK,* LIX (1962; appeared Feb., 1963), 258 f.

[112] One may contrast with the admissions of hermeneutical lethargy from the turn of the century the recent comment by a nontheologian: "The contemporary discussion of the hermeneutical problem is certainly nowhere so vigorous as in the area of Protestant theology." Hans-Georg Gadamer, "Hermeneutik und Historismus," *PhR,* IX (1962), 256.

[113] "The title 'hermeneutics' was familiar to me from my study of theology. At that time I was especially tormented by the question as to the relation between the word of Holy Scripture and theological speculative thought. It was, if you will, the same relation, namely that between language and being, only concealed and unavailable to me, so that I sought in vain on many detours and blind alleys for a guiding thread. . . . Later I found this title *Hermeneutik* again in Wilhelm Dilthey in his theory of those humane sciences which are historiological in character. Dilthey was familiar with hermeneutics

hermeneutics up into his own philosophical vocabulary when he
began to write *Being and Time* in 1923, in seeking to distinguish
his phenomenology from that of Husserl.[114] For Heidegger, hermeneutic was the analysis of the existentiality of existence, i.e.,
of the "existentials" in terms of which existence is to be understood. By deriving ontologically the historicness of *Dasein,* his
hermeneutic provided a foundation for Dilthey's methodology of
the humanities. For if Dilthey had sought to establish a distinctively historic method for the humane sciences that was not borrowed from that of the natural sciences, such a "critique of historic reason" logically presupposed some such analysis of man's
historic being as that provided by Heidegger. Thus, just as Dilthey's concern for understanding had superseded hermeneutics,
in that the problem of understanding is prior to the rules of interpretation, Heidegger's hermeneutic opened up a possibility for
superseding Dilthey.[115]

Yet in the actual analysis of the existentials that followed, Heidegger came to see that "interpretation," which he correctly

---

from the *same* source, his study of theology, especially his study of Schleiermacher." *Unterwegs zur Sprache,* p. 96.

[114] *Ibid.,* p. 95. ". . . Hermeneutical phenomenology . . . the name was
intended to designate a new direction for phenomenology."

[115] "Our investigation itself will show that the meaning of phenomenological description as a method lies in *interpretation.* The *logos* of the phenomenology of *Dasein* has the character of a *hermēneuein,* through which the
authentic meaning of being, and also those basic structures of being which
Dasein itself possesses, are *made known* to *Dasein's* understanding of being.
The phenomenology of *Dasein* is a *hermeneutic* in the primordial significa-
tion of this word, where it designates this business of interpreting. But to the
extent that by uncovering the meaning of being and the basic structures of
Dasein in general we may exhibit the horizon for any further ontological
study of those entities which do not have the character of *Dasein,* this hermeneutic also becomes a 'hermeneutic' in the sense of working out the conditions on which the possibility of any ontological investigation depends. And
finally, to the extent that *Dasein,* as an entity with the possibility of existence,
has ontological priority over every other being, hermeneutic, as an interpretation of *Dasein's* being, has the third and specific sense of an analytic of
the existentiality of existence; and this is the sense which is philosophically
primary. Then so far as this hermeneutic works out *Dasein's* historicality ontologically as the ontical condition for the possibility of historiology, it contains the roots of what can be called 'hermeneutic' only in a derivative sense:
the methodology of those humane sciences which are historiological in character." *Being and Time,* translated by John Macquarrie and Edward Robinson, pp. 61 f.

recognized as the translation of *hermēneia* and thus presumably would equate with hermeneutic,[116] was itself grounded in "understanding," which was the "fundamental existential."[117] Thus his "existentialist interpretation" itself led back from the term hermeneutic to the term understanding. The task logically prior to Dilthey was redefined as that of getting to the basis of "understanding,"[118] and the term hermeneutic faded out of Heidegger's vocabulary.[119]

In the later Heidegger's writing the term hermeneutic re-emerges just long enough to indicate the sense in which it is now heard. Negatively, it does not mean a theory of interpretation, but rather the process of interpretation itself.[120] And it is decisive that interpretation has its focus not in terms of understanding existence, but rather in terms of language. Indeed the term hermeneutic is heard primarily in terms of the meaning of *hermēneia* as "speech." "The term 'hermeneutical' is derived from the Greek verb *hermēneuein*. This refers to the noun *hermēneus,* which can be associated with the name of the God *Hermes* in a game of thought that is more binding than the rigor of science. Hermes is the messenger of the gods. He brings the news of fate. *Hermēneuein* is that exposition that brings news, to the extent that the exposition is itself able to hear the message. Such exposition becomes interpretation of what has already been said by the poets, who themselves, according to the saying of Socrates in Plato's discourse Ion (534 E), 'are messengers (*hermēnēs*) of the gods.' . . . Socrates carries the connection even further in

---

116 *Ibid.,* p. 201.

117 *Ibid.,* p. 182.

118 *Ibid.,* p. 182. " 'Understanding' in the sense of *one* possible kind of cognizing among others (as distinguished, for instance, from 'explaining'), must, like explaining, be interpreted as an existentialist derivative of that primary understanding which is one of the constituents of being and of the 'there' in general."

119 *Unterwegs zur Sprache,* p. 98.

120 *Ibid.,* p. 120. This passage is in the context both of interpreting *Being and Time* and of defining the subsequent "turn" in Heidegger's thought. On the complex problem of the extent to which such subsequent interpretations of *Being and Time* are themselves representative of the position of the later Heidegger, cf. Vol. I of *New Frontiers in Theology,* entitled *The Later Heidegger and Theology* (New York and Evanston: Harper & Row, 1963), esp. pp. 48–56.

thinking of the rhapsodists as those who bring news of the word
of the poets. . . . From all this it becomes clear that the hermeneutical does not mean only the interpretation, but prior to that
already the bringing of the message and the news."[121] Here hermeneutic is primarily the speaking of meaning, and it is a subordinate remark that of course it is a speaking that has itself
understood what it has to say. This priority of proclamation is
the reason the hermeneutic of the later Heidegger is worked out
less under the topic "hermeneutic" than under the topic "language."[122]

Language here seems to have a separate existance from the man who uses it.

Language in the new hermeneutic is not viewed as an objectification behind which one must move in establishing the understanding of existence objectifying itself therein. It is indeed not
man at all who is ex-pressing himself in language. Rather it is
language itself that speaks.[123] It is in this sense that Helmut
Franz warns against the subjectivism involved in letting "not the
exegete as subject, but rather the author as subject dominate.
This subject stands somewhere in isolation and composes texts
with contents, truths, intentions. But such a subject is not seen as
moving and being moved in history."[124] He describes the hermeneutical orientation that avoids this unsuspected form of subjectivism as follows: "The basic thing about a text is not what
the author intended to express in words by following up a given
point of view. Rather, basic is what wills fundamentally to show
itself and have its say prior to or apart from any subjective intent.
The question to the text would then not be the question as to the
[author's] perspective, but rather: 'What shines forth in this
text? What shows itself in this text?' "[125]

[121] *Unterwegs zur Sprache,* pp. 121 f.

[122] The new hermeneutic of Heidegger is most explicit in the volume entitled *Unterwegs zur Sprache,* "On the Way to Language." The titles of the
lectures and essays brought together into this volume are also indicative of
the prominence of the term language in designating the new hermeneutic:
"Language"; "Language in the Poem"; "From a Discussion of Language";
"The Essence of Language"; "Word"; "The Path to Language."

[123] *Ibid.,* p. 20 and *passim.*

[124] "Das Wesen des Textes," *ZThK,* LIX (1962), 190.

[125] *Ibid.,* p. 204.

Such phraseology is not intended to eliminate man from the language process,[126] but merely to emphasize that the subject matter "addresses itself" to man's thought,[127] to which man answers with his words. "Primal thinking is the echo of being's favor, in which what is unique clears and lets it happen that beings are. This echo is the human answer to the word of the silent voice of being. Thought's answer is the origin of the human word, which word first lets language emerge as the enunciation of the word into words."[128]

The subject matter of which language speaks is primarily being. It is man's very nature to hearken to the call of being. "Man *is* actually this relation of cor-'respond'-ence, and only this."[129] In this way language is located at the center of man's nature, rather than being regarded primarily as an objectification of an otherwise authentic self-understanding. For man's nature is defined as linguistic, in that his role is to re-speak, to re-spond, to an-swer, the call of being. "Since flora and fauna are yoked to their respective surroundings, but never set free into the clearing of being—and only this clearing is 'world'—for that reason they lack language. Yet in this term 'surroundings' the whole puzzle of living creatures is compressed. Language in its essence is not the objectification of an organism, nor is it the expression of a living creature. Hence it can never be thought in a way that does justice to its nature by being thought of as a sign or even as a sig-

[126] Cf. the play on words with the German verb *brauchen,* which means both to use and to need. Language, the silent tolling of reality, uses man and indeed needs man's voice as its spokesman. *Ibid.,* pp. 20, 256, and *passim.* This play on words recurs in Ernst Fuchs, *Zur Frage nach dem historischen Jesus, Gesammelte Aufsatze* II, 427.

[127] *Identität und Differenz* (Pfullingen: Günther Neske Verlag, 1957), p. 13. The English translation by Kurt F. Leidecker, *Essays in Metaphysics: Identity and Difference* (New York: Philosophical Library, 1960), p. 13, is here as elsewhere inadequate.

[128] *Was ist Metaphysik?* (Frankfurt a.M.: Vittorio Klostermann, 8th ed., 1960), p. 49. Translation is from the original rather than being derived from the thoroughly confused English translation by R. F. C. Hull and Alan Crick in *Existence and Being,* Gateway Paperback Edition (Chicago: Henry Regnery Co., 1960), p. 358.

[129] *Identität und Differenz,* p. 22. Translation is from the German original rather than being derived from the English translation, *Essays in Metaphysics: Identity and Difference,* p. 21.

nification. Language is the arrival of being itself, both clearing and concealing."[130]

Heidegger's new understanding of language is thus derived from an understanding of man that is not oriented to existentialism but rather to "ontology,"[131] if this term is valid for the distinctively Heideggerian sense of the basic question as to why there are beings at all and not simply nothing—the question as to being. Man is where being's voice is heard and given room. Man is the loud-speaker for the silent tolling of being. When he fulfills this role, he is truly man. It is for this reason that Heidegger regards the poet as mankind's true priest. It is he who names the gods, who speaks forth the world of meaning that being addresses to him; it is he who calls mankind out of the forgetfulness of being into his true role as shepherd of being. It is because of this new understanding of man as being's spokesman that Heidegger's hermeneutic has moved from an interpretation of *Dasein* to an interpretation of poets such as Hölderlin. Indeed Heidegger has become fascinated with such pre-Hellenic heroes as Tantalus, Prometheus, and Sisyphus, who occur in Hellenic mythology as personages to be punished, "tantalized," for having revealed the secrets of the gods—figures whom Heidegger restores to their

---

[130] *Über den Humanismus* (Frankfurt a.M.: Vittorio Klostermann, n.d. [1949]), p. 16.

[131] It should be noted that Heidegger regards "ontology" as referring metaphysically to the science of beings, which obscures the question as to being and is hence to be repudiated. Cf. *Was ist Metaphysik?*, p. 19 (English translation by Walter Kaufmann, *Existentialism from Dostoevsky to Sartre* [New York: Meridian Books, Inc., 1956], p. 217); and the essay "Die onto-theo-logische Verfassung der Metaphysik," *Identität und Differenz*, pp. 35–73 (English translation, pp. 33–67). Hence it is ironic to see him criticized as an ontologist by those who learned from him to transcend traditional ontology. Cf. Carl Michalson's contrast between "Theology as Ontology and as History," *The Later Heidegger and Theology*, pp. 136–156, and Emil Staiger's criticism: "But it must be immediately added that Martin Heidegger does not himself interpret in this way [sc. of *Being and Time*]. He is not concerned to acknowledge that which is unique in a historical figure as unique, although he likes to make use of the ambiguous expression 'let be' for designating the correct encounter of *Dasein* with beings. Rather than ordering the wealth of purely grasped historic life with the aid of his temporal concepts [Staiger's method], he sees in every text—and this is something quite different—only a contribution to his problem of ontology." "Ein Rückblick," *Neue Zürcher Zeitung*, Sept. 27, 1959, Blatt 5, Nr. 2898 (69). In actuality Heidegger's concern with being is an effort to understand reality as historic and linguistic.

original position of honor as hermeneuts of the gods. Thus the primary orientation of *hermēneia* to the numinous messages of the gods emerges in the later Heidegger's hermeneutic, and the role of the new hermeneutic as a new orientation for theology is prefigured by his work.

It was Ernst Fuchs who first translated the hermeneutical discussion from the categories of inauthentic and authentic existence derived from *Being and Time* into the later Heidegger's analogous distinction between the everyday language of the subject-object dilemma and the uncorrupted language of being. From Heidegger Fuchs has learned that man's location in a given historical tradition means that he hears reality in terms of a certain "world," a context of meaning, that he simply takes over from his culture in its language. If "world" is thus experienced in language, and if the term existence suggests that "out there, as world, is to be decided what is to be worked out inside, in man, as *Dasein*,"[132] then the decision with regard to one's self-understanding takes place as a decision with regard to language. Thus language becomes constitutive of self-understanding, rather than merely its secondary objectification.

Helmut Franz clarifies this primacy of language in a commentary on Calvin's phrase "subest locutioni relatio," "relation is subordinate to language": "What precedes every relation and makes such a thing as relation first possible is '*locutio*.' It is not true that the relation, our being involved, is fulfilled and manifested in our being addressed. Rather the opening of an area of 'mutual understanding' as a language area is the primary thing that permits involvement and relations to occur."[133]

Although Fuchs has learned this inherent relation of language to existence in Heidegger primarily with regard to inauthentic existence, he also sees in it a potentiality for a positive theology. For he hears Heidegger's lament about inauthentic language as an indirect witness to true language, somewhat as the law is related to the gospel.[134] "For the lament as *language* no longer be-

---

[132] *Hermeneutik*, p. 67.
[133] "Das Wesen des Textes," *ZThK*, LIX (1962), 198.
[134] Cf. the definition of the relation of Heidegger to theology in terms of

longs to lostness, but rather supplies man with the plus that as the *essence* of language reminds him that he belongs to a communication, a . . . *nearness* to the power at work in language prior to all human participation. For it is not true that man has given birth to language. Rather man is born out of language. That man then has made language a means of usurped existence merely proves that man is accustomed to exist in daily life having missed the mark."[135]

The drag of the past upon man takes place primarily as the language he inherited predisposing him to inauthenticity, so that he is constantly walking in the rut it provides and thus falling into its trap. But this recognition that language is where the past becomes our future can also be stated positively. Indeed such inauthentic language is only the perversion of authentic language, and if authentic language is also part of our past, it can meet us as our future that holds open to us the dimension of our own authenticity into which we can enter. Fuchs finds authentic language in Jesus' language of love, and thus moves from Heidegger into a "christological understanding of language."[136] This is a somewhat different understanding of language from that of Heidegger himself, as detailed study of Heidegger would subsequently indicate,[137] and it is a different grasp of the nature of the new quest of the historical Jesus from that intended by its main proponent at that time, Ernst Käsemann.[138] Yet such observations should not distract attention from the point of major significance in the present context: Fuchs's own combination of these various ingredients emerged as a basically new step in the

---

law and gospel that has increasingly emerged in the school of Fuchs and Ebeling, summarized in *The Later Heidegger and Theology*, pp. 63–76.

[135] *Hermeneutik*, p. 63.

[136] *Ibid.*, p. 78. Cf. the criticism by Helmut Franz, *ZThK, Beiheft* 2, 1961, p. 89: "But is not Fuchs in danger, with this 'solution' of the problem, of dissolving also the inner tension that *maintains* itself in Jesus' language, and indeed that first becomes acute in the very fact that Jesus 'speaks.' "

[137] Cf. *The Later Heidegger and Theology*, p. 71.

[138] Cf. my essay "The Recent Debate on the 'New Quest,' " *The Journal of Bible and Religion*, XXX (1962), 201. Käsemann is currently preparing a critical analysis of the turn the new quest has taken.

development of hermeneutic, of which his *Hermeneutik* of 1954 is the first landmark.

When one opens Ernst Fuchs's *Hermeneutik,* aware that it is the first New Testament hermeneutic since Torm's *Hermeneutik des Neuen Testaments* a quarter of a century before, the contrast between the two works is so overpowering that one is inclined to conclude that they belong to completely different fields and only by mistake came to share the name *Hermeneutik.* Hence it is necessary to point out that there is some continuity between the two volumes, which at least makes it possible to recognize that Fuchs's intention is to move out from the literary genre known as a textbook on hermeneutics. Indeed his point of departure for arriving at his particular understanding of the title *Hermeneutik* is the traditional definition of hermeneutics as the theory of exegesis. "But to the extent that exegetical theology's way of operating in specific cases calls for an accounting as to its presuppositions, there is a need for explicit reflection upon the presuppositions of exegesis. Exegesis too must discuss the communicability of the revelation, but [it must do this] in view of the historical and indeed on the basis of its experiences with the historical. So there is a need for a systematic introduction to the exegesis of the New Testament, in distinction from an introduction in terms of the history of literature. This is the task that we wish to follow up in this *Hermeneutik* with regard to the New Testament. We could equally well have spoken of a 'theological introduction' to the New Testament, but we have not done so since we must go beyond the area of theology in various directions."[139]

Fuchs's *Hermeneutik* is also divided rather traditionally into general and applied (i.e., special)[140] hermeneutic, the latter devoted rather traditionally to a treatment—but what a treatment! —of the various literary and oral forms. Thus Fuchs clearly proposes to be doing what hermeneutics should have been doing, and when one, after reading Fuchs, recalls in Torm the long

[139] Pp. 100 f.
[140] Cf. p. 101.

sections on the language and time of the New Testament, one
can only be amazed that none of the depth dimension that Fuchs
at least exposed to view had even been dimly sensed by Torm.[141]
Hermeneutic is clearly a challenge to hermeneutics that cannot
be simply brushed aside by Biblical scholarship as the responsibility of some other discipline.

Of course the material position of Fuchs's New Testament hermeneutic can best be approached from its point of departure in
Bultmannian hermeneutic, rather than from that of Torm. It is
perhaps relevant in this regard to observe that Fuchs accentuates
the critical side of demythologizing which it shares with *Sachkritik*. "But since this text [sc. John], in spite of its demythologizing intention, still uses mythological terms, its own intention demands its critical analysis, since of course one cannot presuppose
a priori that the evangelist was also able to carry through his intention completely."[142]

It is this critical function in demythologizing that is the con-
necting link with the step Fuchs takes beyond Bultmann. If for
Bultmann the interpreter's own self-understanding is involved in
the hermeneutical process as a pre-understanding, this self-in-
volvement is for Bultmann still subordinated to the purpose of
interpreting the text, which thus remains the ultimate objective
of interpretation. For Fuchs, however, there is a decisive development in the scope of hermeneutic, in that the text in turn
interprets us, and the involvement of our pre-understanding carries beyond its heuristic function in interpreting the text into a
criticism of our own self-understanding in terms of the self-
understanding the text addresses to us.[143] "Who is now the object

[141] Schleiermacher had already related the forms of literary expression
with the transcendental forms in which man perceives, among which forms
time is primary since Kant, so that the hermeneutical recognition of language
and time as structures of man's existence was long overdue. Cf. Dilthey,
"Die Entstehung der Hermeneutik," *Gesammelte Schriften*, V (1924), 327 f.

[142] "Schluss der Vorlesung über das Johannesevangelium, Berlin S.S. 1958
(24.7. 1958)," *Ergänzungsheft* to the *Hermeneutik*, p. 9.

[143] It is indicative of the bond of continuity with Bultmann that Fuchs
works toward his position as an interpretation of Bultmann. "Bultmann's
attempt at demythologizing also takes place as a question, as a critical interpretation of the pre-understanding of being that determines each existence

of demythologizing? Neither God, nor Jesus, nor the world, nor even language oriented toward walking,[144] but rather man caught in a distorted relation to himself, at a standstill, indeed in collapse, who thinks either too highly or too lowly of himself, indeed who does not even know that he lives from a movement that is terribly obscured by his common understanding of space as stationary and of time as only seeming to move. It is not valid to subject the revelation to a stationary space and to a time that only seems to move. Rather one must let oneself be drawn by the gospel back to where space and time make sense in terms of a movement, in terms of a path and walking, as space for others and time for us. For this reason I have in this course replaced Bultmann's program and method of demythologizing with what seems to me a more radical existentialist interpretation, so as to bring the text anew on the road and put it in motion. What resulted was at least an analysis of Jesus' love. It should confirm itself as a movement of our own existence. What in all of this is theory should be brought to an end for now, in order that love itself can begin to speak. What does love say? 'Arise, let us leave theory!' "[145] Such hermeneutic, intended to interpret our existence, flows as directly over into preaching as do passages in Barth's *Romans*.

Since for Fuchs the interpreter's self-understanding is not merely the *pre*-understanding in the hermeneutical process, but is also the *goal* of that process itself, it is not surprising that the concept of a pre-understanding has to some extent been replaced by another concept, that of the "hermeneutical principle."[146] A hermeneutical principle is that with which the text is confronted to call forth from it what it has to say. Put otherwise, a hermeneutical principle is the "place" where the text is to be put

---

(since it is traced out on each existence), i.e., as existentialist interpretation of being." *Ibid.*, p. 12.

[144] "Such an analysis of love [sc. as in John] is however no mythology, since it does not enter in upon concepts *about* love, but rather is intent only upon pointing the way, i.e., is intent on love itself." *Ibid.*, p. 12.

[145] *Ibid.*, p. 13.

[146] *Hermeneutik*, pp. 103–118.

if it is to begin to speak. Put a cat before a mouse and the cat
gets into action and shows what a cat is.[147]

With regard to the hermeneutical principle for theological exegesis, Fuchs observes that it is the confrontation with our need
that reveals what we mean by the term God.[148] Hence, the hermeneutical principle, the "indication of the place for the truth
of the gospel," is the unremitting plaint of Rom. 7:24 as to who
will deliver us from this existence of death.[149] Put otherwise, history, existence in the flesh, is the place of the encounter with
God,[150] and so the hermeneutical principle must be of the nature
of history.[151] The hermeneutical principle is the presupposition
that man has a relation to himself, or, more exactly, the question
as to ourselves.[152] It is ourselves that we place before the text.
The text unfolds itself, speaks up, in what it says about us. Here
one can see interpretation taking place less as "understanding"
than as "language," in that the text interprets itself by what it
has to say about us.

Under "language" Fuchs does not mean simply the act of oral
speaking.[153] "Language is not even necessarily talk. Language is
rather primarily a *showing* or *letting* be seen, an indication in the
active sense: I intimate to you or instruct you what you yourself
should 'perceive' (take notice of or watch out for). . . . That

[147] *Ibid.*, p. 109. Cf. the definition on p. 111: " 'Hermeneutical principle'
designates what bestows on understanding the power and truth of an *occurrence*. It is the *power* of understanding in the birth of *the language naming
the truth*. The hermeneutical principle points out the 'place' of truth." Cf.
also the illustration below, p. 138, of putting a football in front of a person
to see whether he is a person interested in football.

[148] *Ibid.*, p. 110.

[149] *Ibid.*, p. 111.

[150] *Ibid.*, p. 114.

[151] *Ibid.*, p. 116.

[152] *Ibid.*, pp. 116 f.

[153] "Bultmann reproaches me for confusing language (*Sprache*) and speaking (*Sprechen*), since I talk of a language event (*Sprachereignis*) rather than
being satisfied with the expression 'event of speaking' (*Sprechereignis*), which
in his view would be more suitable for what I mean. I am amazed." *Zur
Frage nach dem historischen Jesus,* p. 424. It is to avoid this misunderstanding that I have translated *Sprachereignis* as "language event" rather than as
"speech event."

can take place through a simple movement, even by turning away from another."[154]

It is such "language" that in Fuchs's hermeneutic receives the primary role, which is another point at which he conceives of himself as going beyond Bultmann. "Of course language is directed to man and being is related to existence. Here I do agree with Bultmann. But, on the other hand, both being and man are directed to language. And to this extent we are related to God. . . . The responsibility for speaking resides already in language, not outside it. That is my *thesis*. He who notices recognizes that language 'grants.' <u>Language is not the abbreviation of thinking,</u> but thinking is an abbreviation of language. Language is gift. . . . Like Bultmann, I deny that a person has faith 'at his disposal.' But the reason does not reside in the actuality of sin, but prior to that in the dependence of faith on word, God's word. . . . Hence I took the further step of exhibiting the historicness of existence as the linguisticality of existence."[155]

It is at this point that the term hermeneutic attains the specific profile characteristic of the new hermeneutic, as "faith's doctrine of language."[156] "Being emerges from language, when language directs us into the dimension of our existence determinative for our life. Is that the 'meaning' of the word of God? Then hermeneutic in theology would indeed be nothing else than the 'doctrine of the word of God' (Ebeling), faith's doctrine of language. The reverse also is true: The theological doctrine of the word of God would be the question as to being in the horizon of Biblical language. The content of human historicness would then not be named questionability but rather linguisticality."[157]

[154] *Hermeneutik*, p. 131.

[155] *Zur Frage nach dem historischen Jesus,* pp. 427–429.

[156] *Hermeneutik,* pp. III, 101 f.; cf. below, p. 241.

[157] *Zum hermeneutischen Problem in der Theologie, Gesammelte Aufsätze* I, p. 115. Cf. the definition of reality in terms of language, *Hermeneutik,* p. 130: "Reality is hence not at all simply what is, as we said to begin with in adopting the current view. Rather the real is only that which can become present as language (even though this be in recollection!). What is now unutterable seems on the contrary to be unreal, which does not mean it is or was impossible. Thus reality has not yet been fully defined when we locate it only in the context of beings, but rather as a 'category' it is even more

In this way the problem of understanding aright Biblical history becomes the problem of right language. Bultmann had originally made use of the term *Heilsgeschichte*, "salvation history." Yet he came to reject this term,[158] and Fuchs traces the inadequacy of the *Heilsgeschichte* approach to the inauthentic, objectifying understanding of language it presupposes:

"Faith and faith's *expression* (*Aussage*) are not the same, even though admittedly they condition each other. For faith must always have already been transposed in a quite specific manner into language if it wishes to understand itself as confession, i.e., is to be faith *in* (Jesus Christ). This structure of intentionality[159] (faith *in*) is for us inherent only at the level of language. It does not derive from faith itself, which is originally obedient answer, as we saw.[160] But our language usually has the structure of *logos tinos*,[161] although this structure is not the only one, just as a word can be equally well word from something as word to someone. But faith's *expression* shares in the intentional structure of language and is today characterized by this structure. For example, only in this structure can it be meaningful to insist on the confession to 'objective saving facts,' in which context it is quite irrelevant whether or not the theology that insists on the confession to 'objective saving facts' is aware of the structural dependency, i.e., the *logical* presuppositions, of its expression. Of course as 'theology' it should recognize *which* logic its confessional formulation aids to ascendancy, i.e., to which logic it is submitting itself. Friedrich Gogarten has rightly named this logic the 'subject-object schema.'[162] But the subject-object schema is only *one* of

basically built into the nature of another realm, that of *language*." Ebeling shares the concern for language without departing from an emphasis upon "the all-embracing questionability of the whole" (*ZThK*, LVII, 1960, 350).

[158] This is most explicit in his review of Oscar Cullmann's *Christ and Time*, entitled "History of Salvation and History," in *Existence and Faith: Shorter Writings of Rudolf Bultmann*, translated by Schubert M. Ogden (New York: Meridian Books, Inc., 1960), pp. 226–240 (German ed. *ThLZ*, LXXIII, 1948, 659–666).

[159] It should be pointed out that Fuchs uses the term "intentionality" here to refer to objectification, a usage quite the reverse of that of John Dillenberger, p. 154 below.

[160] *Hermeneutik*, p. 84.

[161] "Word of or about something." Cf. *Being and Time*, p. 201.

[162] *Hermeneutik*, p. 79.

its possible forms. Its basis is intentionality, i.e., its worldliness. 'Objective saving facts' are hence only the reverse of 'objective worldly facts,' i.e., merely an apologetic antithesis, as if God were simply the opposite of the world."[163]

Bultmann himself had met this problem by replacing the term *Heilsgeschichte* with the term *Heilsgeschehen* (or *Heilsereignis*), "saving event." But now that authentic language has come to have such a close association with God's word admitting man to authentic existence, the refinement of terminology can be carried a step further, when Fuchs designates the saving event as "language event" (*Sprachereignis*) and Ebeling as "word event" (*Wortgeschehen*). This terminological development is obvious in such a statement as the following: "All this may be called '*Heilsgeschehen*.' Paul even gives the impression that we had to do with a *Heilsgeschichte*. But one could call the *Heilsgeschehen* a '*Heilsgeschichte*' only as a *Heilsgeschichte* of love. I cannot discuss this further here, for I would have to show Paul's interpretation of Jesus' person to be a genuine interpretation of the historical Jesus, a task that would take us too far afield. It suffices that we retain the *Heilsgeschehen* as a *Wortgeschehen* that happens in the Spirit for faith."[164] Fuchs's use here of the term characteristic of Ebeling rather than of himself indicates that *Sprachereignis* and *Wortgeschehen* are synonyms and that the choice depends upon which Bultmannian term serves as the point of departure, *Heilsereignis* or *Heilsgeschehen*.

Fuchs can illustrate what is meant by a language event by pointing out that one does not name a person brother simply because of a biological fact, i.e., it is not that one is first a brother and then automatically calls the other brother; rather the other becomes brother by my naming him brother. It is the meaningful relationship of brotherhood that is primary, without which the biological tie would be a mockery of the name of brother.[165]

---

[163] *Ibid.*, pp. 93 f.

[164] Fuchs, *ZThK*, LIX (1962), 41. Cf. also his essay "Proclamation and Speech-Event," *Theology Today*, XIX (1962), 341–354.

[165] *Zur Frage nach dem historischen Jesus*, p. 426. Fuchs once made this point in terms of the local color of his Württemberg background by calling attention to the fact that when at the birth of a calf the cow licks down the

The calling of the other "brother" affirms that relationship, lets it be what it is, "justifies" it.[166] Language thus "lets being 'be' temporally, makes it an event."[167] Language can also be termed "admission," in that it admits something into its real being.[168] The language event can also be described as carrying out the assembling function of being to which Heidegger had called attention.[169] Theologically speaking, proclamation is such a language event in which the body of Christ is constituted, assembled. The church as assembly takes place in the language event of proclamation.[170] Here the distinctively Protestant definition of the church in terms of the preaching of the word has been restated in terms of the new hermeneutic's understanding of language.

Fuchs seems to have been the first to introduce the play upon the term trans-lation, as the language of the text conveys its meaning into the language of today. "Truth is always immediate. Hence translating succeeds only by trans-lating (*Über-setzen*) truth to us."[171] Hence Fuchs's close friend in the homiletical field, Manfred Mezger, can begin his "guidance for preaching" with

newborn calf, this is the cow's acknowledgment of the calf as its own, and hence is a "language event."

[166] *Ibid.*, p. 425. Fuchs can refer to his saying "I love you" to his wife as "justifying" her existence.

[167] *Ibid.*, p. 425. Here the term translated "be" is *anwesen*, a term for "being" revived by Heidegger to accentuate the event character of being. Cf. *The Later Heidegger and Theology*, p. 22, and cf. the Greek term *parousia*, meaning presence in the sense of arrival.

[168] The German term is *Einlass*, referring to the granting of entry. Fuchs provides as illustration: "If I . . . say the sheep there are beautiful, I of course refer to the beautiful sheep there. But prior to that I have with this statement also already admitted the beauty of the sheep as that which is and prevails between them and us, in that I entered in upon this occurrence of being." *Zur Frage nach dem historischen Jesus,* p. 425.

[169] "Language picks up the essential trait of being, that it assembles. And the assembling of being *needs* language, *in order to be.* Only in language is being necessarily event." *Ibid.,* p. 425. Cf. *The Later Heidegger and Theology,* p. 59.

[170] *Zur Frage nach dem historischen Jesus,* p. 426.

[171] *Hermeneutik,* p. 109. Cf. also Heinrich Ott's use of the idiom in Vol. I of this series, *The Later Heidegger and Theology,* p. 80, and my discussion of it in the section of the introduction to that volume on "Language and Hermeneutic," pp. 48–56, esp. p. 54. Cf. also my essay "Theology as Translation," *Theology Today,* XX (1964), 518–527.

a section on "the problem of trans-lation: the text and its free-dom," in which the concrete experience of translating the text of the sermon is recognized in its basic hermeneutical relevance for the whole procedure of preaching the text's meaning in the language of today.[172] "Translation does not simply mean finding a word for each word, but rather seeking and finding as well the new place where this text, without detriment to its historical individuality, strikes home to us. The short cut of putting myself in the skin of Moses or Paul is popular but no good, for my name is neither Moses nor Paul."[173] Thus hermeneutic as translation stands in contrast to the Schleiermacher-Dilthey hermeneutic of becoming "contemporary" with the author—reliving his experience.[174] "[Guidance for preaching] includes and tests the whole path of translation over the cleft of the historical distance into our life. Since it sees to it that what was once said is not simply repeated but is to be said anew, it must show what understanding means and make clear how what is understood comes to expression, i.e., becomes sayable, for people listening today."[175] Confronted with such a text as John 20:6 f., the burial clothes neatly placed in the empty tomb, one can neither ignore them as irrelevant to us, nor treat them as symbol or allegory. Rather "the statement of the text is translatable today *only in radically contrary formulation* to that of the text. . . . Guidance for preaching does not consist in sparing the student the trials provided by the text or teaching him some kind of tricks for avoiding the questions traditionally left open or deferred to some vague future for treatment. Rather one must give him courage and charge him to trust the text so unconditionally that the text retains its intention to say something right through the whole procedure of genuinely attempting to translate, especially where—for the sake of the witness intended to create faith—the statement of the text

[172] "Anleitung zur Predigt," *ZThK*, LVI (1959), 377–397, esp. pp. 381–387. Cf. Fuchs's response, "Übersetzung und Verkündigung; Hermeneutisches Korreferat," *Zur Frage nach dem historischen Jesus*, pp. 405–423.

[173] Mezger, *ibid.*, p. 384.

[174] This particular point is that of Hans-Georg Gadamer, *Wahrheit und Methode; Grundzüge einer philosophischen Hermenutik*, esp. pp. 361 ff.

[175] Mezger, *ibid.*, p. 378.

must be repeated *in completely different language,* i.e., in some circumstances *contra versionem explicatam.*"[176]

Fuchs's understanding of language is well summarized in a passage whose own form illustrates the central role of language in hermeneutic. For this summary occurs in an interpretation of the prologue of John, which interpretation takes the form of a discussion of the way to translate it. That is to say, understanding it means naming the words that speak its meaning. Fuchs begins with the famous translation by Faust, "in the beginning was the deed." This is then corrected, on the basis of John 13:34 (the "new commandment" to love), to the translation "in the beginning was love. . . ." Then, in view of 1 John 4:16 ("God is love"), "love" becomes the translation for *theos* rather than for *logos.* "In the beginning was the word, and the word was with love, and the word was love." Then, since this instance of hermeneutic has to do with what hermeneutic itself is, Fuchs continues with a classical formulation of his understanding of language:

"Yet what then does 'word' mean? For we wish to achieve with the term word the expression that is able to grasp Christ once for all. In the supplement to my *Hermeneutik*[177] I made the attempt to understand word as that Yes that forestalls and precedes every No, as the Yes ultimately constitutive of every language event. For word is, after all, language; it speaks, as its very nature. In genuine language do we not, even before any affirmation, say simply this Yes, when we speak? And even more: With our language do we not correspond from the very first to a Yes that grants us entry, entry into that being in which we are with ourselves and yet precisely not left alone? Even though language usually alienates itself from the word, its ground, and builds all sorts of words that are only signs, does it not still in its own-most

---

[176] *Ibid.,* p. 387.

[177] Since in the *Ergänzungsheft* discussion of "word" was in an appendix reproducing the conclusion of a course on John, Fuchs's allusion in the present quotation back to the *Ergänzungsheft* does not involve a contradiction but rather a confirmation of the point made above that this understanding of "word" was worked out in the context of interpreting the Johannine prologue. The same is true of the parallel discussions of "word" in the article "Logos," *RGG,* 3rd ed., IV (1960), 434–440, esp. 439 f., and the passage in *Zur Frage nach dem historischen Jesus,* p. 428.

ground live from that Yes that is the word of all words? To be sure language would then be originally the language of God, and its basic trait would then rightly be named love."[178]

Perhaps nowhere more clearly than here does one hear the sense in which the "saving event" is a "language event," since language, when it is true language, is God's saving word. And perhaps nowhere more clearly than here does one hear the central role of language in a new theology that has its two foci in the historic Jesus and hermeneutic. For the "historic Jesus" is heard not as "objective factuality," but as "word of address"; and "hermeneutic" is heard not as "understanding in speechless profundity," but as "translation into language that speaks today." Thus hermeneutic is the method suited to the historic Jesus, and the historic Jesus is the material point of departure for a recovery of valid hermeneutic.

The nub of Bultmann's opposition to the new quest of the historical Jesus is formulated in his two rhetorical questions: "Does Jesus' eschatological consciousness mediate an eschatological self-understanding to him who perceives it as a historical phenomenon? . . . Does Jesus' claim of authority, perceived as a historical phenomenon, reach beyond the time of his earthly activity?"[179] These rhetorical questions anticipating a negative answer are posed in terms of the method of the original quest, so that the historical Jesus and the proclaimed kerygma are incommensurable. Bultmann even regards his own *Jesus and the Word*[180] as historiography and therefore not as kerygma.[181] But

[178] "Das Christusverständnis bei Paulus und im Johannesevangelium," Das Christusverständnis im Wandel der Zeiten. Eine Ringvorlesung der Theologischen Fakultät der Universität Marburg (Marburger Theologische Studien, ed. by H. Grass and W. G. Kümmel, Bd. 1, Marburg: N. G. Elwert Verlag, 1963), pp. 11–20. Fuch's interpretation of John 1:1 reaches its completion in the translation: "In the beginning was the Yes, and the Yes was love, and love was the Yes."

[179] *Des Verhältnis der urchristlichen Christusbotschaft zum historischen Jesus, Sitzungsberichte der Heidelberger Akademie der Wissenschaften, Philosophisch-historische Klasse, Jahrgang 1960, 3. Abhandlung* (Heidelberg: Carl Winter Universitätsverlag, 1960), p. 17.

[180] Translated by Louise Pettibone Smith and Erminie Huntress Lantero (New York: Charles Scribner's Sons, 1926).

[181] *Kerygma und Mythos,* I, 148; *Kerygma and Myth,* Torchbook ed., p. 117.

when his questions are heard in terms of the language event of
the new hermeneutic, they are subject to a positive answer.[182]
Fuchs and Ebeling would argue that Jesus' word—not just the
Easter kerygma—happens as recurring word today and thus
mediates an eschatological self-understanding to him who hears
it; that Jesus' claim of authority, heard as the word of love,
reaches beyond the time of his earthly activity to speak to us today. If Bultmann can say that Jesus rose into the kerygma,[183]
Fuchs and Ebeling would say that the word event inaugurated by
Jesus' word happens today in the church's proclamation. Thus the
term "kerygma"—which has functioned to separate the church's
proclamation from the historical Jesus—tends to pass out of the
vocabulary of the new hermeneutic,[184] and to be explained and
replaced by the term language event or word event, in which
Jesus' and the church's proclamation belong together.[185] That
this can be asserted not simply as an uncritical harmonization
but as a scholarly viewpoint is due to the fact that theological
scholarship has attained a new methodology, a new hermeneutic,
which traces the translation of meaning in the recurring event of
language.

Hans-Georg Gadamer, Bultmann's leading pupil within the
field of philosophy and Germany's leading authority on herme-

[182] It is thus in terms of hermeneutic that the question of Van A. Harvey
and Schubert M. Ogden, "Wie neu ist die 'Neue Frage nach dem historischen
Jesus'?," *ZThK*, LIX (1962), 46–87, is to be answered.

[183] *Das Verhältnis der urchristlichen Christusbotschaft zum historischen
Jesus*, p. 27.

[184] The turning point in this development is marked by Ebeling's volume
Theologie und Verkündigung, Vol. I of *Hermeneutische Untersuchungen
zur Theologie*, 1962.

[185] Most of Fuchs's contributions to the topic are in the second volume of
his collected essays, *Zur Frage nach dem historischen Jesus*, and in subsequent issues of the *ZThK*. For Ebeling's contributions cf. esp. "Jesus and
Faith,'" *ZThK*, LV (1958), 64–110, also in *Wort und Glaube* (Tübingen:
J. C. B. Mohr, 1960), pp. 203–254, English translation in *Word and Faith*
(Philadelphia: Fortress Press, 1963), pp. 201–246. Cf. also his *Das Wesen
des christlichen Glaubens* (Tübingen: J. C. B. Mohr, 1959), English translation in *The Nature of Faith*, by R. Gregor Smith (Philadelphia: Muhlenberg Press, 1961), Ch. IV, "The Witness of Faith," and Ch. V, "The Basis
of Faith," esp. pp. 70 f., and his essay "The Question of the Historical Jesus
and the Problem of Christology," *Beiheft* 1 of the *ZThK*, LVI (1959), *Wort
und Glaube*, pp. 300–318, English translation in *Word and Faith*, pp. 288–
304.

neutic from the philosophical point of view, has described this hermeneutical development in the Bultmannian school as follows: "In [Fuchs's] essay on 'Translation and Preaching' it becomes clearer to what extent this hermeneutical doctrine seeks to transcend what Bultmann meant by existentialist interpretation. It is the hermeneutical principle of translation that points the direction. It is incontestable that 'the translation should create the same room that the text sought to create as the Spirit spoke in it.' But the bold and yet inescapable consequence is that the word has primacy over the text, for the word is language event. This is obviously meant as the assertion that the relation between word and thought is not that of belatedly catching up with the thought by means of the word expressing it. Rather the word is like a flash of lightning that strikes."[186]

    If the new hermeneutic thus proposes to bridge the gulf between historical and systematic theology in terms of a recurrent event of language that moves from Jesus' word to that of the preacher, then the new hemeneutic has become in fact a new understanding of theological scholarship as a whole. It is this overarching implication moving far beyond hermeneutic's point of departure as a subdivision within Biblical scholarship that becomes most apparent in the work of Gerhard Ebeling. He, like Ernst Fuchs, had studied under Rudolf Bultmann.[187] Yet he began his academic career in the history of doctrine, and moved from there into systematic theology. His dissertation was an investigation of Luther's hermeneutic, and it was thus with the hermeneutical question that he began. And it was indeed from Luther[188] rather than from Bultmann or Heidegger that he re-

    [186] "Hermeneutik und Historismus," *PhR*, IX (1962), 263. The reference in the quotation is to Fuchs's essay "Übersetzung und Verkündigung," *Zum hermeneutischen Problem in der Theologie; Die existentiale Interpretation*, p. 409.

    [187] Ebeling studied in Marburg from the Summer Semester of 1930 through the Winter Semester of 1931–32. Then he studied in Berlin, which was his home, and in Zürich, where he completed his doctorate under Fritz Blanke in 1938.

    [188] In his programmatic essay on "The Significance of the Critical Historical Method for Church and Theology in Protestantism" of 1950 (*Word and Faith*, p. 23), Ebeling lists among the works appearing just after World War I responsible for the theological shift at that time "Karl Holl with his

ceived most directly the correlation between word and faith that
has become the focus of his theology. Already in his dissertation
he had stated:

"The relation between faith and word in the process of understanding and interpretation is not a relation that moves from the
subject to the word, but rather from the word to the understanding subject. Faith adds nothing new to the word, but is the becoming effective of the word as that which it claims to be—as
God's word. If faith does not correspond to the word, it is not
only not believed but also not understood. For it is not in the
least grasped in its real nature and significance. This correlation
between word and faith belongs to the word not on the basis of
its general structure as word, but rather as witness to the incarnation of the Son of God, in which it is this incarnate One who is
encountered in the present. In all words of Scripture we have to
do with nothing other than the incarnate Son of God, Jesus
Christ. The effect of this is that not a single word of Scripture is
understood if it is not grasped in its correlation to faith. God's
word comes into view as God's word in no other relation at all
than that of faith. Hence the relation between word and faith is
unique, unrepeatable and indivisible. The relation between word
and faith is the only contact between God and existence. The
understanding of the word in faith is thus nothing other than the
christological interpretation of Scripture. To the inseparable togetherness of the two natures in Christ there corresponds the
never-ending togetherness of word and faith."[189]

---

collection of Luther essays." Among these was one on "Luther's Significance
for the Advance of the Art of Interpretation," written in 1920, which Ebeling
considers as sharing in the reawakening of interest in the hermeneutical
problem. Cf. Karl Holl, *Gesammelte Aufsätze zur Kirchengeschichte*, Vol. I,
Luther (Tübingen: J. C. B. Mohr, 1921, 7th ed., 1948), pp. 544–582.
Ebeling's own dissertation, published in the series *Forschungen zur Geschichte
und Literatur des Protestantismus*, X, 1 (1942; 2nd ed., 1963), under the
title *Evangelische Evangelienauslegung; Eine Untersuchung zu Luthers Hermeneutik*, reflects his point of departure in Luther's hermeneutic. Cf. also
Ebeling's articles "Die Anfänge von Luthers Hermeneutik," *ZThK*, XLVIII
(1951), 172–230; "Luthers Psalterdruck vom Jahre 1513," *ZThK*, L (1953),
43–99; "Luthers Auslegung des 14. (15.) Psalms in der ersten Psalmenvor-
lesung im Vergleich mit der exegetischen Tradition," *ZThK*, L (1953), 280–
339.

[189] *Evangelische Evangelienauslegung*, 1st ed., pp. 382 f.

When Fuchs (born in 1903) and Ebeling (born in 1912) were together at the University of Tübingen just after World War II, there grew up not only a unique personal friendship but also a material unity of position that has made of the new hermeneutic a single school of thought with a shared leadership. Ebeling began as did Fuchs with the subject matter of his own field, which in his case was church history. He entered the postwar discussion with a programmatic document proposing a basically new understanding of church history as "the history of the interpretation of Holy Scripture."[190] This hermeneutical understanding of church history gives this discipline a more direct relation to the theological enterprise as a whole than it had had, for example, in the Barthian system.[191]

When in 1950 the leading German theological periodical, the *Zeitschrift für Theologie und Kirche,* was reopened with Ebeling as its editor, he began with a programmatic essay that recast the whole of theology in terms of hermeneutic.

"The question of hermeneutic forms the focal point of the theological problems of today. A brief glance at the individual theological disciplines can elucidate this assertion. That Old Testament and New Testament scholars come up against the problem of hermeneutic in a special way is obvious at once. But the same is true also of the discipline of church history—here, indeed, in two respects: first in so far as it is likewise continually concerned with the interpretation of sources, but then also and above all because of course the process of exposition of Scripture that goes on in the history of the church presents the hermeneutical problem in its full compass, and thus the question of the theological grasp of the nature of church history opens straight into

---

[190] *Kirchengeschichte als Geschichte der Auslegung der Heiligen Schrift* (Tübingen: J. C. B. Mohr, 1947).

[191] Cf. *Church Dogmatics,* I, 1, translated by G. T. Thomson (New York: Charles Scribner's Sons, 1936), 3: "Thus as *Biblical* theology, theology is the question as to the *foundation,* as *practical* theology it is the question as to the *aim,* as *dogmatic* theology it is the question as to the *content,* of the language peculiar to the Church." Then in fine print: "*Church history* so-called answers, from the point of view of Christian language about God, to no question that need be put independently, and is therefore not to be regarded as an independent theological discipline. It is the indispensable *auxiliary science* to exegetical, dogmatic, and practical theology."

the basic problem of hermeneutic. The difficult problem of theology's systematic method can be properly solved only when it is likewise set in the light of the question of hermeneutic. For resting on the exposition of Scripture and the history of theology, dogmatics has the task of bringing the church's teaching into contact and discussion with contemporary principles of thought, there to submit it to critical sifting and present it in its full inner coherence. Thus here the struggle for the momentarily required translation of the kerygma is brought to its issue in the most comprehensive way—whereby, however, the hermeneutical question in its basic methodological significance is also momentarily brought to a decision. And it is likewise plain that for so-called practical theology, above all in its teaching on sermon, instruction, and pastoral care, the hermeneutical question presents the one central problem underlying all questions of detail, in so far as the *applicatio* must not stand unrelated and all on its own alongside the *explicatio*. More particularly also in the study of missions, with its difficult questions (so highly instructive for theological work as a whole) of translating the Biblical message into the languages of totally different civilizations, the hermeneutical problem proves to be of fundamental significance."[192]

This lead essay on "The Significance of the Critical Historical Method for Church and Theology in Protestantism" also faced squarely the issue of the positive significance of critical scholarship for the church. This too Ebeling worked out in terms of hermeneutic, as the freeing of the word event from impediments. He has summarized his thesis as follows:

"Criticism is an element of integration in the effort to understand the text. For the sake of what the Biblical text seeks to bring to understanding, criticism is directed against everything that obstructs this hermeneutical function of the text. It is levelled in principle against distortion of the text—whether distortions in the form of the text resulting from the process of transmission, or distortions in the understanding of the text resulting from

[192] *ZThK*, XLVII (1950), 11 f., *Wort und Glaube*, pp. 12 f. [*Word and Faith*, pp. 27 f.].

traditional prejudices, inappropriate systems of interpretation and unsuitable approaches to the problem, or distortions of the matter itself with which the text as a Biblical text has to do, resulting from confusion in the linguistic medium of the text. The purpose of the critical historical method therefore lies ultimately in the interpreter's self-criticism in view of all the conceivable possibilities of deceiving himself as to the aim of the Biblical text."[193]

If the basic hermeneutical task of translating meaning from one culture to another had been laid hold of by Bultmann primarily in terms of the shift from a mythopoetic culture through enlightenment into a postmythical world, Ebeling opens this translational task of hermeneutic out into the total theological enterprise. Here he revives Dietrich Bonhoeffer's call for a "non-religious interpretation of Biblical concepts" suitable for a "world come of age."[194] Thus in Germany Ebeling has become, like R. Gregor Smith in Scotland, John A. T. Robinson in England, and William Hamilton in the United States, the theologian who has carried out the legacy of Bonhoeffer.

In this way Ebeling has achieved a hermeneutic that has embraced the doctrine of the word of God and become the focus to a total theological position. The new hermeneutic is a new theology, just as were dialectic theology and Ritschlianism before it. Indeed it is Ebeling's conviction that theology itself *is* hermeneutic, for it consists in translating what the Bible has to say into the word for today.

Perhaps the maturest statement of the material theological position of the new hermeneutic is the following attempt by Ebeling to summarize his position in a way that clarifies misunderstandings that had arisen:

"The criticism to make against a theology that has become traditionalistic and positivistic is not that it abides by the given, the tradition. Quite the contrary. It is precisely under the ap-

---

[193] *Wort und Glaube,* p. 451 [*Word and Faith,* p. 428].
[194] "The 'Non-religious Interpretation of Biblical Concepts,' " *ZThK, LII* (1955), 296–360; *Wort und Glaube,* pp. 90–160 [*Word and Faith,* pp. 98–161]; cf. also the brief essay entitled simply "Dietrich Bonhoeffer," *Wort und Glaube,* pp. 294–299 [*Word and Faith,* pp. 282–287].

pearance of especially loyal allegiance to the tradition that *de facto* it is given up. For it is 'presented' as *traditum* and thus as *praeteritum,* rather than by responding responsibly in pointing into the future with a word happening today, so that what is transmitted, the *traditum,* can take place as *traditio,* the act of transmitting. The *traditum* becomes what it is transmitted for only when it enters in upon the act of transmission, i.e., when the text fixed in letters becomes the spiritual occurrence of the oral word. The thesis that the object of dogmatic theology is not to be defined as a textual object is not intended to make the text irrelevant, but rather to be what really lets it count. Dogmatic theology completes the task of interpretation not in the sense of a method competing with historical exegesis, but rather in the sense of a turn, called for by the subject matter itself, from the historical to the dogmatic way of understanding.[195] In dealings with the text *its* being interpreted by us turns into *our* being interpreted by the text. The interpretation of the text in the sense of an objective genitive becomes an interpretation of the text in the sense of a subjective genitive. Instead of the text being that which is to be interpreted and is in need of interpretation, what the text is there for emerges as that which is to be interpreted, clarified and delivered. For the text is not there for its own sake, but rather for the sake of the word event that is the origin and hence also the future of the text. Word event is the event of interpretation taking place through the word. Hence the text is there for the sake of the event of interpretation, which is the text's origin and future. For the word that once happened and in happening became the text must again become word with the help of the text and thus happen as interpreting word. What happens in the word event can thus be called interpretation, since it is the essence of word to clarify what is obscure, to bring light into darkness, and thus, if it is the word that concerns every man absolutely, to name the reality of man's being as what it truly is. The depths of such event of interpretation are of course only fully grasped when it is recognized that this bringing into truth is at the same time the exposure and the alteration of reality.

---

[195] Cf. below, pp. 93 ff.

Thus the object of dogmatic theology is the word event itself, in which the reality of man comes true."[196]

One of the most significant aspects of this new theology is that it stands within the context of a new assessment of the nature of the liberal arts in general. It was Dilthey's recognition of hermeneutics as the methodology of the humanities, deepened by Heidegger, that gave to the hermeneutic of Bultmann critical rapport with the cultural life of our times. For Bultmann was doing in terms of Biblical interpretation what, e.g., the Heideggerian philosopher Hans Jonas was doing in terms of gnosticism and Emil Staiger in terms of German literature.[197] But in the present situation Dilthey and increasingly Heidegger are being superseded by the Heidelberg philosopher Hans-Georg Gadamer, a former pupil of Heidegger and Bultmann, whose *magnum opus* grounds the humanities in a hermeneutic oriented not to psychologism or existentialism, but rather to language and its subject matter.[198]

Hans-Georg Gadamer

Gadamer criticizes Dilthey to the effect that his orientation to the individual's psychic structures as the context for interpreting the text produces a hermeneutic not fully commensurate to historic reality. "The basis upon which [Dilthey] sought to erect a construction of the historic world in the humanities is the recog-

---

[196] *Theologie und Verkündigung,* pp. 14 f.

[197] *Die Zeit als Einbildungskraft des Dichters* (Zürich: Atlantis Verlag, 1939, 2nd ed., 1953). It is significant that Staiger, whose indebtedness to the early Heidegger is quite explicit (cf. "Ein Rückblick," *Neue Zürcher Zeitung,* Sept. 27, 1959, Blatt 5, Nr. 2898 [69]), has come increasingly into an antithetic relationship to the later Heidegger. Cf. "Ein Briefwechsel mit Martin Heidegger," *Die Kunst der Interpretation: Studien zur deutschen Literaturgeschichte* (Zürich: Atlantis Verlag, 1955; 2nd ed., 1957), pp. 34–49. To a considerable extent this is the antithesis of the professional literary critic to the philosopher's interpretations of literature sometimes lacking in professional exactitude; but it is also to some extent the tension between an interpretation in terms of the existence whose temporality comes to expression in literature and an interpretation in terms of language in which being speaks. The presence of Professor Staiger at the University of Zürich immediately gives to Ebeling's hermeneutic a universe of discourse shared with the humanities. The practical relevance of this rapport is enhanced when one recalls that many theological students, planning to teach in the public schools, divide their studies between theology and literature.

[198] *Wahrheit und Methode: Grundzüge einer philosophischen Hermeneutik* (Tübingen: J. C. B. Mohr, 1960). Cf. also his essay "Vom Zirkel des Verstehens," in the *Festschrift Martin Heidegger zum siebzigsten Geburtstag* (Pfullingen: Neske Verlag, 1959), pp. 24–34.

nition that experiences are characterized by inwardness, so that
here there is no problem of knowing the other, of knowing what
is not myself, such as was at the basis of the Kantian approach.
Yet the historic world is no experiential relation such as is history,
e.g., in autobiography, where it portrays itself in the inwardness
of subjectivity. Historic relation must ultimately be understood
as a relation of meaning that basically transcends the experiential
horizon of the individual."[199] Gadamer's own positive alternative
begins to emerge in the following critical appraisal of Dilthey:
"His point of departure, the taking of 'experiences' into oneself,
could not build the bridge to historic realities, for the great historic realities—society and the state—are actually already determinative prior to every 'experience.' Self-reflection and autobiography—Dilthey's point of departure—are not primary and
do not suffice as a basis for the hermeneutical problem, since they
re-private-ize history. In reality history does not belong to us but
we to it. Long before we understand ourselves in retrospection we
understand ourselves as a matter of course in the family, society,
and state in which we live. The focus in terms of subjectivity is
a distortion. The individual's self-reflection is only a flash within
the unbroken flow of historic life. Hence the individual's pre-
judgments, much more than his judgments, are the reality of his
being."[200] This historic "prejudice" with which our experience
is loaded is primarily our language.

Gadamer's pupil Heinz Kimmerle[201] has traced this deficiency
in Dilthey, upon whom the modern development of hermeneutic
had been built, back to Schleiermacher, from whom Dilthey derived his hermeneutic. Dilthey's inadequacy with regard to the
"historic world" is due to Schleiermacher's inadequacy with regard to "language"—as indeed the new focus on language in
hermeneutic is an effort to do justice to the historic aspects of
hermeneutic. Dilthey's Schleiermacher was, however, not the
whole Schleiermacher, for Friedrich Lücke's edition of Schleiermacher's hermeneutics omitted the early manuscripts as too frag-

---

[199] "Hermeneutik und Historismus," *PhR,* IX (1962), 243.
[200] *Wahrheit und Methode,* p. 261.
[201] His unpublished dissertation of 1957 was on "The Hermeneutic of
Schleiermacher in the Context of His Speculative Thought."

mentary for publication, whereas Kimmerle maintains that Schleiermacher increasingly departed from an earlier, hitherto unknown, hermeneutical position, and progressively fell into the defect Gadamer detects in Dilthey. "The late Schleiermacher tends (from 1819 on) more and more toward a different, a psychological, understanding of individuality. The specific linguistic expression is no longer related to language as the general dimension, but rather to the totality of the individual life that produced it. He is primarily concerned to explain (reproduce) how an individual speech or act is an element of the whole life (by means of what he called psychological interpretation). The individual's life experience becomes the hermeneutical principle that guides the effort at understanding."[202]

Kimmerle has published a new edition of Schleiermacher's hermeneutical writings in which for the first time the early fragments are made available to the public. It is Kimmerle's thesis that they show Schleiermacher to have oriented the hermeneutical task originally to language, and thus to be materially a precursor of the new hermeneutic. "The decisive productive thought of Schleiermacher's hermeneutic, as it comes to expression primarily in the early sketches, resides, however, in its strict and conscious orientation to the concrete procedure of living speaking. In Manuscript I there is the statement: 'All that is to be presupposed in hermeneutics as well as all that is to be found is language alone. Where the other objective and subjective presuppositions belong must be found from the language' (p. 8); and in Manuscript II much the same is said and actually in a more explicit way: 'Everything that (can) be the task of hermeneutics is part of a sentence' (p. 11)."[203]

[202] Kimmerle, "Hermeneutische Theorie oder ontologische Hermeneutik," *ZThK*, LIX (1962), 116.

[203] Friedrich D. E. Schleiermacher, *Hermeneutik,* newly published from the manuscripts and introduced by Heinz Kimmerle, *Abhandlungen der Heidelberger Akademie der Wissenschaften, Philosophisch-historische Klasse, Jahrgang 1959, 2. Abh.* (Heidelberg: Carl Winter Universitätsverlag, 1959), p. 17 of the Introduction. Gadamer uses the first of these previously unknown statements by Schleiermacher as the motto at the head of Pt. III of *Wahrheit und Methode,* p. 361. Christoph Senft, in reviewing Kimmerle's edition of Schleiermacher's *Hermeneutik* (*PhR*, X, 1962, 288–290), suggests that the hermeneutic of the younger Schleiermacher, which Kimmerle identified, may

Gadamer's own point of departure is the recognition that much of truth has not come to us by means of scholarly method and yet commands our acknowledgment as true. His approach is "to seek, wherever it is to be found, the experience of truth that transcends the area under the control of scholarly methodology and to investigate the legitimation peculiar to it. Thus the humanities unite with kinds of experience that lie outside science: the experience of philosophy, of art, and of history itself. All these are kinds of experience in which truth that cannot be verified with the methodical means of science makes its presence known."[204]

It is his interest in the philosophical legitimation of such ways of knowing that lie outside science that leads Gadamer to hermeneutic. "In my opinion the contemporary relevance of the hermeneutical phenomenon resides in the fact that only by penetrating into the phenomenon of understanding can such a legitimation be provided."[205] The result is a new approach to understanding. "Understanding is itself not to be thought of so much as an action of one's subjectivity, but rather as entering into an occurrence of transmission in which past and present are constantly being mediated. That is what must gain acceptance in hermeneutical theory, which is much too dominated by the idea of procedure, method."[206]

Gadamer does not simply set up a theory about understanding, but rather investigates the conditions under which understanding does in fact take place. Thus, aspects of hermeneutic that may not otherwise have been regarded as of principal significance for scientific interpretation emerge, in view of their constant presence in the interpretation that really takes place, as basic ingredients that must be recognized as such. One of these neglected aspects is the temporal gulf between text and interpreter. One reason it

---

have been consistently retained by Schleiermacher in later years, contrary to Kimmerle's own assumption. Yet one should be cautious in rewriting history to make it conform to the current view.

[204] *Wahrheit und Methode,* pp. xiii f.

[205] *Ibid.,* p. xiv.

[206] *Ibid.,* p. 275. The term "occurrence of transmission" (*Überlieferungsgeschehen*) is analogous to Ebeling's term "language event" (*Wortgeschehen*). Both involve a continuing occurrence rather than a single event.

had not been given constitutive importance in previous hermeneutic is that it had been usually bridged in terms of some unhistoric element common to both the past and the present. Dilthey described this as follows: "The possibility of universally
valid interpretation can be derived from the nature of understanding. Here the individuality of the interpreter and that of his
author do not stand over against each other as two incommensurable facts. Both have been formed on the basis of universal human nature, and therein is made possible man's capacity for
community in speech and understanding."[207] Heidegger's existentials seemed to make such common ground available even on
the assumption of the historicness of existence, so that his pupil
Hans Jonas could boldly refer to this common ground of existentials as the "metaphysical *a priori*" of the history of ideas.
"The phenomena in question . . . , to the extent authentic fundamental existentialist phenomena are involved, are also still
available to us in such a way as to permit us to measure what
was said then by the phenomena themselves."[208] And yet in
retrospect Jonas has recognized that the Heideggerian existentials
were not themselves beyond the historic flux, but were indeed historically conditioned and not universally valid. "When, many years
ago, I turned to the study of gnosticism, I found that the view-
points, the optics as it were, which I had acquired in the school
of Heidegger, enabled me to see aspects of gnostic thought that
had been missed before. And I was increasingly struck by the
familiarity of the seemingly utterly strange. . . . The fitness of
its categories to the particular matter was something to ponder
about. They fitted as if made to measure: *were* they, perhaps,
made to measure? At the outset, I had taken that fitness as simply
a case of their presumed general validity, which would assure
their utility for the interpretation of any human 'existence' whatever. . . . Thus the meeting of the two, started as the meeting
of a method with a matter, ended with bringing home to me that
existentialism, which claims to be the explication of the funda-

---

[207] "Die Entstehung der Hermeneutik," *Gesammelte Schriften,* V (1924),
329.
[208] *Augustin und das paulinische Freiheitsproblem,* 1930, p. 6.

mentals of human existence as such, is the philosophy of a particular, historically fated situation of human existence: and an
analogous (though in other respects very different) situation had
given rise to an analogous response in the past."[209]

In a somewhat similar way Kimmerle criticizes the use of the
existentialist analysis of Dasein to bridge the historical distance
between text and interpreter: "Has here historical relativity been
thought through in a sufficiently radical fashion? Is it not possible
that a *metaphysical* entity has been introduced here as a hermeneutical principle, an entity that does not stand up to a
Kantian-type epistemological critique applied to history? Dilthey
himself wished to put alongside the Kantian 'critique of pure
reason' a 'critique of historical reason.' Would not such a critique
have to insist radically that every period can really only be understood in its own terms, from its own center, without reference to
any trans-temporal instance? The idea of individual life, no matter
what general formulation is given it, cannot provide the principle
for understanding each particular phenomenon in all periods of
time, nor even for the historical context in general in which we
ourselves stand. The analysis of Dasein as being in the world is
metaphysicized, contrary to its own self-understanding, when it is
expected to provide the schema of categories for every scholarly
effort at understanding."[210]

Gadamer sees as of fundamental hermeneutical significance the
fact that the interpretation of documents of the past involves a
separation in time that no assumed "contemporaneity" can really
overcome, and hence that the interpretation is always a translation from one situation to another. One always understands the
text, if not better, at least differently than does the author himself. "Every historian and philologian must reckon with the fundamental openendedness of the horizon of meaning in which he
moves as he understands. Historic tradition can only be understood by recalling the basic continuing concretizing taking place
in the continuation of things. Similarly the philologian who has

[209] "Epilogue: Gnosticism, Existentialism, and Nihilism," *The Gnostic
Religion* (Boston: Beacon Press, 2nd rev. ed., 1963), esp. pp. 320 f.
[210] "Hermeneutische Theorie oder ontologische Hermeneutik," *ZThK*, LIX
(1962), 120.

to do with poetic or philosophic texts knows about their inexhaustibleness. In both cases it is the continuation of the occurrence that brings what is transmitted into new aspects of meaning. New actualization in the process of understanding involves the texts just as much in an authentic occurrence as is the case with events when they are involved in occurrence by their own continuation. That is what we designated the 'effective history' aspect within hermeneutical experience. Every actualization in the process of understanding can be aware of itself as a historic possibility of what is understood."[211]

The fact that the interpreter has an interest in his subject matter that no assumed "objectivity" of method has ever fully succeeded in eliminating points to another often neglected but nonetheless basic hermeneutical insight: The subject matter of hermeneutic is the *relation* between the interpreter and the text he is studying, the "interest," the material issue involved. The objective of understanding is material agreement. "Understanding is always the process of welding [the interpreter's and the text's] horizons that only seem to exist independently."[212] The interpreter assumes the text is answering some question, and attributes to the text adequacy to reveal that question. Thus the interpreter enters into the text's dimension of meaning and seeks to make sense of what it says. Hence Gadamer speaks of an "anticipation of perfection" as an aspect of the hermeneutical circle. One anticipates not only that there is a consistent view in the text, but also that it is true to the subject matter, until the text itself no longer permits such an assumption. At that point critical operations must begin because the text is no longer "intelligible." "Understanding means primarily to understand each other on the subject matter, and only secondarily to clarify and understand the view of the other person as such."[213] It is significant that Gadamer places as a motto at the head of this section of his book the following quotation from Luther: *"Qui non intelligit res, non potest ex verbis sensum elicere"*—he who does not

---

[211] *Wahrheit und Methode,* p. 355.
[212] *Ibid.,* p. 289.
[213] *Ibid.,* pp. 277 f.

understand the subject matter under discussion cannot elicit the meaning of the words.[214]

Gadamer's position has been questioned as to the scholarliness of interpretation of this kind by the leading contemporary exponent of the Dilthey tradition, the Italian historian of law Emilio Betti. To him Gadamer replies in a letter, later cited and expanded in an essay, as follows:

" 'Basically I do not propose *a method,* I only describe *what is.* I do not think one can seriously contest that the situation is as I describe it. . . . E.g., you too, when you read a classic study by Mommsen, immediately detect in what period all that could have been written. Even a master of historical method is not able to remain completely free from the prejudices of his time, his social environment, his national position, etc. Is that to be taken for a deficiency? And even if it were, I regard it as a philosophical task to reflect as to why this deficiency is never absent wherever something is done. In other words, I regard *acknowledging what is* as the only scholarly way, rather than taking one's point of departure in what should or might be. In this sense I try to think beyond modern science's concept of method (which retains its limited validity), and to think, in explicit universality, what *always* happens.'

"But what does Betti say to that? That I reduce the hermeneutical problem to the *quaestio facti* ('phenomenologically,' 'descriptively'), and do not pose the *quaestio juris* at all. As if Kant's posing of the *quaestio juris* to pure natural science had been intended to prescribe how it should really be, rather than attempting to justify the transcendental possibility of natural science as it was. In the sense of this Kantian distinction, thinking beyond the humanities' concept of method, which my book attempts, poses the question as to the 'possibility' of the humanities (which certainly does not mean what they really ought to be!).[215]

This emphasis upon analyzing the possibility of interpretation as it in fact takes place, and thus upon the analysis of what is, is designated by Gadamer as an "ontological turn in hermeneu-

214 *Ibid.,* p. 162.
215 "Hermeneutik und Historismus," *PhR,* IX (1962), 249.

tic."[216] "This *ontological* turn in hermeneutic signifies its elimination as a doctrine of a special art or method. It makes the theory of understanding into a central philosophical problematic."[217]

This new turn in German hermeneutic was introduced into the theological discussion at the meeting of "Old Marburgers" in October, 1962, which was devoted to hermeneutic. Gadamer insisted that it is not a self-understanding that comes to expression in language. Word is "selfless," and what the Biblical author is talking about transcends his self-understanding. What language has to say must be sought in terms of its subject matter, so that the word "disappears" into what it has to say. To be sure, what the word has to say does not lie outside language as understood by the new hermeneutic—a point made by Heidegger and conceded by Gadamer. Yet it is this dialectic between language and its subject matter (*Sprache* and *Sache*) rather than that between mythological language and the existential self-understanding it objectifies, which designates the point at which the hermeneutical discussion in Germany now stands.

The involvement of Heidegger and Gadamer in the new hermeneutic points to the fact that this hermeneutic provides the prospect not only of a new grasp of the nature of the theological task, but also of the place of theology in the university. It is the purpose of the present volume to investigate the extent to which this new hermeneutic provides as well an adequate point of focus for theology in the context of higher education in America.

[216] Pt. III of *Wahrheit und Methode* is entitled the "Ontological Turn in Hermeneutic [worked out] in Terms of Language" (pp. 361–465).
[217] Kimmerle, "Hermeneutische Theorie oder ontologische Hermeneutik," *ZThK*, LIX (1962), 121. The title of Kimmerle's essay expresses the same alternative.

2. Word of God and Hermeneutic[1]

University of Zurich

I

The subject "Word of God and Hermeneutic" combines two concepts which are perhaps more representative than any others of the approach that has determined theological thinking in the last four decades, and that still determines it today and also must determine it in order to be faithful to the Reformation. For by concentrating on the word of God the Reformation conferred on the problem of hermeneutic a significance which, in spite of Origen and Augustine, it had never attained before. One might also say: a significance which had never before been perceived in these dimensions. For the *Catholic view of tradition* was in point of fact an answer to the hermeneutical problem—holding as it does that the revelation testified in Scripture cannot be correctly understood without the tradition presented in the church.

[1] The paper was first read at the editorial conference of the *ZThK* on April 18, 1959, at Sindlingen, and then repeated on May 10 at the Interfac 1959 (Swiss Conference of Reformed Students of Theology) at Vaumarcus (Neuchâtel) and on June 3 at the University of Heidelberg on the invitation of the Faculty of Theology.

For what follows cf. my article "Hermeneutik" in *RGG*[3] III, pp. 242–262.

How profoundly I agree with Ernst Fuchs and how much I owe to him from many years' exchange of views can be seen from the many connections between this paper and the recently published first volume of the collected essays of Ernst Fuchs: *Zum hermeneutischen Problem in der Theologie; Die existentiale Interpretation* (Tübingen: J. C. B. Mohr, 1959).

[This paper also appears in *Zeitschrift für Theologie und Kirche*, LVI (1959), 224–251; *Wort und Glaube* (Tübingen: J. C. B. Mohr, 1960), pp. 319–348; English translation by James W. Leitch, *Word and Faith* (Philadelphia: Fortress Press, 1963), pp. 305–332. It is here reproduced with the kind permission of Fortress Press. Eds.]

For in the strict sense this tradition is interpretative in character, even where in less strict terminology it is accorded a supplementary function.[2] Now although the exclusive particle *sola scriptura* was directed against this Catholic view of tradition, yet the so-called *Scripture principle of the Reformers* did not really consist in a reduction of the sources of revelation, a quantitatively narrower definition of the norm. Rather the *sola scriptura*, as opposed to the hermeneutical sense of the Catholic principle of tradition, was itself already a hermeneutical thesis. Holy Scripture, as Luther puts it, is *sui ipsius interpres*.[3] Incidentally, that is strictly speaking also the point of the orthodox doctrine of verbal in-

[2] *Tridentinum Sess. IV,* Denzinger 783, 786; *Vaticanum Const. dogm. de fide. cath.* cap. 2, Denzinger 1787, 1788. On the discussion on the interpretation of these texts see R. J. Geiselmann, "Das Konzil von Trient über das Verhältnis der Heiligen Schrift und der nicht geschriebenen Traditionen. Sein Missverständnis in der nachtridentinischen Theologie und die Überlieferung dieses Missverständnisses," in *Die mündliche Überlieferung: Beiträge zum Begriff der Tradition,* edited by Michael Schmaus (Munich: Hueber, 1957).

The different verdicts on the question whether the tradition has to be assigned interpretative or supplementary character hang together with the divergence of views on the nature of interpretation. But according to the view of the Roman Church the tradition naturally contains nothing that contradicts Scripture and is not provided for at least in germ in it. The concept of development, on which the discussion of the Catholic concept of tradition concentrates itself, therefore involves the hermeneutical problem.

[3] Luther's first explicit discussion of the sole authority of Scripture (in *Assertio omnium articulorum,* 1520: *WA* 7, pp. 96 ff.) is exclusively concerned with the problem of Scripture exposition. It is a question of the correct understanding of the rule (introduced as an objection to Luther himself, but claimed by him against the Roman view): "The Holy Scriptures are not to be interpreted according to one's own mind" (96.10 f.). "It is therefore an obvious error that by the sentence, 'the Scriptures are not to be interpreted according to one's own mind,' we are commanded to put aside the sacred Scriptures and seek after and believe the commentaries of men" (96.35–37). Rather, the truth is: "The Scriptures are not to be understood except *by* that Spirit by which they were written, which Spirit can nowhere be found with more immediacy and liveliness than in these very Scriptures themselves which the Spirit has written" (97.1–3). The exclusive sense of the "sola scriptura" is thus aimed against the alleged insufficiency of Scripture on the hermeneutical side: ". . . so that [the Scripture] *per se* is most certain, most easy, most open, interpreting itself (*sui ipsius interpres*), proving, judging, illuminating everything of everyone . . . (referring to Ps. 119: 130:) here clearly the spirit has imparted illumination and teaches that understanding is given only through the words of God (*per sola verba Dei*), just as one would enter through a gate or opening or (as they say) from a first principle from which he has to start into light and understanding" (97.23–29).

spiration and of the *affectiones scripturae*, its *auctoritas, perfectio*, and *perspicuitas*.[4] That Holy Scripture is *sui ipsius interpres* was not a second point added to the *sola scriptura*, but only made explicit its hermeneutical sense. It is not as if the Scripture principle of the Reformers were joined by a hermeneutical principle, but rather *the Scripture principle of the Reformers is*, rightly understood, *nothing else but a hermeneutical principle*. It says: Scripture is not obscure, so that the tradition is required in order to understand it. Rather, Scripture possesses *claritas*, i.e., it has illuminating power, so that a clarifying light shines from it, among other things also on the tradition.[5]

Now it is true that the consequences of this hermeneutical sense of the *sola scriptura* were not sufficiently clearly recognized during the Reformation itself, and still less in *orthodoxy*. Both in the understanding of "word of God" and also in the conception of hermeneutic this showed itself in a certain lack of clarity and later even in grave errors. Luther, it is true, was aware that the proposition of the *claritas scripturae* demands a distinction be-

---

[4] The consistent development of the early Protestant doctrine of verbal inspiration took place under pressure of the Catholic argument that the very concept "canon" already presents the authority of tradition, and the "sola scriptura" is thus a contradiction in terms inasmuch as this "principle" is in fact a confessional statement of the church. In face of that, the sufficiency of Scripture also in regard to the very point of the authorization of Scripture had to be expressed with the utmost sharpness. The hermeneutical sense of the doctrine of verbal inspiration (which then caused so much confusion precisely in the hermeneutical field) becomes very clear from the conclusion that the pointing of the Hebrew text must also be inspired since the unequivocal meaning of the text seemed to depend on it.

[5] On Luther's doctrine of the *claritas scripturae* cf. esp. *De servo arbitrio* (1525), *WA* 18, pp. 606.1–609.14; 652.23–653.35 (= Clem. 3, pp. 100.34–103.22; 141.1–142.19). "For it should be settled as fundamental, and most firmly fixed in the minds of Christians, that the Holy Scriptures are a spiritual light far brighter even than the sun, especially in what relates to salvation and all essential matters. But because we have been so long persuaded of the opposite, by that pestilent dictum of the Sophists, that the Scriptures are obscure and equivocal, we are compelled to begin by proving this very first principle of ours, by which all else must be proved (a procedure which to philosophers would seem irrational and impossible!)" (*WA* 18, p. 653.28–35 = Clem. 3, p. 142.11–19; cf. J. I. Packer and O. R. Johnston, trans., *Martin Luther on the Bondage of the Will* [Westwood, N.J.: Fleming H. Revell, 1957], p. 125). Cf. R. Hermann, *Von der Klarheit der Heiligen Schrift: Untersuchungen und Erörterungen über Luthers Lehre von der Schrift in De servo arbitrio* (Berlin: Evangelische Verlagsanstalt, 1958).

tween the unrestricted clarity of the *res* of Scripture and a partial obscurity of its *verba*[6]—a distinction which, when pursued further, makes a problem of the relation of word of God and Scripture. But the later efforts to safeguard the Reformers' position led to the orthodox identification of Scripture with the word of God. That jeopardized alike both the Reformers' concept of the word of God and the Reformers' understanding of the *claritas scripturae*.[7] And the lack of clarity in regard to hermeneutic took its toll in exegesis and dogmatics. Exegesis found itself again, as before, under the domination of the dogmatic tradition which was

[6] "I certainly grant that many *passages* in the Scriptures are obscure and hard to elucidate, but that is due, not to the exalted nature of their subject, but to our own linguistic and grammatical ignorance; and it does not in any way prevent our knowing all the *contents* of Scripture. . . . You see, then, that the entire content of the Scriptures has now been brought to light, even though some passages which contain unknown words remain obscure. Thus it is unintelligent, and ungodly too, when you know that the contents of Scripture are as clear as can be, to pronounce them obscure on account of those few obscure words. If words are obscure in one place, they are clear in another. What God has so plainly declared to the world is in some parts of Scripture stated in plain words, while in other parts it still lies hidden under obscure words. But when something stands in broad daylight, and a mass of evidence for it is in broad daylight also, it does not matter whether there is any evidence for it in the dark" (*WA* 18, p. 606.22–37 = Clem. 3, p. 101.20–38; Packer and Johnston, *op. cit.*, pp. 71 f.).

[7] In order to emphasize that the *res* of Scripture can remain *mysteria,* but that the grammatical sense of Scripture can nevertheless be clear to anyone, Luther's observations on the *claritas scripturae* are in orthodoxy seemingly turned upside down: "The Holy Scripture is called 'clear' not on account of its content, but on account of words. For even content lacking clarity can be proposed in clear and perspicuous words (Hollaz). We distinguish between the clarity of the content revealed in Scripture and the lucidity of the words by which the revealed content is denoted. We are speaking about the latter, not the former, since we acknowledge that in Scripture there are contained many abstruse mysteries, inscrutable to the human mind, especially in this life. But we deny that these contents are presented in Scripture in obscure speech and ambiguous words" (Quenstedt). Quoted according to H. Schmidt, *Die Dogmatik der evang.-luth. Kirche,* 7th ed., 1893, p. 46; translation, *The Doctrinal Theology of the Lutheran Church,* C. A. Hay and H. E. Jacobs [Philadelphia, 1889], pp. 85 f.). To be sure, it is not a case of direct contradiction, when we consider Luther's distinction between *externa* and *interna claritas* and notice that the statements quoted from the early Protestant dogmatic theologians concentrate in essence on the problem that Luther puts under the head of *interna claritas*. Nevertheless, there are highly significant changes of emphasis, which of course could be brought out only in a detailed analysis of the early Protestant doctrine of Scripture and of Luther's (not completely thought out) doctrine of the *duplex claritas* (and *obscuritas*) *scripturae*.

always decisive in case of doubt. And dogmatics fell back into its traditional form, without sufficient attention being paid to the significance of the Scripture principle for the method of dogmatics.

Thus it is not only the close connection of the subjects word of God and hermeneutic that has its origin in the Reformers. The heritage of the Reformation also includes where the concept word of God is concerned the latent tension with Holy Scripture, and in regard to hermeneutic the tension between exegesis and dogmatics which is at first likewise latent. And because of that the close conjunction of word of God and hermeneutic was in jeopardy of being transformed by criticism into its opposite. This became clear in the *theology of the modern age*. Using the lever of hermeneutic, it first brought out the tension between exegesis and dogmatics, as also between Scripture and the word of God, and finally called in question the concept of the word of God itself. It was the concentration on the word of God at the Reformation that had conferred such importance on hermeneutic. And now in the modern age hermeneutic threatened to lead to the dissolution of the word of God. If we still bear in mind the internal links indicated with the Reformation, then such a condensed formula may perhaps be applied to the problem of modern theology, without implying an irresponsible condemnation of the development in theological history that has here taken place.[8]

The more recent decided *transition to a theology of the word of God* was in danger of regaining this Reformation theme at the cost of thoughtlessly overlooking the hermeneutical problem. In point of fact, too, some theological oddities did get out of hand, and what is much worse, a late by-product was the intensification of the stuffy atmosphere of a narrow churchiness. Yet we must not judge by such incidental accompaniments. The return to the theology of the word of God resulted from a passionate wrestling with the hermeneutical problem. The various prefaces to Barth's *Romans* are impressive testimonies to that.[9] We are assured that

    [8] Cf. *RGG*[3] III, pp. 253 f.
    [9] Above all the prefaces to the 1st (1918) and 2nd (1921) eds. I quote from the 5th impression of the revised version (Munich: Chr. Kaiser Verlag, 1929).

it is not to be a case of breaking with modern, critical historical hermeneutic, but only of necessary corrections to it. "The critical historical people are not critical enough for me," said Barth.[10]

This critical advance seemed indeed to have purely theological motives, but fitted completely into the general contemporary movement of the hermeneutical problem. In contrast to the traditions of the earlier part of the modern age, the hermeneutical interest had slackened since about the middle of the nineteenth century. But in the debate with positivism and historism the problem of hermeneutic was more deeply and more and more widely involved and so acquired new acuteness. Thus it was not unconnected with general, comprehensive historic changes when in the theology of the last decades the subject of hermeneutic came so much into the foreground once more—and that, too, in critical reflection on the inadequacy of modern hermeneutic hitherto.

But now, it is no accident that the prevailing *dissensus* within theology arose at this point. It is usually marked for simplicity by the names of Barth and Bultmann. In the framework of the present sketch of the problem it seems to present itself as follows: On the one side, the passion for the word of God tends toward disparagement of the hermeneutical problem; on the other side, the interest in the hermeneutical problem appears to jeopardize what is said of the word of God. But we must be very much on

[10] *Ibid.*, p. xii. 1918: "The critical historical method of research into the Bible is right enough: it aims at a preparation for understanding, and that is never superfluous. But, if I had to choose between it and the old doctrine of inspiration, I would definitely take the latter: it has the greater, profounder *more important* right, because its aim is the work of understanding itself, without which all preparation is worthless. I am glad not to have to choose between the two. But my whole attention has been directed to seeing *through* the historical to the Spirit of the Bible, who is the eternal Spirit" (*ibid.*, p. v). 1921: "I have been called a 'declared enemy of *historical criticism.*' . . . But what I reproach them with is not the historical criticism, the right and necessity of which on the contrary I once more explicitly recognize, but the way they stop at an explanation of the text which I cannot call any explanation, but only the first primitive step towards one, namely, at establishing 'what is said' . . . ." (*ibid.*, p. x). The basic hermeneutical impulse of so-called dialectical theology, as it comes to expression in these prefaces of Barth's, has not lost anything of its drive even after four decades. Cf. also R. Bultmann's remark from the year 1924: "It is no accident that the latest movement in theology was not born from the matrix of orthodoxy but in point of fact from liberal theology" (*Glauben und Verstehen* [Tübingen: J. C. B. Mohr, I, 1933, 1]).

our guard against drawing the differences too crudely. It is correct at all events to say that Barth and Bultmann form a very different estimate of the theological relevance of the hermeneutical problem and that this is connected with a difference also in their view of the word of God. Yet Barth has not by any means surrendered his initial hermeneutical impulse, but has let it lead him on to the path of his *Church Dogmatics*. For if his direct treatment of the hermeneutical problem is relatively meager, the *Church Dogmatics* presents over and above it an implicit answer to the hermeneutical problem.[11] On the other hand, Bultmann's continuous concern with the theme of hermeneutic has no other aim than to be the methodological vindication of a theology of the word of God.[12]

The differences are thus bound up with what they have in common. Common to both is that in opposition to historism and psychologism they address themselves to the specific "matter" of theology. But in distinction from the objective approach of the *Church Dogmatics* Bultmann considers the understanding to belong to the matter itself. That is why for him the problem of the preliminary understanding acquires such importance. Common to both is, further, the tendency to surmount the dualism of historical and systematic theology. But while in Barth the methodological tension is set aside altogether and the separation of the disciplines is reduced to a certain practical division of labor, Bultmann finds that precisely where methodology is concerned the element of tension remains, yet so that each theological discipline contains it within itself. Common to both is, lastly, that on no account will they return to the orthodox distinction of *hermeneutica sacra* and *hermeneutica profana*. Barth, however, brings out the unity of hermeneutic by claiming general validity for the hermeneutic dictated by the Bible,[13] while Bultmann on the contrary

---

[11] The hermeneutical problem in Barth (as far as his intentions are concerned) has been taken up without remainder into the discussion of the subject matter of theology.

[12] Perhaps—in addition to the concept of the kerygma which is central for Bultmann's theology—I may recall as an illustration of this fact that the essay on demythologizing ends: "The word became flesh."

[13] "Where does the theory of hermeneutical principles just sketched come from? Well, the very fact that although in itself it is surely as clear as day,

approaches the hermeneutical problem in theology from definite standpoints provided by general hermeneutic.[14]

The discussion of the word of God and hermeneutic appears today to have become bogged down. But it is not by any means over and done with and, as it seems to me, has not even advanced to final alternative answers. One could attempt to take the conversation further by a detailed analysis of the controversy we have just fleetingly touched on between Barth and Bultmann. Yet it seems to me more helpful to approach the phenomena themselves by way of a few remarks on the structure of the problem our subject involves.

II

Whatever precise theological definition may be given to the *concept of the word of God,* at all events it points us to something that happens, *viz.,* to the movement which leads from the text of Holy Scripture to the sermon ("sermon" of course taken in the pregnant sense of proclamation in general). As a first definition of the concept of the word of God the reference to this movement from text to proclamation may suffice. For this is in fact according to Christian tradition the primary place of the concept of the word of God. We here set aside questions that

---

yet it does not after all enjoy general recognition, shows that it can hardly have been derived from general reflections, i.e., from reflections that are possible in a general way, upon the nature of man's word, etc., and thus from a general anthropology. Why do the reflections that are possible in a general way upon the nature of man's word not usually lead to the propositions just stated? I would answer: because special care is taken not to let the theory of hermeneutical principles be dictated, as has of course happened here, by Holy Scripture. . . . It was with the only possible exposition of Holy Scripture in mind that we laid down the principles of exposition just given. Certainly not in the belief that they are valid *only* for the exposition of the Bible, but fully believing that *because* they are valid for the exposition of the Bible they are valid for man's word *in general,* and that they thus have a claim to *general* recognition. . . . There is no such thing as special Biblical hermeneutic. But precisely the general, and only valid hermeneutic must be learned by means of the Bible as the testimony to revelation" (*Die Kirchliche Dogmatik* [Zollikon-Zürich: Evangelische Verlag AG., 1/2, 5th ed., 1960], 515; cf. *Church Dogmatics,* 1/2 [Edinburgh: T. & T. Clark], 465 f.)

[14] "The interpretation of the Biblical Scriptures is not subject to any different conditions of understanding from any other literature" (*Glauben und Verstehen* II, 1952, 231) [*Essays Philosophical and Theological* (London: SCM Press, 1955), p. 256].

probe behind that—why the Holy Scripture that presses for proclamation or the proclamation that takes its stand on Holy Scripture should be marked out in particular above other things as
word of God; or what form of the word of God to some extent
precedes Scripture; and whether the word of God is not found
also outside the relation of text and sermon. For according to
Christian conviction the answers to all these questions can be
truly known only in connection with that movement from the
text to the sermon. But it is of decisive importance to choose this
movement as the starting point for the definition of the concept
of the word of God.

The criticism usually made of the orthodox doctrine is that it
identifies Scripture and the word of God without distinction. And
the correction then made is to say, instead of "Scripture *is* the
word of God," something like, "Scripture *contains* or *witnesses
to* the word of God." In other words, one refers to a factor distinct from Scripture which has to be sought within or behind it.
There is no doubt some truth in that. Yet the decisive short-
coming of the orthodox position lies in the fact that Holy Scripture is spoken of as the word of God without any eye to the
proclamation,[15] and thus without expression being given also to

---

[15] The orthodox understanding of the word of God is completely dominated
by the aspect of the becoming Scripture of God's word. The written word of
God is *monon kai oikeion* the principle of theology (Joh. Wolleb, *Loc. theol.
Prooem. De natura Theologiae,* ed. Cott. II, 8). We acknowledge, therefore,
no other principle of theology than the written word of God. (Joh. Wolleb,
Christ. Theol. Compend., Praecognita Can. V). Orthodoxy too, of course,
knew of the *verbum Dei* as *viva vox,* and indeed knew both of the necessity
of preaching by word of mouth and also of the historic priority of the *verbum
Dei non scriptum.* For the rest, the strong emphasis on the *verbum Dei scriptum* can surely be understood and approved of insofar as it was a case
of deciding the question of the normative authority unequivocally in favor
of Scripture and disputing the normative significance of an oral tradition
that vaguely develops and uncontrollably claims a hearing alongside of
Scripture. For that reason not only the necessity but also the dependability
of Scriptural fixation had to be emphasized. Yet in doing so, all too little
attention was paid to the tension that exists between the character of the
verbum Dei as spoken word and the character of writtenness. Here we see
a startling divergence from the Reformation. Luther, as is well known, insisted that the gospel is really oral preaching: ". . . in the New Testament
the sermons are to be spoken aloud in public and to bring forth in terms
of speech and hearing what was formerly hidden in the letter and in secret
vision. Forasmuch as the New Testament is nothing else but the unlocking

and revealing of the Old Testament. . . . That, too, is why Christ himself did not write his teaching, as Moses did his, but delivered it orally, also commanded to deliver it orally and gave no command to write it. . . . For that reason it is not at all the manner of the New Testament to write books of Christian doctrine, but there should everywhere, without books, be good, learned, spiritually minded, diligent preachers to draw the living word from the ancient Scriptures and constantly bring it to life before the people, as the apostles did. For before ever they wrote, they had preached to and con verted the people by word of mouth, which also was their real apostolic and New Testament work. . . . That books had to be written, however, is at once a great failure and a weakness of spirit that was enforced by necessity and not by the manner of the New Testament" (*Kirchenpostille* 1522, *WA* 10/1, 1, pp. 625.12–628.8. Further, *WA* 10/1, 1, pp. 17.4–18.1 and 10/1, 2, pp. 34.12–35.3. Cf. G. Ebeling, *Evang. Evangelienauslegung* [Munich: Evangelischer Verlag Albert Lempp, 1942], pp. 365 ff.; H. Ostergaard-Nielsen, *Scriptura sacra et viva vox* [Munich: Chr. Kaiser Verlag, 1957]. On the distinction between Scripture and spoken word depends not only the right understanding of the difference between the Old Testament and the New Testament, but also—as a presupposition of that, though not identical with it —the right understanding of the relation of law and gospel. For the distinction of law and gospel concerns their *efficacia,* and that in turn goes with a difference in their word character. The difference between written and spoken word, however, is no purely formal one. Reading aloud what is written does not yet produce spoken word in the sense Luther means here. He is concerned with the insight into the difference of law and gospel and can be rightly interpreted only in the light of the distinction of law and gospel. "For the preaching of the gospel ought to be far different from the preaching of the law. The law was written on tablets and was a dead writing, a tablet enclosed within limits and therefore not sufficiently efficacious. But the gospel is committed to the living and most free voice poured out into the ears of the hearers. Therefore it has greater power for conversion" (*Enarr.* 1521: *WA* 7, p. 526.12–16). It is symptomatic of the impoverishment of the understanding of the word in orthodoxy that those insights were completely lost from sight. It was no longer borne in mind that to the essence of the word belongs its oral character, i.e., its character of an event in personal relationship, that the word is thus no isolated bearer of meanings, but an event that effects something and aims at something. In Joh. Gerhard I find the point of view we have just discussed mentioned only once, but significantly enough in the form of a Catholic objection which is rebutted. Gerhard (*Loci theol. loc* I *De script. s.,* cap. 2, q. 3, ed. Cott. II, 30) quotes among other things remarks of the Catholic apologetic theologians Lindanus (The nature of the evangelical word clearly shrinks back from writing and letters) and Pistorius (The apostles did not write out of an intention to do so, but on account of unexpected necessity). The orthodox understanding of the *verbum Dei as verbum scriptum* stood on its own in isolation from the proclamation that is to take place, and so shrunk to an unhistoric understanding of the word. From the standpoint of Luther it is obvious that that endangered both the right distinction between the Old and New Testaments and also the right distinction of law and gospel. These critical considerations are not mentioned in the otherwise so praiseworthy book by Bengt Hägglund, *Die Heilige Schrift und ihre Deutung in der Theologie Joh. Gerhards: Eine Untersuchung über das altlutherische Schriftverständnis* (Lund: C. W. K. Gleerup, 1951).

the future to which Holy Scripture points forward as its own future. On closer inspection the concept of the word of God certainly seeks to be interpreted in a still more comprehensive sense in terms of event. Yet that results from the basic starting point in the process of the text becoming proclamation. The question as to the real nature of this event must therefore be at least one essential element in the doctrine of the word of God.

Now whatever the precise definition that may be given to "hermeneutic," as the theory of understanding it in any case has to do with the word event. And indeed, like every science, it ultimately has a practical aim, as an aid to the word event, *viz.,* as guidance on how a word that has taken place comes to be understood. That is not intended by any means to simplify hermeneutic by reducing it to a collection of rules. But even when the hermeneutical problem is entered into radically, teaching about understanding must give proof of itself by serving the understanding, be it only in providing a critical indication of its limits.

Now if in the word of God we have a case of the word event that leads from the text of Holy Scripture to the proclamation, then the question is whether hermeneutic can be expected to help toward that happening rightly. Here doubts arise at once. Can the event of the word of God be served at all by scientific methods? Must the hermeneutical approach as such not at once have a destructive effect on the concept of the word of God, as also on the corresponding concept of the Holy Spirit? But doubts, too, of a less radical kind also call in question the service of hermeneutic here. Does not hermeneutic deal only with an exposition which is subject to scientific criteria? Even then there are, as is well known, already great methodological difficulties. Now insofar as the sermon is preceded by a scientific exposition of the text, hermeneutic may also have significance for it. But then the question remains what the scientific exposition contributes to the sermon and what distinguishes it from the exposition that takes place in the sermon itself; whether it is appropriate to contrast the latter as "practical" exposition with the scientific kind and so withdraw it from the strict standpoint of hermeneutic, or to distinguish it as *applicatio* from the *explicatio* and thereby deny that the sermon in its essential nature is exposition at all, however much it may contain textual exposition. Yet is it not bringing the event of the word of God into dangerous isolation from word events in general if we withdraw it from the reach of hermeneutic? Indeed, is it not the case that the concept of the word of God can be used at all only when hermeneutical justification can be given for it? But what does "hermeneutic" then mean? Let us therefore attempt first of all a more precise clarification of the concept hermeneutic.

III

According to the common view there is a sharp distinction between exegesis as the process of exposition itself and hermeneutic as the theory of exposition. And here indeed it is assumed that verbal statements are the object of exposition, i.e., the thing requiring exposition. According to the several kinds of verbal statement, general hermeneutic may be differentiated into various special hermeneutic, though of course without departing from the comprehensive framework of general hermeneutic.

This customary view of hermeneutic requires correction in various respects.

1. On the threshold of the Enlightenment the *distinction of general and special hermeneutic* had taken the place of the very differently articulated orthodox distinction of *hermeneutica sacra* and *hermeneutica profana*.[16] The basic proposition that

16 It was still retained in pietism, where also for the first time the concept hermeneutic coined in the middle of the seventeenth century (cf. *RGG*[3] III, p. 255) had made possible the formula *hermeneutica sacra*. Joh. Jak. Rambach defines this (with characteristic emphasis on the requisite subjective presuppositions): "Taken in a first sense, it is a practical faculty by which the Christian, equipped with a good mind and with the tools of a good mind as they might be at his disposal and aided by the light of the Holy Spirit, investigates the meaning of the Scripture from the Holy Scripture itself, to his own benefit and salvation. In a second sense, 'sacred hermeneutic' is a practical habit by which the theological doctor, sufficiently equipped with the necessary tools, under the guiding light of the Holy Spirit, is made capable of legitimately investigating the meaning of Scripture, and, after this investigation, of explaining it to others and applying it wisely so that in this way the glory of God and the salvation of men is promoted" (*Institutiones hermeneuticae sacrae*, 1723). J. A. Ernesti, on the other hand, gives

Holy Scripture is not to be differently interpreted from other books[17] seemed, it is true, now to allow of only one single science of hermeneutic and to relieve theology of any special discussion of the hermeneutical problem, indeed even to forbid it. But owing to the colorlessness and abstractness of the proposition of a general hermeneutic, it did not exclude the introduction of various special hermeneutic applied and related to concrete subjects, as long as these various special hermeneutic remained subject to, and derived from, general hermeneutical criteria. Indeed, modern hermeneutic developed at first almost entirely in the form of special hermeneutic of such kinds,[18] in the construction of which theology played an outstanding part along with classical philology and jurisprudence. It can even be said that the principle of a single science of hermeneutic worked itself out in practice as the principle of an increasing hermeneutical specialization.

For theology this meant in the first instance that, although specifically theological hermeneutic disappeared, there arose within theology various hermeneutics in different degrees of specialization, such as Biblical—Old Testament or New Testament—hermeneutic, or (the demand for this at all events has already been made) in such a way that each Biblical book requires a special hermeneutic.[19] We must not let ourselves be deceived about the real nature of this state of affairs by, say, the fact that such extreme specialization was never realized, and that Biblical—Old or New Testament—hermeneutic owing to the theological dignity

---

a general definition of hermeneutic: "Hermeneutic is a science which leads a man to the subtlety both of understanding and interpreting the sentences of any author, or a science which hands down an account of the meaning, to be both discovered and explained with subtlety, of all words" (*Institutio interpretis N.T.,* 1761).

[17] For the first time in J. A. Turrentini (*De sacrae scripturae interpretandae methodo tractatus bipartitus,* 1728): "There is no method of interpreting Scripture other than that of other books."

[18] An early exception is: J. M. Chladenius, *Einleitung zur richtigen Auslegung vernünftiger Reden und Schriften,* 1742.

[19] "Today we know that it is only the kind of material and the special interest we take in it that puts a peculiar stamp on hermeneutic. Now we must make, and fulfill, the demand to set alongside the special hermeneutic for the New Testament as a whole also an individual hermeneutic for each New Testament book" (E. von Dobschütz, *Vom Auslegen des NT* [Göttingen: Vandenhoeck und Ruprecht, 1927], p. 16).

of these books at once gives the impression of theological hermeneutic. Strictly, however, the basic conception is that there is no such thing as theological hermeneutic. For the differentiation in hermeneutic is held to be justified indeed from the standpoint of different literary complexes, but not on the basis of particular, nonuniversal epistemological principles such as those of theology. Thus hermeneutic in theology became the methodology of definite individual disciplines—*viz.*, the Biblical ones—and therewith at once the boundary separating them from dogmatics, which as such had nothing to do with hermeneutic.

The fact that in contrast to this, historical and systematic theology today join hands in the hermeneutical problem and hermeneutic has expanded to become the methodology no longer merely of individual theological disciplines but of theology as a whole, is to a great extent a distant result of Schleiermacher. For his pioneer view of hermeneutic, as the theory of the conditions on which understanding is possible, modified the relation of general and special hermeneutic in a twofold way.

First, a special hermeneutic must now take strict account of what can here be *differentia specifica*. The view which Schleiermacher himself here put forward in detail[20] is doubtless obsolete.

[20] "The answer, then, to the question whether and how far New Testament hermeneutic is of a special kind is as follows. On the linguistic side it does not appear to be special, for here it is to be related in the first instance to the Greek language. On the psychological side, however, the New Testament does not appear as a unity, but a distinction has to be made between didactic and historical writings. These are different types (*Gattungen*), which certainly demand different hermeneutical rules. Yet that does not yet give rise to a special hermeneutic. All the same, New Testament hermeneutic is a special kind, but only in relation to its compound linguistic ground or the Hebraizing character of its language. . . . For when a spiritual development takes place in a people, then there also arises a new linguistic development. Now as every new spiritual principle has a formative effect on language, so also has the Christian spirit. But that does not in other cases give rise to any special hermeneutic. If a people begins to philosophize, then it displays a vast linguistic development, but it does not require any special hermeneutic. The new Christian spirit, however, appears in the New Testament in a hybrid language, in which Hebrew is the stem in which the new thing was first thought, but Greek was grafted on to it. For that reason New Testament hermeneutic is to be treated as a special kind. As the mixture of languages is an exception, and not a natural condition, so too New Testament hermeneutic as special hermeneutic does not derive from general hermeneutic in the regular way" (D. F. Schleiermacher, *Hermeneutik und Kritik mit*

His basic demand, however, is still valid. The view emphatically advanced today by Bultmann, that the difference as to what one is after in the interrogation (*Woraufhin der Befragung*) has differentiating character in the hermeneutical sphere,[21] is a first step toward clarification of this side of the hermeneutical problem— a step that is capable of being developed and certainly also stands in need of further development. This provides, without relapsing into an alleged *hermeneutica sacra*, the possibility of speaking of a hermencutic related to theology as a whole, which on the basis of the specifically theological approach works out structures and criteria of theological understanding that apply in theology not only to the exegetical but also to the dogmatic understanding. It is absolutely necessary that this should then be done in demonstrable connection with a general theory of understanding. The nature of the connection, however, raises difficult problems.

The other impulse which Schleiermacher gave to the further history of hermeneutic is today discernible above all in a surprisingly *extended use of the word hermeneutic*. It is not only that hermeneutic can now be spoken of in sciences in which it was not possible before and which do not have to do with texts at all but with phenomena—for example psychology. Rather, the development from Schleiermacher via Dilthey to Heidegger shows that the idea of a theory of understanding is on the move toward laying the foundation of the humanities, indeed even becomes the essence of philosophy,[22] that hermeneutic now takes the place of the classical epistemological theory,[23] and indeed that fundamental ontology appears as hermeneutic.[24]

besonderer Beziehung auf das NT, ed. F. Lücke, *Sämtliche Werke* I, 7 [Berlin: G. Reimer, 1858], pp. 27 f.).

[21] R. Bultmann, "Das Problem der Hermeneutik," in *Glauben und Verstehen* II, esp. pp. 217 f., 227 ff. [*Essays Philosophical and Theological,* pp. 240 ff., 252 ff.]; *Geschichte und Eschatologie* (Tübingen: J. C. B. Mohr, 1958), pp. 131 ff. [*The Presence of Eternity* (Edinburgh: University Press, 1957), pp. 113 ff.]. It would be well to raise the problem of a systematic statement of the possibilities as to what one is after in the interrogation, as also of the criteria of its application.

[22] O. F. Bollnow, *Dilthey: Eine Einführung in seine Philosophie* (Stuttgart: Kohlhammer, 1936; 2nd ed., 1955), pp. 24 f., 212 f.

[23] Cf. W. Wieland, article "Erkenntnistheorie," *RGG*³ II, pp. 559 ff.

[24] M. Heidegger, *Sein und Zeit* (Tübingen: Max Niemeyer Verlag, 9th

Thus outside of theology, too, hermeneutic today is breaking through the old, narrow bounds of philological or historiographical hermeneutic, or is plumbing their depths. For theology the hermeneutical problem is therefore today becoming the place of meeting with philosophy. And that always involves at the same time both community and contrast. This confirms once again that in an approach so radical as this there is point in speaking of theological hermeneutic without in any way refurbishing the division into *hermeneutica sacra* and *profana*.

2. The customary view that *hermeneutic is the theory of the exposition of texts* already seemed a moment ago to have undergone correction in that phenomena can also be objects of exposition. If we followed that further, then we should doubtless have to limit it to phenomena insofar as they have to do with the linguisticality of existence, and are thus "texts" in the wider sense. Hermeneutic would then also remain related to the word event. But what is now to be held against the usual view is something other than that.

It is usually taken for granted that the reason why hermeneutic has to do with the word event is that verbal statements pose the problem of understanding. Now however much the need for hermeneutic does in fact arise primarily from difficulties of understanding in the word event, it is nevertheless completely false to take this situation as the point of orientation for one's basic grasp of the relation between word and understanding and of what is ultimately constitutive for hermeneutic. The superficial view of understanding turns matters upside down and must therefore be completely reversed. *The primary phenomenon in the realm of understanding is not understanding* OF *language, but understanding* THROUGH *language*. The word is not really the object of understanding, and thus the thing that poses the problem of understanding, the solution of which requires exposition and therefore also hermeneutic as the theory of understanding. Rather, the word is what opens up and mediates understanding, i.e., brings something to understanding. *The word itself has a hermeneutical*

ed., 1960), pp. 37 f. [*Being and Time* (London and New York: SCM Press, 1962), pp. 61 f.].

function. If the word event takes place normally, i.e., according to its appointed purpose, then there is no need of any aid to understanding, but it is itself an aid to understanding. It is to my mind not unimportant for the proper grasp of the hermeneutical problem whether we set out from the idea that a verbal statement in itself is something obscure into which the light of the understanding must be introduced from elsewhere, or whether, on the contrary, we set out from the fact that the situation in terms of which and into which the verbal statement is made is something obscure which is then illumined by the verbal statement. This starting point opens up three important perspectives for the question of hermeneutic.

First, interpretation, and therefore also *hermeneutic,* is *requisite* only in the case *where the word event is hindered* for some reason or other. But for that reason also the hermeneutical aid can consist only in removing hindrances in order to let the word perform its own hermeneutical function. And the removing of hindrances to understanding can usually likewise take place only by word. For hermeneutic is of course not a departure from the linguistic realm in order to understand language, but a deeper penetration into the linguistic realm in order to understand by means of language.

From the point of view that it is a question of removing hindrances, we can now also grasp that the scope of the hermeneutical task can vary in extent. There is relative justification for restricting ourselves to what immediately concerns the grammatical and philological understanding of a text. We can include in the realm of the hermeneutical task also the very much wider problem of historical understanding. We can extend hermeneutic also to the understanding of what confronts us with the task of understanding, by encountering us in the present. And we can thus, moving ever further afield, relate hermeneutic to the problem of understanding as such, i.e., to the problem of the ultimate conditions under which it is possible for understanding to take place at all. We are not, of course, left to choose at will. How radically we have to consider the hermeneutical problem depends on the extent to which lack of understanding arises.

Secondly, because hermeneutic can make room only for the word's own hermeneutical function, and thus because, as we could also say, hermeneutic only serves the word's own intelligibility, the content and *object of hermeneutic is the word event as such.* For where a word happens, understanding is made possible. If hermeneutic, in order to be an aid to understanding, has to reflect on the conditions under which understanding is possible, then it has to reflect on the nature of words. *Hermeneutic as the theory of understanding must therefore be the theory of words.*

If that is formulated with the help of Greek by saying that hermeneutic is the theory of the Logos, then within the limits of Greek thinking that would doubtless seem very reasonable.[25] For the Logos which holds equal sway in things and in the knowing subject himself is the condition of the possibility of understanding. The Logos is for the Greek a hermeneutical principle. It is a question, of course, what relation responsible hermeneutic today could adopt toward this Greek conception of hermeneutic. However little explication we have as yet given to our references to word event and linguistic event, there is nevertheless obviously a considerable difference from the Greek Logos concept. Yet for all that, wherever the subject of hermeneutic is taken up, contact with the problems of Greek thinking is surely *conditio sine qua non.* For the taking up of the hermeneutical problem has its origin in Greek thinking. And however far we may diverge in our view of the word event, hermeneutic will never be able to enter into complete opposition to the Greek Logos. Otherwise, it would have to be denied altogether that hermeneutic is an undertaking which makes sense.

And lastly, if what is constitutive for hermeneutic is the word that does not require to be made understandable but itself opens up understanding, then hermeneutic, just because it has to do with the word event, has always to do at once with the thing that is to be brought to understanding by means of the word event. For that reason it is false to hold that hermeneutic is restricted to pure matters of form. For *in that hermeneutic addresses itself di-*

---

[25] Cf. Kleinknecht on the Logos in Greek thought and Hellenism, *ThWNT* IV, 76 ff.

rectly to the word, it addresses itself directly to the reality that comes to understanding through the word. True, to speak of the formal character of hermeneutic is right enough in a way, if it is borne in mind that "formal" is the designation of a relation, so that the selfsame thing which in one regard is a definition of content can in another respect be a formal definition.

That hermeneutic must always in some way or other have a bearing on actualities, is a thing I now merely indicate by mentioning a few symptoms in a disconnected list: We can get to the root of understanding only when we encounter what is not understood and what cannot be understood. We can know about the nature of words only when we come upon what is underivably given and is beyond the reach of words. Words produce understanding only by appealing to experience and leading to experience. Only where word has already taken place can word take place. Only where there is already previous understanding can understanding take place. Only a man who is already concerned with the matter in question can be claimed for it.

The significance of this for the grasp of the hermeneutical relationships is that the hearer's relation to the verbal statement must always be coupled with a corresponding relation to reality (to which incidentally there is added a third, at least potential relation to his fellow men, in order to verify his understanding by joint understanding). It follows for the hermeneutical removal of hindrances to understanding that apart from difficulties of understanding that can be removed by the manifold means of philological and historical interpretation, there are also difficulties of a kind that have their ground in the relation to the matter in question and to overcome which we must therefore also begin with that relation.[26]

26 Luther knew about that: "The things (*res*) are preceptors. One cannot make sense of the words if he does not understand the things (*res*). Therefore Munsterus often errs because he does not understand the things (*res*). I myself have explained more passages through knowledge of the things than the grammarians by other knowledge. If the lawyers were not to understand the things (*res*), nobody would understand the words. Therefore, the study of the things (*res*)—that's the thing" (*WA Table Talk* 5, p. 26.11–16, No. 5246). "There remains only the grammar (*grammatica*) which has to give way to theology. For the words are subject to and have to give way to

3. A third correction of the common view relates to the seemingly so straightforward and sensible *distinction between exegesis* or interpretation *and hermeneutic*. It is true that this distinction brings us into certain difficulties with the wide use in Greek of *hermēneuein,* which of course is really a synonym of *exēgeisthai* and *interpretari.*[27] But why should a terminology of somewhat arbitrary coining, such as appeared in the seventeenth century with the concept hermeneutic, not be left as valid?

Now I think all the same that the basic meaning of *hermēneuein,* to bring "to understanding," which combines the various meanings "state," "expound," and "translate," accords very well with the real sense of hermeneutic. Indeed, I hold it moreover to be in the nature of the case that the words interpretation and hermeneutic at bottom mean the same. True, it is at first sight one thing to interpret and another to reflect on the method of interpretation. We do not expect the same of New Testament exegesis as of New Testament hermeneutic. Yet how is hermeneutical insight actually acquired? Where does hermeneutic itself find the basis of its knowledge? If hermeneutic is the theory of understanding, then how, we must surely ask, does understanding itself come to understanding? If hermeneutic as the theory of understanding is the theory of words, how then does "word" itself come to expression so that there can be a theory of words? If hermeneutic is to be an aid to understanding, an auxiliary in the word event, then where is understanding opened up in such a way that aid to understanding is to be expected from that quarter? Where do words so encounter us, where do words so take place, that therein the word event itself comes into view? If, as we have made clear, "word" itself is a hermeneutical principle, i.e., is that from which understanding proceeds and in which it has its origin, then hermeneutic as the theory of words must thus arise from the word event itself. *Hermeneutic therefore, in order to be an aid to interpretation, must itself be interpretation.* Here

---

the things (*res*), not the things (*res*) to the words, and the utterance rightly follows the meaning, and the letter follows the spirit" (*WA* 5, p. 634.14–16; *Op. in ps.*).

[27] *RGG*[3] III, p. 243.

we have the famous hermeneutical circle in its methodological significance for hermeneutic itself.

The question that is now constitutive for hermeneutic—the question where we are encountered by *the* word event which becomes the source of the understanding of word events, which is thus of relevance for fundamental ontology, and which we have to hold to in order to achieve hermeneutical insight—is a question which obviously calls for ultimate decisions and therefore also, as we must suppose, gives rise to ultimate differences. For although hermeneutic is meant to serve understanding, and therefore assuredly also agreement, yet it is part of the phenomenon of understanding that the ground of the understanding, being a point beyond which no further questioning is possible, confronts us with a decision. Comprehensive differences of understanding, such as those for example between the confessions, are therefore of a hermeneutical kind and by their antithetical character point the ultimate limits of the possibility of agreement, just because they touch upon ultimate mysteries of the ground of understanding. This much, however, can be said in general terms on the question of what has to be the guiding light of hermeneutic: it must be a word event in the comprehensive sense that it embraces both linguistic tradition and encounter with reality. Only by facing up to both of these together can hermeneutical knowledge be acquired.

IV

Our observations on the nature of hermeneutic, which were meant to take us beyond the common view, have remained still in abstract generalities and have also still left aside entirely the question of theological hermeneutic. In the short space at my disposal I can neither develop the first step I have indicated toward a hermeneutical theory of "words" and thereby make it concrete, nor enter into all the many important theological problems which now present themselves again the more forcibly for having been left out of account meantime. Any reasonable man will pardon that, provided I add a few pointers at least to bring us to the *basic problem of theological hermeneutic*. I do so in three steps, by remarking on the relation between general and theological hermeneutic, on the relation between word and word of God, and finally on the point with which we started—the relation between text and sermon.

1. In our introductory deliberations the question arose whether the word of God and hermeneutic do not stand to each other in a relationship of outright hostility, so that faith in the word of God would forbid the hermeneutical approach and the hermeneutical approach would destroy the concept of the word of God. The central point in our deliberations on hermeneutic—*viz.*, that "word" itself has a hermeneutical character and hermeneutic is the theory of "word"　now suggests as a corresponding proposition: *theological hermeneutic is the theory or doctrine of the word of God*. The seeming simplicity of this step, however, must not allow us to overlook the problems it involves. For in fact the very point in dispute is whether and how far there is room for the two propositions alongside of each other.

[margin note: Relations between general and theological hermaneutic]

This much, however, must be clear: If the concept of the word of God is to be taken strictly, then of course the word of God must be ascribed hermeneutical relevance for theology, i.e., the word of God must then in itself be a source of theological understanding; and the structure of the understanding peculiar to theology must result from the essential structure of the word of God. The fact that hermeneutic of such a kind, as a theological doctrine of understanding, is then a doctrine of the word of God and consequently already *materialiter* interpretation of theological statements, is surely hardly an objection. It is no more so than the fact that then hermeneutic is ascribed the role of a basic theological methodology and its restriction to the methodology of individual theological disciplines—*viz.*, the exegetical ones—is set aside.

On the other hand, we must explicitly consider the rightness of the proviso we have just made in regard to these statements. Is *the concept of the word of God to be taken strictly*, i.e., does it mean *word in the proper sense*, or is the word of God a mythical concept and therefore only symbolical in character, and is the speaking structure that belongs to the so-called word of God consequently also that of mythical speaking and the structure of understanding that belongs to it that of mythical understanding? This is the decisive point for determining whether the word of God allows of conjunction with the idea of hermeneutic with its roots in the Greek concept of the Logos. For the mythical as such does not tolerate that conjunction. *In face of the mythical, hermeneutic must become demythologizing.* For we have departed from mythical thinking the moment we adopt the hermeneutical approach. That Christian faith has adopted the hermeneutical approach is indeed identical with its having assented to the possibility and necessity of theology. And that again was expressed in its asserting an association between the Biblical concept of the word of God and the Logos concept of Greek philosophy. It is true that in doing so the considerable difference between the two was largely obliterated. But an interpretation in terms of pure antithesis would not do justice to the significant fact that what the Bible means by "word" does not, for all its differences, put out of commission what the Greek understands by "word," while on the other hand the Greek conception of hermeneutic, with its root in the Logos idea, allows of being corrected in the light of the Biblical understanding of "word."

This is true in the first instance quite apart from the concept of the word of God. For in what the Bible understands by "word" and (not unconnected with that) in the characteristic way the Biblical thinker's understanding works and in what he understands by "reality," experiences are comprised and dimensions of understanding opened up which permitted of an exceedingly fruitful encounter with Greek thought. But now the concept of the word of God forms no exception to that, insofar as "word" here does not mean any special, supernatural word (and incidentally, God does not mean any separate, special Reality), but true, proper, finally valid word.[28] For that reason theological her-

[28] On what follows cf. the chapters "The Communication of Faith" and "The Word of God and Language" in G. Ebeling, *Das Wesen des Christlichen Glaubens* (Tübingen: J. C. B. Mohr, 1959; 2nd ed., 1960), pp. 102 ff., 243 ff. [*The Nature of Faith* (Philadelphia: Muhlenberg Press, 1961), pp. 84 ff., 182 ff.]

meneutic can find itself over wide areas in agreement with non-theological hermeneutic, but where the hermeneutical problem reaches the ultimate ground of understanding, it must enter into conflict with all nontheological hermeneutic—not in order to defend its own special right to independent existence, but in order to maintain responsibly to all comers in the field of hermeneutic the fact that God's word is the ultimate ground of understanding because it is here in the last analysis that word is encountered as word and understanding as understanding. For the claim to truth which is made here means truth absolutely. And for that reason it always combines both things: agreement with all truth and opposition to what everyone is expected to reject as untruth.

2. The point we have just mentioned, the *relation between word of God and word in general,* requires some further elucidation. It is a cardinal error in theology when God is spoken of as a part of reality and when for that reason God is thought of as something additional to the rest of reality. The inference is that we should first of all have to speak of God and the world in themselves as two separate entities side by side and only then of their relationship as one of mutual supplementation or of mutual competition. But the fact is that God cannot be spoken of in theology without the world thereby coming to expression as event, and the world cannot be spoken of in theology without God thereby likewise coming to expression as event.

This cardinal error by which theology is constantly threatened is also the ground of the fundamental misunderstanding according to which God's word is, so to speak, a separate class of word alongside the word spoken between men, which is otherwise the only thing we usually call word. God's word is here said to be not really word at all in the sense of the normal, natural, historic word that takes place between men. It is said that if it would reach man, then it must first be transformed into a human word, translated as it were from God's language into man's language —a process in which, as in every process of translation, we have naturally to reckon with certain foreshortenings and distortions. These shortcomings are then exculpated by means of the idea of accommodation, or the process is interpreted as analogous to the

[margin handwritten note: The Word of God is not in a special class separated from the word of man.]

incarnation: As God finally took the highest, or lowest, step of becoming man, so (it is said) God's word earlier, and in another form of course also later, becomes at least a human word. But this is a conglomeration of dreadful misinterpretations which cannot here be submitted to detailed critical analysis. Let me make only this one brief remark: When John 1:14 says that the word became flesh, that surely means (interpreted of course in very abbreviated terms) that here word became event in a sense so complete that being word and being man became one. But that does not allow of any analogical transference to the relation of two kinds of word—let us say for the moment, in order to lay bare the metaphysical misunderstanding it contains, of heavenly word and earthly word. When the Bible speaks of God's word,[29] then it means here unreservedly word as word—word that as far as its word character is concerned is completely normal, let us not hesitate to say: natural, oral word taking place between man and man.

The Bible can, of course, radically contrast God's word and man's word, but not in regard to the question of the verbal or, to put it still more sharply, spoken character of the word concerned, but rather in view of the question who is the real speaker of it: God, who is *verax*, or man, who is *mendax*.[30] Thus the point of the contrast is whether the word event is one that is misused and corrupted by man, or whether it is one that is sound, pure, and fully realized—which is what is meant to be the destiny, and indeed the natural destiny, of words in human society. And that implies at the same time a contrast in what the word produces: whether it is a destructive and deadly word or one that brings wholeness and gives life. The full theological bearing of this difference, however, can come to light only when word is really taken as word, and when it is clear that God and word

[29] Cf. G. Bornkamm, "Gotteswort und Menschenwort im NT," in *Studien zu Antike und Urchristentum (Ges. Aufs.* II), *Beitr. zur evang. Theol.* 28 (1959), pp. 223–236; R. Hermann, *Gotteswort und Menschenwort in der Bibel: Eine Untersuchung zu theol. Grundfragen der Hermeneutik* (Berlin: Evangelische Verlagsanstalt, 1956).
[30] Rom. 3:4.

are no more contradictory than man and word, but on the contrary it is "word" that unites God and man.

To make that clear would require a comprehensive analysis which must certainly take its bearings on the word of God, yet in such a way that in so doing the whole range of experience with words is kept in view and called upon. Here of course it would then be necessary for the profound *difference between the Greek and Hebrew understanding of word, truth, and reality*[31] to be examined—*viz.*, that (in accordance with the different etymology) Logos on the one hand means "coherence,"[32] and on the other hand *dabar* means that in which a thing shows itself:[33] on the one hand a timeless, on the other, a historic understanding of word. And no doubt it is only the latter that really lays hold of what words mean for man's existence between God and the world. Word is, taken strictly, happening word. It is not enough to inquire into its intrinsic meaning, but that must be joined up with the question of its future, of what it effects. For ultimately the questions as to the content and the power of words are idenical. Word is therefore rightly understood only when it is viewed as an event which—like love—involves at least two. The basic structure of word is therefore not statement—that is an abstract variety of the word event—but appraisal, certainly not in the colorless sense of information, but in the pregnant sense of participation and communication.

That helps to clarify the question of why words are required at all. It is a long way off the mark when "word" is understood as

[31] H. von Soden, "Was ist Wahrheit? Vom geschichtlichen Begriff der Wahrheit," in *Urchristentum und Geschichte,* I (Tübingen: J. C. B. Mohr, 1951), 1–24; L. Köhler, *Der hebräische Mensch* (Tübingen: J. C. B. Mohr, 1953), pp. 117 ff.; Thorleif Boman, *Das hebräische Denken im Vergleich mit dem griechischen* (Göttingen: Vandenhoeck und Ruprecht, 1952; 2nd ed., 1954), esp. pp. 45 ff. [*Hebrew Thought compared with Greek,* translated by J. L. Moreau (Philadelphia: Westminster Press, 1960), pp. 58 ff.]

[32] *ThWNT* IV, 78.34.

[33] Whether this attempt to formulate the specific character of the Hebrew understanding of word can be justified also from the etymological standpoint is admittedly questionable. On the disputed etymology of *dabar* cf. O. Grether, *Name und Wort Gottes im AT, Beih. zur ZAW* 64 (1934), pp. 59 ff.; O. Procksch, in *ThWNT* IV, 89 f.; T. Boman, *op. cit.,* p. 52 [p. 65].

a technical means of rational intercourse. Certainly it must serve as that, too; and if we traced that idea to its roots, then we should doubtless also come upon the decisive point. More appropriate is the more comprehensive answer for which our discussion has already paved the way: word serves understanding. Where word happens rightly, existence is illumined (and that naturally always means existence in association with others). We could, however, still go a step further and in seeming tautology say: word serves speaking. And the mocking counterquestion whether it is really such a serviceable thing would have to be met and mastered by a "Yes indeed!" If the word is the thing which shows what the speaker is, then we should have to say: the precise *purpose which the word is meant to serve is that man shows himself as man*. For that is his destiny. And for that reason word is absolutely necessary to man as man. For his destiny is to exist as response. He is asked what he has to say. He is not destined to have nothing to say and to have to remain dumb. His existence is, rightly understood, a word event which has its origin in the word of God and, in response to that word, makes openings by a right and salutary use of words. Therein man is the image of God.

Man fails toward man, and so for that very reason also toward God, in the right use of words. This fact lends urgency to the search for that word which is a true, necessary, salutary, remedial, and therefore unequivocal and crystal-clear word, for the word which, because it accords with man's destiny, corresponds to God, that is, the search for the word by means of which one man can speak God to another so that God comes to man and man to God. That salvation is to be expected solely from words and is therefore at one and the same time a wholly divine and a wholly human thing—these are no paradoxes and whimseys.

This opens up a deeper insight into the nature of the word event. As communication word is promise. It is most purely promise when it refers to something that is not present but absent—and that, too, in such a way that in the promise the absent thing so to speak presents itself; that is, when in word the speaker pledges and imparts himself to the other and opens a future to him by awakening faith within him. The conjunction of God, word, faith, future as the prime necessity for the good of man's human nature requires to be understood as a single vast coherent complex and not as some sort of chance conglomeration to be accepted on positivist terms.

This word event takes place, Christians confess, in the gospel. It is savingly related to the word event which always proceeds from God and strikes the foolish man as the law which kills. But for that reason, too, it is only in the light of the gospel that we can grasp what God's word really means and how far the law is God's word. For God's word must not on any account be reduced to a formal concept which would be indifferent toward any intrinsic definition of the word of God.[34] For God's word is not various things, but one single thing—the word that makes man human by making him a believer, i.e., a man who confesses to God as his future and therefore does not fail his fellow men in the one absolutely necessary and salutary thing, viz., true word.

3. There is no need to state here the reasons *why* the proclamation of the word of God appeals to Scripture, and Scripture thus becomes the text of the sermon. I would merely go on to add in conclusion an explanation of *how* that happens, in what sense Scripture is the text of the sermon, and thus how *text and sermon* are related to each other.

We begin with the question: What is the aim of the text? It aims at all events to be preserved, read, and handed on—and that, too, in the service of the proclamation. Here of course we should at once have to make differentiations, not only between Old and New Testament texts, but also in both cases between different degrees of explicitness with which the aim is proclamation. The question of the aim of the text could indeed be shifted from the individual text to the Biblical canon as such. It

---

[34] Cf. Ebeling, "Erwägungen zur Lehre vom Gesetz," *Wort und Glaube*, pp. 255 ff., esp. pp. 277 ff. [translated by James W. Leitch, *Word and Faith*, pp. 247 ff., esp. pp. 265 ff.].

would of course be a question whether the original intention of the canon would be done justice to by asserting that it aims at being a collection of sermon texts. But above all in face of the individual text it would be a doubtful proceeding to ignore that text itself where this basic question is concerned. It should not be supposed that any and every text in Holy Scripture is in itself a sermon text. What is claimed to be a sermon text must at all events seek to serve the proclamation of the word of God. Yet it would not be right to say: *The text* seeks to be proclaimed. Apart from the fact that such a direct, authoritative aim is present in relatively few texts, that way of putting it would also be fundamentally wrong. For it is not *texts* that are to be proclaimed. Rather it is God's word that is to be proclaimed, and that is one single word, but not words of God,[35] not a variety of different texts.

Indeed we must put a still sharper point on it: If the word character of God's word is taken strictly, then it is absurd to designate a transmitted text as God's word. We say this not out of contempt for its content or for its being written, but rather precisely out of respect for both. It is of course entirely true of sermon texts by and large that they are concerned with proclamation that has taken place, and to that extent—if it was right proclamation—with past occurrence of the word of God. Naturally the form of direct speech on God's part cannot here rank as criterion. It is significant that with Jesus (apart from Christian imitations of the prophets) the stylistic form 'Thus saith the Lord' ceases—a fact well worth bearing in mind for the doctrine of the word of God. But if it is a case of proclamation that has taken place, then we shall have to say of the sermon text: Its

---

[35] L. Köhler in his *Theologie des AT* (Tübingen: J. C. B. Mohr, 1936), p. 90 [*Old Testament Theology*, translated by A. S. Todd (Philadelphia: Westminster Press, 1957), pp. 106 f.] draws attention to a "linguistic point that is usually neglected. What the prophets are given to deliver is always called *the* word of Yahweh. It is never called *a* word of Yahweh, in fact that expression probably never occurs at all. Each individual revelation is called not a word, but *the* word of Yahweh, so that when a string of individual messages follow each other, each of them can be introduced by the formula: 'then the word of Yahweh came.' Thus in each individual revelation the whole word of God is always expressed."

aim is that there should be further proclamation—and that, too, with an ear open toward the text, in agreement with it and under appeal to it.

The process from text to sermon can therefore be characterized by saying: Proclamation that has taken place is to become proclamation that takes place. This transition from text to sermon is a transition from Scripture to the spoken word. Thus the task prescribed here consists in making what is written into spoken word or, as we can now also say, in letting the text become God's word again. That that does not normally happen through recitation should surely be clear. If the concept of exposition can now be applied to this process, then we should have to say it is a question of interpreting the text *as word*.

But is the application of the concept "exposition" here not questionable? This misgiving is in fact justified. Yet we must be very careful in giving place to it. For it is manifestly true all the same that the movement from the text to the sermon is a hermeneutical process in which, indeed to an eminent degree, it is a case of understanding and bringing to understanding. It would undoubtedly be wrong to assert that this movement from the text to the sermon does not come within the scope of the hermeneutical problem as posed by that text. For if its aim is that what it has proclaimed should be further proclaimed, then the hermeneutical task prescribed by the text in question is not only not left behind when we turn to the sermon, but is precisely then for the first time brought to its fullest explication. The problem of theological hermeneutic would not be grasped without the inclusion of the task of proclamation; it is not until then that it is brought decisively to a head at all. And that, too, because the Biblical texts would not be rightly heard unless they were seen to present us with the task of proclamation.

As it happens, the coming to a head of the hermeneutical problem in this way is not by any means peculiar to theology alone. We have an analogous case in legal hermeneutic. The *problem of legal hermeneutic* would be inadequately characterized if we left out of account the question of how to master the task of understanding that arises from the relation between the legal sources and the task of giving legal decisions in the present—in such a way, namely, that the traditional legal sources point the way to legal decisions in the present and thus become an illuminating source of understanding for the complications of the present legal case. It is true that one can also stop at a purely historical interpretation by examining the traditional legal sources with regard to the situation in which they arose and the sense in which they were then meant. Yet it cannot be called a falsification of the hermeneutical task when the legal sources, so far as they are presently still in force, are examined with regard to their bearing on this or that legal case. Certainly the text makes an unconditional demand for historical interpretation. But the so-called application to the present case is nevertheless not something entirely independent of that. For the judge must be expected to give a legal decision according to the laws that are presently valid. It is expected that in encountering the present concrete case the received text as an illuminating, clarifying, guiding word will become the source of legal understanding and therefore too the source of legal decision. Thus not merely the source of past legal decision, but as the source of past legal decision it becomes the source of legal decision in the present. Certainly the accents shift where hermeneutic is concerned. But they allow of only relative separation from each other. The man who has no interest in giving legal decisions will be a poor legal historian. And the man who does not trouble himself with historical interpretation jeopardizes the purity of his legal decisions in the present.

The reference to this analogy would require to be further developed in order to bring to expression the difference between it and the problem of theological hermeneutic. But neither is a special case. Rather, both make clear the structure of the hermeneutical problem in general, since in every case historical understanding joins with some form or other of expectation of further present understanding, interest in the past unites with interest in the future (as also conversely interest in the future with interest in the past). The relative distinction between the two hermeneutical aspects can perhaps also be given terminological expression as follows: The sermon as such is in point of fact not *exposition* of the text—whereby exposition here means the concentration on the historical task of understanding. For to understand this text as a text means to understand it in its historical givenness as proclamation that has taken place. Now of course the sermon certainly does presuppose intensive efforts toward such understanding of the text. How could it otherwise appeal to it? And it contains also according to the particular circumstances a greater or less degree of explicit interpretation of the text. But the sermon as a sermon is not exposition of the text as past proclamation, but is itself proclamation in the present—and that means, then, that *the sermon is* EXECUTION *of the text.* It carries into execution the aim of the text. It is proclamation of what the text has proclaimed. And with that the hermeneutical sense of direction is, so to speak, reversed. The text understood by means of the exposition now helps to bring to understanding what is to attain understanding by means of the sermon—which is (we can here state it briefly) the present reality *coram Deo,* and that means, in its radical futurity. *Thus the text by means of the sermon becomes a hermeneutical aid in the understanding of present experience.* Where that happens radically, there true word is uttered, and that in fact means God's word.

The real rub in the hermeneutical problem, as it presents itself for theology, consists in the connection between exposition of the text as proclamation that has taken place and execution of the text in proclamation in the present. The *concept of existentialist interpretation* has been employed to characterize this fundamental hermeneutical problem. The efforts toward a closer definition of it are still going on.[36] I think the concept can be meaningful and helpful if it brings out the fact that existence is existence through word and in word. Then existentialist interpretation would mean *interpretation of the text with regard to the word event.* There, in my opinion, lies the decisive starting point from which to direct historical exposition toward the utmost fulfillment of its task, and precisely in so doing to gain criteria for the inner hermeneutical connection between text and sermon.

[36] See above all E. Fuchs, *Zum hermeneutischen Problem in der Theologie,* pp. 65 ff.

The hermeneutical principle would then, in accord with what we said earlier, be the word event itself. For hermeneutic, we said, is the theory of words. And we can now designate as identical with that, because merely the radicalization of it, the fact that theological hermeneutic is the doctrine of the word of God, but that for that very reason there can also be doctrine of the word of God only as theological hermeneutic. In view of that the hermeneutical principle could be given various precise definitions. With an eye to the real sphere of the word event I suggest for consideration the formula: <u>The hermeneutical principle is *man as conscience*</u>. I refrain here from further attempts to ground and elucidate that. For a principle should surely be something that is obvious of itself, or at all events gives guidance and proves its fitness in use.[37]

---

[37] This does not rule out the need to form an exactly defined *concept* of conscience. Let me merely recall, as against the superficial objections that are to be expected on the ground of the dominant rules of theological language, that for Luther *"theologice"* was synonymous with *"in conscientia"*: (on Gal. 51.) "It is freedom from law, sins, death, from the devil's power, from the wrath of God, from the last judgment. Where? In the conscience. Thus, I am justified, since Christ is the liberator and makes men free, not carnally, not politically, not diabolically, but rather theologically (*theologice*), i.e., only in the conscience (*in conscientia*)" (*WA* 40/2, p. 3.5–8).

3. The New Testament and the Hermeneutical Problem

ERNST FUCHS
University of Marburg

As children in my native province of Württemberg we learned a series of Bible verses each year at school. That was my first contact with the New Testament. The Old Testament suited my father better. He was of the opinion that the Old Testament portrayed life as it is. He thought the New Testament was almost too sentimental. Jesus was a noble man, nothing more, the victim of a hard world.

Like many other sons, I did not believe every word my father said. But it is possible that I would not have accepted very much of the New Testament had I not chanced into the classroom of Professor Adolf Schlatter as a very young student at Tübingen. I was at the time a law student, not a theology student; but I had learned Greek, and so I was able to follow his lecture. Professor Schlatter was just then interpreting the Gospel of John. Now the Greek of this Gospel is quite easy to understand. That helped me out. But what especially struck and pleased me was the professor himself. He had the courage to express along with the text his own conviction and the experience of his own life. He enthralled me so much that I could not keep from going back day after day to his lecture; and the next semester I could not resist hearing his exposition of the Gospel of Matthew, which incidentally was Schlatter at his best. Finally, almost against the will of my father, I gave up law and become a theological student.

Please do not misunderstand me—I did not go through a conversion experience. For a long time I had been familiar enough with godly persons, and I respected them. I cherished no partic-

ular doubts and was happy over every pious word, if it made
sense. To be sure, I always posed this condition, and I hope I still
do today: Pious words should not be stupid. When the Apostle
Paul praises the foolishness of God to the effect that it is wiser
than the wisdom of men, he certainly does not mean God is
stupid, but rather that man cannot subsume God's revelation under human wisdom. Consequently, we should be willing to be
surprised. And if the same Paul often presents himself as if he
acts as a fool in the eyes of the world, that is painful irony. Faith
is not stupid, faith is itself a kind of wisdom. Hence faith deepens
human wisdom to an extent one would never expect. I learned
this from Professor Schlatter. The voluminous *Theologisches Wörterbuch zum Neuen Testament* published in Stuttgart is dedicated
to his memory. Many New Testament scholars are collaborating
on this lexicon. It is itself an indication of the fact that what faith
effects is not negligible.

A still greater impression than that of Professor Schlatter was
made on me by the Marburg Professor Rudolf Bultmann. I met
him in 1924, in a period in which Bultmann was again grappling
with Schlatter, under whom he too had studied during his student
days. But this study of Schlatter was not taking place without
criticism. Schlatter had all too freely passed over critical historical
work on the New Testament. Bultmann, however, had grown up
with the critical historical method and had mastered it. Yet Bultmann too was not fully satisfied with this method of interpreting
the text. Meanwhile, Karl Barth had risen as a new star on the
theological horizon, and Bultmann turned to him with a passion.
But Barth too was no master of historical criticism. Bultmann had
to work out his own path. He was helped by the fact that shortly
before, in 1923, the philosopher Martin Heidegger had come to
Marburg. Heidegger captivated Bultmann, because both scholars
looked to the Greeks, and Heidegger himself at that time took
great interest in the development being introduced in theology by
Karl Barth. A new academic era had begun.

Now imagine for a moment the young student with all these
influences working upon him: Schlatter, Bultmann, Heidegger,
and, behind the latter two, Karl Barth. And this is the way it was

with many others of Bultmann's students. Would it not take a long time for there to be any results? Of course. But that was not all. In Germany there arose a new and brutal régime which terrified the world and the German nation as well. Even the church was put in a completely new situation, since it was severely persecuted. The enemies of the church brought about what the professors would perhaps never have achieved, or at least only very slowly. There arose a new interest; or, better, a really new life became evident in the church. Many persons, whom one has often lost track of in subsequent years, became inwardly more alive than they had ever been before and accepted the pain of persecution. That time is continuing today under reversed circumstances. Not all have stood the test—indeed, that was not to be expected. And it was not only theologians who stood the test. It was especially average people in the local congregation who did so. But one thing profited in each case. This was the New Testament. In day-by-day living we also learned to read it differently from before. To be sure, the problems remained to a large extent the old problems. But we were now able to see the work of our teachers with sharpened eyes, simply because the time compelled us to do so. And since we had such good professors, new insights emerged, which appear to us as the fruit of the work of our great teachers. It is this which I want to report to you.

I would like to picture the matter as I see it. Others may then give their own contribution. This is why I took the liberty of such a personal introduction.

I. Questions Emerging from the Theology of Bultmann

People in Germany ask me _why I have pushed the "historical Jesus" so decidedly into the foreground_. Is this sliding back into a past liberalism? Is the historical Jesus our business at all? Does not Christian faith believe in the Resurrected One, in Jesus Christ as its Lord? May one as interpreter of the New Testament go back behind the "proclamation" of the New Testament? If the historically interested scholar may do such a thing, is it befitting for the theologian? Must one not make this choice: either one arrives at the historical Jesus, but without faith in him as Lord, or one holds firmly to faith in Jesus Christ as Lord, and then the historical Jesus belongs to a past time prior to this faith?

Now I do not wish to talk my way out of these questions by saying the resurrected Lord is, after all, neither a ghost nor a mythical figure, but precisely the historical Jesus (to whose history there belongs more than just his life prior to the crucifixion, of course). I do not propose to begin by taking this way out, for it could very well be that all that was ascribed to Jesus after his crucifixion does not at all fit the historical Jesus, but fits much better those men who wanted to believe in him. Even faith can embellish. Why could it not have embellished the historical Jesus too? Of course, one could still ask whether such embellishment was not actually appropriate to, and worthy of, Jesus. But this answer would hardly correspond to the intention of Christian faith. For Christian faith means to speak of God's act, not of the embellishing acts of man. If God embellished Jesus, that would be something else again.

On the other hand, it seems to me that the following observation takes us further. Granted, Christian faith has in mind Jesus Christ as Lord, and thus it intends to be faith in Jesus Christ. Granted, this faith arose only after the crucifixion of Jesus. Granted, too, faith in Jesus Christ believes about itself that such faith is not man's work but God's act, so that faith appeals for its truth to God's Holy Spirit and not to man (1 Cor. 2:4 f.). This is the point in the apostolic appeal to the "Scriptures" (1 Cor. 15:3–5). But granting all of that, will one not have to ask all the more: *How does it happen that the Gospels want to narrate words and deeds of the historical Jesus, as Matthew, Mark, and Luke have clearly done?* To be sure, what is at issue is not how many of these words are "authentic" and which acts of Jesus actually happened. Rather, what is decisive is the fact that such things should be narrated at all. What does this interest of the evangelists in the historical Jesus mean? Certainly form-critical research has shown that the evangelists made their traditions of narratives and sayings serve the purpose of preaching faith. But

does this really answer the question? Why did they not, like the
Apostle Paul, confine themselves to the "kerygma," the proclamation of the crucified and resurrected Lord? If they had done that,
they would not have been able to write Gospels, at least not those
which we have in the canon today. Not even the Gospel of John
could have been written. Although this Gospel offers but little
about the historical Jesus, it intends in its own way to do nothing
other than the three other Gospels: it intends to bring the historical Jesus, the son of (Mary and) Joseph, near to us (John 6:42).
These evangelists are certainly not modern historians, not even
Luke. Much of what they say does not stand up under historical
criticism. But *they all have in mind the historical Jesus,* that man
who, at the time when he was crucified, had lived and had been
known and loved by men such as Peter. And they say of him that
Christian faith applies to him. Are they thereby carrying out a
correction of the primitive Christian kerygma, for example the
Pauline kerygma? *Or have we understood this kerygma inaccu-
rately? We would do well to think in terms of the latter possibility.* In any case, we cannot deny that *the Gospels intended to
include the historical Jesus in the kerygma* and that for this purpose they appealed to what he said and did. This is true in principle, as well as in detail, of both the Gospel of John and the
other three. *Could our conception of the historical be in need of
correction? This is indeed my opinion.*

Of course I do not deny that there are historical facts, nor do
I deny that historical criticism is a good way to establish facts.
One cannot treasure too highly the empirical, the factually prova-
ble. Anyone who has flown even once in an airplane sees this point.
Here in the airplane only facts count. Hence a crash is an awful
thing which always makes everyone sad. This is also true in the
area of the New Testament. I do not think we should rank the
facts lower. Rather I think *we should note facts even more carefully than we are accustomed to do in the practice of exegesis
and preaching.*

This poses *a new problem, the problem of hermeneutic.* Bultmann called it *the problem of demythologizing* the New Testament message. The problem applies to the mythical statements in

[margin note: The Historical Jesus is important because the Gospel writers felt he was important]

[margin note: But the mythological statements of the N.T. must be "demythologized."]

the New Testament. No one can deny that there are such state-ments: Jesus is conceived of as a pre-existent heavenly being. After his resurrection he rules together with God at God's right hand. During his lifetime he can walk on water like a spirit. He was con-ceived by the Holy Spirit without male participation. And so forth.

Bultmann says that the interpreter must not "eliminate" these statements, but rather should "interpret" them. But how does one do that? In any case not by declaring that such statements refer to facts of a peculiar kind which do not occur otherwise, miracu-lous facts that bear the peculiar mark of God's work upon them. Of course such an explanation is not completely worthless. For *we really do need to think about how one can speak of God and his works.* If for no other reason, this is necessary because the New Testament says quite emphatically that God "raised" the crucified Jesus. But it is advisable not to come to this task too hastily. We must first prepare ourselves for it. And this preparation can be done best by first making clear the task of "interpretation," espe-cially of interpreting statements that are undoubtedly mythical, such as talk about Jesus' pre-existence.

Of course there lurks here an awkward difficulty. Bultmann's procedure is to investigate the "understanding of existence" in mythical conceptualizations. For this purpose he distinguishes be-tween the mythical conceptualizations, on the one hand, and the self-understanding that is supposed to be expressed with the help of those conceptualizations, on the other. *The mythical concep-tualizations make use of "this-worldly" media when they wish to point out God's work.* They speak as if one could come down from heaven like a dove, etc. So they do not distinguish between this life and the beyond—that is to say, they make the distinction only in such a way that the beyond functions like a kind of pro-longation of this life. But that is only a deficiency in their way of conceiving things. *What they really intended to say is more, namely, a distinction in principle between this side and the be-yond,* between God and man. The exact *boundary* lies less in the conception than in the man himself who talks about it, yet cannot speak about it the way he would like. So Bultmann investigates the so-called "anthropological" presuppositions of these mythical conceptualizations. Then they become valuable. For they now show how such persons view themselves and their relation to God. They show themselves to be *attempts to speak of God,* but *by means of man's understanding of himself as God's work.* And here Bultmann is right. If such mythical conceptualizations permit one to sense something of how man understands or should understand himself, do we not then gain access to those conceptualizations? Not that we should in turn repeat them! But do we not gain a guide as to how we could understand ourselves? Consequently, *we are called upon to examine what alternatives we have for understanding ourselves at all.* And this examining is to take place with the help of the self-understanding of persons who in those times thought they needed to speak mythically in order to express their self-understanding correctly. *The interpretation of the conceptualizations is turned into the interpretation of our own existence—which has now become the hermeneutical task.*

   The awkward difficulty in Bultmann's program thus resides less in the New Testament manner of speech than in the New Testament compelling us to examine our self-understanding by learning (even though with the help of those mythical statements) *to inquire in principle as to our alternatives for understanding ourselves.* This difficulty is less of a theoretical than of a practical nature. One likes to seek help in the ambiguous insistence that we should accept only such statements as require of us *"engagement."* This means we should accept as true only that which we acknowledge as valid for our own person. Not that a person should force himself to accept something that he would not accept as true on his own initiative! No, each person should accept as true precisely that which he recognizes as valid for himself since he knows his own life to be determined by it. Only thus does a person "repent," for only thus does he come to himself, like the prodigal son in the parable. And when that happens, the word of forgiveness or grace may also reach him, if it is preached to him. *Now he understands what it means when it is said that he himself is God's work* (Eph. 2:10). And then he also understands how he is to evaluate his own works in the future. So this would be *engagement* in the sense

[margin note, handwritten:] Interpretation of N.T. mythology demands, first of all, understanding of ourselves.

[margin note, handwritten:] Each person should accept that which he recognizes as valid for himself.

of the New Testament text. Is that all? No, that is not all. It is clear that *such a person will in the future understand not only himself or his works differently from before, but also the world.* He will want to have as though he did not have (1 Cor. 7:29–31). And as a consequence he will hold God to be the power that concerns not only himself but also the whole world. Indeed, he will learn to distinguish between God's giving and taking, and he will take to heart such thoughts as those expressed so tellingly in Thornton Wilder's play *Our Town. The beyond does indeed begin several lengths earlier than we perhaps had thought.* It begins already in ourselves. Man is not simply master of his fate or of his life. *Man is dependent on the time which is apportioned to him.* Hence Bultmann can say that man is not at his own disposal. But man should know about not being at his own disposal. He should hear about it in time and reflect on it, for he is *responsible* for the time given to him. So man is a being "in time and yet beyond time,"[1] beyond, since he is not at his own disposal, yet in the here and now, since he knows this and is responsible for it in his present. *Precisely this being beyond time in time is the encounter of man with God.*

Once again: Is that all? It is not all. It is the beginning. If there were no more to say, we would have been led up only to the point of faith. We will be grateful for being led this far. But *faith in its turn has experiences. And these experiences reveal to us new facts which could not yet come up for discussion in the concept of demythologizing.*

II. The Experiences Faith Has

I do not mean to say that Bultmann's program of demythologizing comes anywhere near exhausting the wealth of his theology. Yet *I cannot resist directing one question to Bultmann at this point.* With many other scholars, he holds the opinion that Jesus awaited the kingdom of God in the near future.[2] A few scholars

[1] Rudolf Bultmann in "Optimismus und Pessimismus in Antike und Christentum," Yearbook for 1959 of the Reuchlin Society of Pforzheim, p. 35.
[2] Rudolf Bultmann, "Das Verhältnis der urchristlichen Christusbotschaft zum historischen Jesus," *SBHA,* Phil.-hist. Klasse, 1960, no. 3, pp. 11 f.

have pointed a way out by attempting to define as inauthentic all the Son-of-Man sayings in which this personage is a heavenly being, leaving to Jesus only the proclamation of the kingdom of God. One of my pupils (E. Jüngel), in a study he has recently completed, attempts to show that Jesus conceived of the kingdom of God as something which determines the present, whereas under the concept of the Son of Man he did not await the near God of the kingdom of God, but rather the God still distant from us. Thus Jesus' preaching of the kingdom of God would have us think of God's grace, and Jesus' expectation of the Son of Man would have us think of God's judgment. I hold this thesis to be interesting and defensible. But be that as it may, *would not Jesus' expectation for the future also have to be demythologized? Was it correct at this point simply to hold fast to a conception attributed to Jesus (a mythical conception of course), in order then to hang on it the problem of the "delay" of the parousia?* Is something negative, something which could never come to pass, supposed to have brought the whole development into action? *With what right does one elevate over against that the preaching of the resurrection of Jesus as something different, as the message of an act of God?* Would then two quite different things have been mixed up with each other: 1) as a backdrop, a mythical expectation which failed; 2) the claim of an act of God, *instead* of the expected concept and presumably not derivable from it? Would then the mythical expectation have been corrected by *God's* act at Easter? *Can one still call such a procedure demythologizing?* Would it not be more nearly correct to demythologize the so-called "Easter faith" as well, and prior to that Jesus' expectation?

Perhaps at this central place in the kerygma one should attempt rather to correct *a deficiency in the program of demythologizing itself.* The deficiency is that *the reference to the self-understanding of the persons does not suffice, if or so long as one looks only at the beginning of their new self-understanding.*

One could arrive at much the same point by asking: *How is the Easter faith to be distinguished,* for example, *from faith in the forgiveness of sins,* as it is expressed in the parable of the prodigal son (or, better, the parable of the prodigal sons, Luke 15:11 ff.)?

Could one perhaps say that *the Easter faith proclaims to all the world what previously was believed only quietly in silence?* And could one say this is because Jesus' person, even after his crucifixion, pressed forward of its own accord into the center of the stage? But would that not mean that *such faith in forgiveness even prior to the crucifixion had its own consequences?*

Is not one consequence the inference we should draw, *namely, that the imminent expectation attributed to Jesus does not suffice to describe Jesus' message?* For how else would it have been possible for Paul to try to direct Easter faith back into the course of faith in forgiveness (although in terms of grace rather than of forgiveness, a term not prominent in Paul)? Before one establishes which experiences were connected with the Easter faith (even though one rightly says: the experience of the word of God), one must first ask *which experiences were related to the faith which Jesus had had in mind and had encouraged* (if indeed one should not say Jesus rendered faith possible!). And this faith was not a faith in some kind of imminent expectation—that idea was doubtless in current circulation ever since the emergence of John the Baptist and was a matter of course, so to speak, even without faith. Rather it was, for example, *faith in the forgiveness of sins,* in the *working* of the kingdom of God *already in the present,* as it was celebrated by Jesus with his disciples and other persons also at meals, so that for him John's baptism of repentance was apparently no longer the crucial point. If John called for a break with the former way of life, *Jesus already celebrated the beginning of the new life,* a life already within the kingdom of God. Hence *Jesus' position competes* in a most peculiar way *with the so-called "Easter faith,"* so that one must ask whether the term "Easter faith" fits the situation at all. One should rather say "Easter confession." Yet, as we have said, faith's experiences themselves must be investigated in more detail before we can say much about the Easter experience.

What experiences does faith have? This question finally brings me to the point decisive for my theological work. Naturally one can say: *the experience of the forgiveness of sins.* Of course. *What then? Does faith have no further experiences?* Must one now leap over to the Easter statements? That would be odd. Bultmann likes to emphasize that faith is "self-surrender." Of course that is right, so long as it is a matter of faith having to be ready to surrender every securing of its own existence. For faith clings to God. Faith knows that man is one upon whom God has bestowed his goodness and that the time given us reminds us again and again of our being recipients of God's goodness. To the extent that the world of the visible and available tempts man to cling to the visible, faith must maintain "distance" from the visible. To this extent faith is and remains self-surrender. Otherwise faith would destroy the nature of our life as a gift of God. One could also put it this way: Otherwise faith would no longer be faith in God the Creator, who is at the same time our Redeemer when the world presses us down. So he who loves his neighbor will in faith try to show him by his acts who helps man and what endangers man. At this point faith has much in common with a genuine humanism. But these are not yet the characteristic experiences of faith.

In prayer too—for example, in the Lord's Prayer—the genuine experiences of faith initially appear less in the content than in the fact that one prays at all. Then of course the content becomes indicative. The petition "Thy kingdom come" is less indicative of an imminent expectation than of the fact that one still prays for the coming of the kingdom at all, when one is actually standing already within it. How does that come about? *Is there an experience of faith which could destroy the beginning of the kingdom of God? Indeed there is.* A very simple reflection will readily make that clear.

If a person believes that his sins are forgiven, then he will have the strength and the freedom to love his neighbor. If that happens, the neighbor is not only helped, but the help itself now becomes a factor which affects my contacts with my neighbor. It is not only the evil works which come between us! The good ones also have their effect. And *it is these good works, which faith is able to do and does in fact do, which promptly come between our neighbor and ourselves, indeed between us and our faith.* We see something which we had not previously seen in that way. This is not yet the glory of Jesus. But it is the power and authority of faith, as it works itself out in good works. And it is this *seeing* which *com-petes* with faith. *It can, like the Easter experiences, become stronger than faith. But in this way faith becomes vulnerable.* For setbacks will be unavoidable, since the environment hostile to faith reacts to just such works, for example with jealousy or hate. This too is to be counted among the consequences of Jesus' preaching itself. One can still detect such a consequence in the malicious criticisms, such as that expressed in Matt. 11:19, where Jesus is reproached for the company he keeps. But it is also clear that these direct consequences of Jesus' preaching are played down in the narrative. They are no longer of interest, since the shadow of the cross far exceeds all that.

It is not until the Apostle Paul's debate with his fanatical oppo-nents, for example in Corinth, that the problem becomes clearly visible. Paul is able to support his position by emphasizing the importance of weakness as the correct norm for understanding his office. Yet even in his case the significance of such passages for the experience of faith is obscured by the shadow of the cross, namely, that he, once a persecutor, has himself become a perse-cuted missionary. Does it not become clear in such cases that *espe-cially the beginning of the kingdom of God or of faith leads again and again into hardships which cause one to pray—now with real urgency—for the coming of the kingdom, whose overwhelming power faith has already tasted?* And will not faith rightly look to the place from which it expects help? And what other place could that be than the place where Jesus himself became the victim of the world? The disciples obviously thought of Jerusalem. Paul understood more deeply and thought in principle of Jesus' cross, and thus of the dead whom God would—soon?—raise, since the dead now, because of Jesus, belonged together with the living, the believers.

But what did faith hold to if it did not want to fall back into "conceptualization"? The experiences that faith had with its works and their consequences were not the only experiences of faith. *Are we going on a wrong track when we bring together the interest in the historical Jesus,* as it comes to light in the Gospels, and *the experiences faith had?* How then had the experiences of faith become concrete in contacts with the historical Jesus? We have already spoken of Jesus' meal. It is now time to look to Jesus' preaching itself. For faith, reflected for example in discipleship, arose as a result of his preaching. So *his preaching may reflect basic experiences of faith* as well. Indeed this is the case. And what was said earlier about prayer applies here too; *what is decisive is not in the first place the content, but that Jesus spoke at all.* Only then are we to come to grips with the content of his preaching.

Now the sense in which this preaching is intended to be understood becomes clear. It is not a conglomeration of more or less unrelated views, but it is first of all word, language, *exhortation*, as Bultmann rightly says. What is the essential thing in this exhortation? Among other things it surely is this: *A person is called upon to listen and is told he has to listen with regard to himself.* Certainly this exhortation takes place so one will respond. And certainly the name for this response is faith. But even more takes place. The exhortation has not done its service merely in that Jesus has spoken to someone. *Jesus also gives his hearer the exhortation to take along with him on his way!* This does not mean Jesus would not have expected one to listen to him immediately, without delay. Certainly he can put his hearer to the test by making him decide immediately, as in the case of the rich young man in Mark 10:17–22. Yet *Jesus bestows his word upon his hearers as a gift*. He formulates it so that *the hearer has something to hold to in the future also, as if a model of faith were given him to take along.* Of course Jesus himself later entered with his person into this position and as the crucified became the model of faith. But we can still detect that this was earlier so decidedly the case with regard to the most characteristic words of Jesus that other persons could readily create new and similar sayings. For this reason the question of authenticity is not so important as one supposes. It is enough that a saying becomes recognizable as a model of faith, so that we have the right to regard the saying as characteristic for Jesus, if this is not excluded by other considerations.

Hence there belongs with faith a word that not only calls forth faith but also accompanies it. *Faith has a particular relation to language that is all its own. This experience is the most character-istic experience of faith.* We now turn to it in what follows.

III. Word and Faith

What do we mean when we say "word"? Theologians think first of the "word of God" which in the beginning created heaven and earth, or of the Logos which became flesh, as the Gospel of John says. But that is not our intention here. We are thinking, for example, of the parables of Jesus. Yet here too, wrong opinions creep in. One assumes parables are there primarily to make something clear to people of low intelligence, or to express something overwhelming in handy form, or to expand something easily overlooked, so that one will look at it and pay attention to it. All that does not concern us here. Instead we take our point of departure in the phenomenon of language.

What is language? We leave it to the philosophers to "define" it. Instead we want to describe what we mean. What do you say to the following thesis: *At home one does not speak so that people may understand, but because people understand!* This is the statement that I wish to use as my point of departure.

Of course I do not deny that one can also discuss at home. In general one must concede that home is often only a kind of prolongation of school or college. He who has become accustomed for so many years to move among teachers and pupils will continue that style at home, especially if he graduated from school with honors. I realize that the Communists deny that today there is any such thing as home. They, and not only they, hold home to be an antiquated bourgeois arrangement. Nonetheless, there are families in which children grow up and where people try to spend a treasured part of the daily schedule with each other. Women know that and men desire it. Here then everything runs according to its own rules of play, whether we are happy or not. Here people understand each other in their joys and in their problems; here people know each other. And here is where the statement applies that people speak together because they understand each other and not in order to understand each other. Of course there also occurs such a thing as a sickening silence.

Since we are indeed philosophizing a bit, let me emphasize that one further insight belongs to a full understanding of this situation. What is this language of the family all about? One can say it is about all that which causes joy and gives rise to problems. From this one could infer that in the family language has to do with the members of the family. This is true, of course. But this does not yet say the crucial thing about language. Rather, *the language of the family has to do with that trait of language which in general composes its essential feature: with time*. The mother usually announces with her words the time, as time to get up, to eat, to work, to play, to go to sleep, etc. She says: "Come!", "Go!", "Watch out!", etc. Or she uses her words to fill up the present, by telling a story, etc. I hope families also sing together. This is a "pastime" that is possible, thanks to language. Here a "mutual understanding" always prevails, whether we get along well together or not. Unfortunately, people often understand each other better when they argue than when they are happy, so that games easily degenerate into fights. Then one hears: "You *are* a . . . ," etc.! All this is announcing the time. That is what language is there for. *What is distinctive about language is not the content of the individual words, not the thought or the designation, but rather its use, its application, its concentration upon the time and thus upon the distinction of times.*

In order to understand better this effect of language we should look more carefully at time as well. At least in the family, time is essentially not a constant of measurement, not a unity without limits. Instead it is pluralistic. *Time is always time only as a given time, as time for this or time for that, so that at the same time different times are present.* For the one child it is time to go to sleep, for the other it is time to go to the theater, for a third it is time for some specific work, and perhaps all at the same time in the evening at eight. This use of the term "time" is not a figurative secondary usage, but rather the primary and genuine usage. Of course simultaneous times permit a common dating. But the dating—eight in the evening in the illustration given above—actually fails to say what time has begun or ended in each individual case. I suspect one would have to say that time always is, was, or will be present, but within limits of differing extent and related to different areas. However, for our purpose it suffices to point out that the content of a time thus determined is always more or less presupposed, since one knows all the more what it is just now the "time for": Now we are sitting at the table—"Stay seated!" etc. *So this is what language announces. It does not create something new, but it announces what it is time for.* Language presupposes that there is this time at home, in one's home town, in the environment with which one is *familiar*. Language protects it, and thus vouches for this sphere. If this sphere diminishes, then there disappears also the normal capacity for language. Language then becomes standardized and is only a means of information, as in science. On the other hand, language is intensified where the home and family must be protected or are threatened or destroyed. Genuine tradition can hence be detected by its intensified language—for example, by the presence of a dialect. Here language is emotional. Its understanding of time ranges between song and shout. But it always says what it is time for. It says it even to the point of death. For death says to the survivors: "Now you speak!" Yet the survivor will probably lament, since the time for mourning has come.

Without a doubt Jesus speaks in this sphere of provincial and family life as it takes place in peaceful or normal times. It is from this life that he takes the examples for his parables. One observes the people walking along the street and knocking on the window, one hears the loud voice of their festivities. The farmer goes to his field, sows, and harvests. The wife plants the small plot of land adjoining her house. There are the rich and the poor, the honest and the frauds; there is happiness and need, sadness and thankfulness. But all that is not only milieu, not only "source material" for a poet (in case poets speak at all about source material, which may be only what historians of literature talk about). Jesus does not use the details of this world only as a kind of "point of contact"; instead, *he has in mind precisely this "world."* He can address it as an "adulterous generation." Are the people his enemies, his opponents? Actually they are not. When the evangelists usually have the Pharisees appear as Jesus' opponents, this is an unhistorical cliché. It is Jesus himself who insists as emphatically as possible on God's command being in force, just as does the Pharisee.

But at this point special care is called for. *What does it mean to insist on God's command being in force?* In our field of research today one likes to talk about a "sharpening of the Torah" by Jesus, and one has in mind such things as the antitheses of the Sermon on the Mount as they are formulated or transmitted by Matthew (5:21–48). What then does it mean to say: "Do not be angry," "Do not commit adultery," "Offer no resistance," "Love them"? May one no longer give legalistic orders as "those of old" were commissioned to do? Does God contradict himself? Are there only now genuine commandments? Oh no! There were always commandments. And those of old understood God very well. Or has misuse become too glaring? Does Jesus, like an Immanuel Kant, mean to penetrate through a sea of external, casuistic obligations to a simple, inner commandment of duty, which each can always keep fresh in his soul and meditate upon? Does Jesus simply desire a "good" will? Oh no! What was done by that master in the vineyard or the father of the two sons in killing the fatted calf—that was not just good will. Does Jesus even more simply desire "decision," that decision to believe without which true brotherly love is often not possible, that self-surrender of which Bultmann speaks so persistently? Yes, that is what Jesus desires. Yet it will be good to recall that brotherly love can be practiced also without faith and indeed is practiced everywhere from time to time. So, does Jesus then desire a continuing love? Of course! But all that would be primarily only a sort of obedience, and to this extent only a new obedience and less a new content. But one can hardly overlook the fact that Jesus' requirements have a new content. What is this new content, this new "What" that is not only a new "How"? Bultmann is also right in understanding Jesus' requirement "eschatologically": *Since a new time has dawned, the time of the final revelation of God, Jesus desires true obedience in a new situation and for this new situation*. This is said by parables such as that of the farmer who found the unexpected treasure or the merchant who sold everything for the one precious pearl (Matt. 13:44–46), or sayings such as the *logion* about not looking back when one puts one's hand to the plow, and the difficult saying that the dead should bury their dead (Luke 9:62, 60). Perhaps one must rise up even against one's own family, as Jesus himself did (Luke 14:26; Mark 3:33), and take one's cross upon oneself (Luke 14:27).

The evangelists call this "following after" Jesus. But with this term *the center of the matter* has not yet been fully reached. This center is better designated *"being called into the kingdom of God,"* as the (threatening?) parable of the banquet shows (Luke 14:16–24). This calling is clearly expressed by the beatitudes at the beginning of the Sermon on the Mount (Matt. 5:3–10). Matthew precedes the call with the word "repent" (Matt. 4:17). Hence one is tempted to conceive of Jesus either as a second and last John (Matt. 3:2), or as the "dignitary" of the last hour, who is to bring our relation to God into order once for all. Yet it is easily overlooked that Jesus exposed all his hearers to offense at his own person (Matt. 11:6). One should not make light of this observation by noting that Jesus' hearers, especially in the parables, were his "enemies," who would not have wanted to submit to Jesus' lofty position. Jesus' offense is to be understood in a different way. Jesus conducts himself as a man like other men, and, in contrast to the collection of miracle stories in Matt. 8–9 or even in contrast to Matt. 11:5, he does not accredit himself at all by working miracles. If they nevertheless take place, they are not signs of a special nature of Jesus' person, but rather of the special new time (Luke 11:20). So one should pay attention only to the signs of the time (Luke 12:54–56). On the other hand, the content of this language is as old as the behavior of the birds in the heaven and the adornment of the lilies of the field (Luke 12:24, 27 f.). Hence everything depends now quite exclusively on the hour itself (Luke 12:57–59). Jesus' preaching is exactly like his conduct, his whole appearance: it is quite simply *the announcement of the time itself,* the *new* time of the kingdom of God. Jesus has as little interest in being something special in his own person as has the Apostle Paul in Corinth (2 Cor. 12:11). Jesus has no office, but rather only a single commission. To this extent he is comparable to John the Baptist. But, in distinction from the Baptist, Jesus announces the new time not because it is coming but because it is here. And it is about this that he calls for faith—that is, for decision. This decision places him who enters in upon it on the side of God and the miracle of *divine* action (Matt. 17:20). But *what the believer does as a consequence happens in the same context of daily living that Jesus in his sayings and parables brings so persistently and tangibly to expression! This is the offense.*

We should not block out access to this very simple situation by making a problem of faith. A saying such as "I believe, help my unbelief" (Mark 9:24) surely refers to an exceptional case. Actually, Jesus calls for an unambiguous faith, a faith without ups and downs (cf. also Mark 9:23). We should not object, "Where is this faith to be found?" He who believes in a theology will—if only because of logical errors in his theology—hardly ever come to a faith without ups and downs, unless he mistakes faith for a principle. For Jesus, faith is by no means a principle; instead, it is quite simply a practical obedience that is willing to be told that *now the time has come in which God comes forward as God.* Jesus has in mind the concrete revelation of God. But he means it not as a kind of future, not as something still to be awaited, which is not yet even here at all; instead, it is present, as in the parable of the lost sons, or better, the parable of the loving father (Luke 15:11 ff.). Of course for Jesus, just as for the prophets of the Old Testament, God is the almighty creator of heaven and earth, who is able to make the dead alive (cf. Mark 12:18–27). For him that is no problem at all. If he wanted, Jesus could simply say that if the woman has had seven men, she will be resurrected seven times. But such thoughts are beside the point, since they do not do justice to God's presence. *This presence connects our action with God's action.* Certainly our action and God's action are strictly to be distinguished, so that we should not have care, since God cares (cf. Luke 12:22 ff.). But if I believe that, if I enter in upon it, my action as love flows from love to God (Mark 12: 28–34). For I can really love God from now on, I can *rejoice* in him, since *Jesus has made God present for me. And how has he done that? Through his words, which now lie like Christmas presents on the table.* What we should put on—so to speak, what we should clothe ourselves with—are indeed Jesus' words themselves. And *clothed in them we should henceforth carry on our daily life.* It will have become a completely new life. What then does this faith believe in?

IV. WHAT FAITH BELIEVES IN

I have just asked what, then, this faith believes in, this faith that is offered to us and required of us in Jesus' words, when we once put ourselves in the position of Jesus' hearers.

This faith does not believe directly in Jesus. Primitive Christianity after Jesus' crucifixion was the first to do this, in proclaiming Jesus as resurrected, exalted to the lordship over the world (Phil. 2:9–11; Rom. 10:9 f.; Acts 2:36). It was first in primitive Christianity that one began to embellish Jesus' person with honors and distinctions, in order to proclaim him as God's Son. In Jesus' preaching it was different. Here we ourselves were embellished, namely, with Jesus' words. Did one then believe at that time in the kingdom of God? That too would not be the correct expression. The kingdom of God was there, of course; one did not need to believe it (Matt. 12:28; and even Matt. 11:5). But this kingdom was there in a different way from the way primitive Christianity later conceived of it, after Judaism's apocalypticism had again gained a stronger influence on the followers of Jesus (for example, in Paul or prior to Paul, so that the apostle only touched upon this tradition, 1 Cor. 4:8; 15:51 f.; 1 Thess. 4:13 ff.). The kingdom of God was present *with Jesus* in daily life. For that is where it really wanted to do its work, according to Jesus' words: right within the "adulterous" generation. *Did one then believe in Jesus' preaching? That is the way one should put it.* For Jesus' word did put one in decision; it required decision, and required it right now (Luke 14:15 ff.).[3] *One believed in the present as the new time of the kingdom of God.* Yet this time worked itself out not only in Jesus' words, but, on the basis of these words, in daily life. And this daily life achieved its clarity from the same traits of language that life has at home, in the family, back home. To put it precisely, does this not imply that when one entered in upon Jesus' words *one believed in this daily life itself, one believed Jesus' preaching made our life again a life in that same intimate fellowship which gave rise to our language as the language of this intimate life?* That is my impression. I do not mean that Jesus interpreted our life optimistically. But I do mean Jesus preached that God the creator enters into the present there, that he wishes to bring his divine power into action precisely where we have to live our life. This is at the place where language occurs, in the time for language—namely, in the daily fellowship of our home-like world, which is yet corrupted into such an alien world by sin, false commands, and lies. *If God went to work here, then man had to live accordingly, that is all.* And since God had long since created the world, everybody knew what that meant.

In Europe today one is involved in the criticism of traditional metaphysics. That way of thinking did once lead men, for example, to discover America, since experience was subordinated to thinking in order to test experience. That is Platonism. Now in what I am about to say I am certainly exposing myself to the suspicion of being a Platonist. But perhaps Plato was not as wrong as people today would have us believe.

For *there are theological problems that are not human problems at all, but rather divine problems, God's problems.* At least it appears that way to us, as soon as we strike upon these problems. And *with this I come to the most important thing relative to the New Testament; I come to the "kernel" of Christian faith.*

I am quite aware that the objection is raised to my presentation of Jesus' preaching and its understanding of faith that here the

---

[3] See on this text Eta Linnemann, "Überlegungen zur Parabel vom grossen Abendmahl," *ZNW,* LI (1961), 246–255.

primitive Christian kerygma, the Easter kerygma, has been by-passed. Now let us look into this.

We would like to presuppose that Peter and a few others actually saw Jesus at that time—the Easter gospel, just as Paul lists it (1 Cor. 15:1–11). We also wish to avoid raising the question about the empty tomb this time. The question is after all quite a different one: What difference has the resurrection made? Is one not ashamed of insisting so loudly on the resurrection, after almost two thousand years of church history have shown the situation mankind is in? We should indeed be ashamed, if we wish to stand up for Christianity. Of course faith should oppose evil. But this should not be done only against outsiders. We also have to stand against ourselves! Yet this is still not the problem I have in mind.

What seems to me more and more urgent has to do with the *sacrament*. To be sure, I reserve the explication of the sacrament for later publications. Yet this much should be clear: *The sacrament directs man to precisely that sphere in which he is not at his own disposal*. What kind of sphere is that? A sphere of magic? Hardly. Rather, if the historical Jesus is to be involved, it is *the same sphere of the word in which Jesus moved*. Yet this was *the sphere of our daily life!* What does this area have to do with the sacrament? A great deal, I say, although I do not wish to get myself involved in liturgical movements. For *our daily life has to do with death*. Here is the point where our daily life intersects with the death of Jesus, so that we gain new factors in common between Jesus and ourselves.

Before we pursue this phenomenon further, we must of course consider again an observation that is at first independent of faith. We all too readily associate that which endangers our daily life with evil. Then the problem of theodicy arises—that is, puzzling over the question why good gets along so poorly and evil gets along so amazingly well. One can console oneself with the statement that only the end will decide. And this end can be delayed or drawn threateningly near, as one wishes. All right. But for the present moment that helps but little. The poor are usually poor too long to be able to be happy in spite of it, and the rich are rich too long to wake up and come to themselves. Nonetheless, even this aspect of the matter belongs to the phenomenon that I have in mind.

I have in mind this: *Just as faith endangers itself through its achievements, the good often leads to unhappiness.* That need not be occasioned by evil deeds. Let us assume quite simply the not unusual case of a loved one, for example a child, who is taken from us by death. Why cannot mothers separate themselves from the graves of their children? This is the phenomenon I have in mind.

Must we not say that the living and the dead are not as easily separated as one often assumes, even though the memory of the dead does in fact dim with the course of time? But should they be separated at all? I do not deny that they often should be separated. And yet death often is really unbearable and leaves wounds that do not heal. *Death can make life more unbearable than an evil deed does.* Death belongs to daily life. It is a guest in our inn, perhaps often even the innkeeper, a bartender and drink mixer. And we become acquainted with it in this way.

But did not Jesus call for *love,* because *now in the time of the kingdom of God it has become universally possible? What then does love say to death?* Does love keep silent about it? I do not think so. It is less the predictions of the passion (which are not historical, Mark 8:31, etc.) than his *parables* themselves which in reality *resist death. They lead into eternal life.* Is it not so? Do they not speak, as Bultmann puts it, "on this side and beyond time"? And if they do that, are they not actually talking about one time, *the time when God sets himself not only to provide a beginning, but with the beginning to assure the continuation and the end,* as Paul emphasizes (Phil. 2:13)? Has not the gospel in the Beatitudes of the Sermon on the Mount, by designating certain persons as blessed, already reached the moment when the future has begun to usher in its time and let it start running off— as if a button were pushed which put everything in motion? *But what should be set in motion when that happens*—that is to say, *when faith happens?*

If one describes faith from outside, one can say it is a "circle." From outside, one cannot decide whether faith gives rise to what it believes or whether faith is the result of what it believes. *Faith is always activity and passivity alike.* But where does that come from? This structure of faith hardly comes from faith itself. For faith does not reflect upon itself, but rather holds to its "object." Thus in our instance, namely, in Jesus' view, it believes that the time of the kingdom of God has come. Faith will not say of itself that it gives rise to this time. And yet this seems to be the case, although no one can be certain in denying that faith is aroused by the time in which it has faith. *Where does this back-and-forth in faith belong? It really belongs in love. For love is always activity and passivity alike* and quite consciously rejoices over this situation. But this means that love keeps itself in motion. It too is something which is not really at man's disposal. It can become his only as event.

Hence *love is properly called a work of God.* Its problem is not itself, but rather the fact that *in the case of humans love strikes upon conditions that the human is not up to, since he must die.* If someone asks what love is, one must say to him: You will certainly know what love is when the time for love has come! The general question as to love posed by Plato, and also the question as to the time for love posed by New Testament theologians such as Paul (1 Cor. 13), do not seem yet to reach the truth that concerns Jesus. It seems to me that he was concerned with the further fact that *the time has come for love to prevail among us humans.* Would that not have to be the time when God makes the dead alive? When he calls that which is not present to be present (Rom. 4:17)? Has not then the time come when the decision is made as to who will belong to those present and who to those absent? And would not those present be present like the children, and those absent be absent like the children's enemies (Matt. 18:2 f., 6 f.)? Then indeed we would be "in the father's house"—namely, at home. But would that not mean that love knows no impediment, that one can say it is irreversible? Then *God's problem would be the problem of how to see to it that love prevails. And under no circumstances would that be our task.* Is this the meaning of the faith that moves mountains, the faith that takes comfort in the might and power of God, that indeed insists on this power in the present because it—believes?

But how then would the *world* appear? Yet is not this too a problem "for God," not for man? Is not this the problem that the New Testament implies by proclaiming Jesus' lordship? What then is the decisive thing about this lordship of Jesus? Is it not this, that after Jesus became Lord it was unavoidable that the Holy Spirit come (Gal. 4:4, 6)? Does not this insight lurk behind the formula "through our Lord Jesus Christ" (Rom. 5:1, 11)? And when through this lordship the Holy Spirit is given to us in "our hearts," because the love of God is poured out in us, does love have to do with something other than the life-giving activity of this Spirit, the activity of God (2 Cor. 3:6; Rom. 5:3-5)? *Is not letting love simply reign as God's work precisely what faith in Jesus involves itself in?* What then could separate us from it (Rom. 8:26 f., 37–39)? And did this power of love bypass Jesus? *If it began to speak in him, then "it was necessary" for it also to work itself out in him.* That is the tenor of 1 Cor. 15, as in all the Pauline statements to the effect that Jesus gave himself for us (Gal. 1:4; 2:20). His cry on the cross cannot be understood other than his sayings; here *love cried.* Those who saw Jesus exalted to the right hand of God as Lord of the world—were they wrong? Did those who had been Jesus' disciples have any other alternative than to say for their part now, after Jesus' death, what *God* had to say in view of Jesus' cross?

Thus everything comes to a head in this: *If Jesus made the voice of love count, and thus made God himself count, then he wanted his hearers to do this too.* Whether they could or could not doubtless had to remain an open question for a while. But when Jesus had been executed, the time had come for it to be *decided* whether the disciples would in their turn speak, like Jesus, in God's stead. They did—but they did in such a way that it remained clear that even a Paul had to speak in God's stead by appealing to Christ (2 Cor. 5:20).

I take it to be the same problem, irrespective of whether it was Jesus or the apostles after him who said what God wanted to have said. *God's revelation consisted simply in God letting men state*

God's own problems in their language, in grace and judgment. So one illuminates the other. Jesus illuminates the apostles' talk and their talk illuminates Jesus' task. *This is why I have in my own way renewed the question of the historical Jesus.* Jesus himself had been God's word to which all clung, for Jesus did not want to be or to be understood as anything other than God's word, which entered into his daily life and began here its work. He was this word, for *he let himself be heard at precisely that place where God himself had begun to speak. Jesus was God's word, if at that time the time for this word had come! And that is what faith in Jesus believes, by believing in the historical Jesus. This alone is the true meaning of "Easter faith."* Jesus and those who believe through him belong forever together. For this reason they believe in him by confessing him as God's word, indeed as God's "verb," God's "time-word."[4]

V. The Hermeneutical Problem

Now after all this, how does the hermeneutical problem present itself? How do I come to understand? You will have noticed that to a large extent I have avoided the terminology which has become customary among us in Germany—for example, in the Bultmannian school. This terminology is probably in need of revision anyway. What I too would like to retain is the concept "existence." One formerly understood this term to mean simply that which is in existence, reality, in distinction from the essence. Thus one distinguished between the content (essence) and the actualization of the content (existence). But with regard to man this distinction did not stand up. If, for example, man is that being which can "involve" himself, then the actualization belongs to the content of man's life.

This version of the concept "existence" could be understood ethically. Then the issue would be whether a person makes the good the content of his life, so that the person in question actualizes himself as a good man.

---

[4] [The German word for "verb" means literally "time-word," and it is this literal meaning upon which the text here plays. Tr.]

This pattern is also at the base of the well-known distinction between "indicative" and "imperative" in the Pauline ethics of justification, as Bultmann has described it. In this case what is at issue is that a person actualize faith. He would do this if he were willing to give up attempting by his own works to bring about his existence, the actualization of his life; rather, at this point he would "surrender" himself, that is, submit himself to God and by so doing actualize faith, which means simply holding to faith in all situations of life. *This person would then leave it to God to make of him what God wished.* And in this way *he would be in a position to love his neighbor selflessly and still not ask the impossible of himself.*

I do not wish to say that this description completely grasps Bultmann's position. But at least this much should be said, that basically the "gift of faith" and "task of faith"[5] are here simply understood as a unit, since faith reveals itself fully only to him who risks it as self-surrender in the service of his neighbor. But does not the same hold true of "the good"? Does not "the good" open itself only to him who surrenders himself completely to it? The only distinction would be that in the case of "the good" I am tormented by temptation as to whether I am capable of this surrender, whereas faith believes that this temptation has been taken from it. The exciting question is simply this: Who is able to believe, that is, how does a person get to faith? But it is precisely this question which seems to me of secondary importance. Instead, the decisive question in the New Testament is this: *Why are we capable of faith?* If the New Testament did not point constantly to God's work, the call to faith would be asking the impossible of us all. For if there were faith only in isolation, it would certainly be no more a match for the world than the human body is a match for a car that runs it down on the street. One could not justify encouraging people to believe unless one could say to them that God is not idle and does more than man. Hence *faith appeals to "God's work."*

[5] [This formulation for the interrelation of indicative and imperative is occasioned by a play on words in the German "Gabe und Aufgabe" that is lost in English. Tr.]

The concept "existence" is able to suggest this situation, if one uses this concept somewhat differently from Bultmann's usage. Now it is no longer primarily the question of how I as a person come to myself and the like; rather this question is deferred. In an age in which jobs are always available at an employment agency it is of course not very easy to make my concept of existence intelligible. When a person knows he can always find a job, he hardly asks about his existence. Of course if unemployment is on the rise, then the problem becomes more apparent—then one understands better that it is perhaps less a matter of jobs than whether one can "establish oneself"[6] somewhere. That is what people used to say. For example, if a merchant opened a shop, he said he had established a livelihood[6] for himself. In earlier times the individual had to arrange that for himself. In those days one did not yet have the tremendous industrial concerns of today. So it was clear that a person always had to hold to something from which he could live—not only to money, but also to a position he had worked himself into in order to earn a *steady* income, as the farmer holds to his farm to live from it by living and working on it.

This situation is actually still prevalent today, although we no longer notice it so readily and naturally. So *I can really understand a person only when I know where he must carry on his life so as to live*. Even his inclinations reflect this structure. If I want to know whether someone is a football player, I have only to bring a football near him. Then I can tell at once whether he is a football player or not. This is existence. *Man always has something outside himself and always lives "with" something that so determines him that his life cannot be fully grasped without this something* (e.g., the football). And in this sense *faith lives with God and from God. Without God one does not understand a believer.* One must understand what he finds in God, why he holds to God. Then one understands the believer and his faith. Neither conscience nor self-examination suffices to understand one who is a

---

[6] [The German idiom means literally "establish an existence," and thus provides the play on words presupposed in this illustration but lost in translation. Tr.]

believer in the New Testament sense. One must know *what this believer finds in God. And it is of this that the New Testament provides information.*

The difficulty is not a false methodology, but a lack of conscious experience, and this on the part of the exegete of today. We cannot conceive of there being a life after death. We assume we are obligated to fit the divine within the limits of our scientifically investigated world of facts. And of course that does not succeed. A science subject to the control of the experiment is not up to that. Such science can at most ruin the world, since its last experiment brings the end. But this science is basically stupid. It discusses its limits too little. And science itself cannot discuss its limits, since it has already toned down the concrete and only acknowledges what leads to the experiment. But our life does not take place in experiments. The catastrophes of our life announce their presence much earlier, in daily *living*. And they show up where words "fail us," as one says, since for example our fellow man has withdrawn himself from us. But it is precisely at this point that one should also speak of *death*. I do not deny that Bultmann's hermeneutic correctly takes death into account. But, as I have here attempted, *one should see death in the context in which it becomes apparent in daily life*. This is not in the least only the biological context; nor is it only the context of the fear of war which today dominates so many people. *Death is to be understood within daily life as it affects language,* and indeed for each of us. *In death man is silenced; even the survivor can be put to silence.* Yet that is not everything. Nor is it true that modern man is only a challenger (for example of nature), an attacker whom death strikes into silence. Instead, death itself is a challenge. *What is challenged by death is our love.* Death seems often to intensify it, but more often to disprove it. *Death says to us that we are not capable of love, and in this way it also claims that love itself is not equal to our life in the world.* He who lets himself be influenced by this is misled into obeying not love, but a law of the jungle where the stronger eliminates the weaker. This is the language with which death threatens. And hence death is the *ultima ratio,* the last word of governments *and* of private individ-

uals. Death mocks our existence by branding it as all too preliminary and tempts us to overstep our limits. *One need only replace
the word "death" with the Pauline word "law,"* and then every
informed person will recognize immediately that our reflections
are quite Biblical, well-known to the theology of the New Testament. And *hermeneutic should make use of this discovery.*

Now if our situation is different from the way death teaches us
it is—that is to say, *if love is right—then death is wrong.* And
then death cannot be the true "limit" of our life. *One must draw
the consequences of all this. That is the hermeneutic which I envisage. I concentrate on language.* And I concentrate on it
as it is challenged by death. Death at the grave mocks the
survivors: "Now you speak!" And to this one must answer:
"Love is the victor!" This statement is a postulate. And this postulate is the postulate of faith: Love wishes for me, precisely when I
am confronted with death, that I believe that love is victorious,
not death. That is not possible without God. But with God it is
a matter of course. This is the way Jesus thought. But Paul did
not think differently.

So you believe in a life after death? To this question of the
natural scientist, faith answers: "Yes, I believe it; because God
has said A, he will also say B." And to be strengthened in this
faith I seek where God has said A. *I look to all the possibilities of
genuine love.* And now I for my part shade the natural sciences
out of daily life, and *I train myself in the genuine language of
daily life.* There certainty prevails. And there, in that atmosphere
of respect with which genuine persons avoid prying into the secret
of God, I can overcome, say, the deep pain owing to the loss of
loved ones. Here I experience that *to love's A there is again and
again love's B.* And I depend on this arrangement. I train myself
in it. Then there is a point in talking of God's work.

All of this is simply a movement of language. I have already
said that, strictly speaking, *language brings only announcements
of the time.* Now I can add that *time primarily determines everything we call a "work."* If we would realize often enough that our
works are dependent on their time—one cannot always harvest
nor always sow—then we would also recognize more clearly the

limits of our works, and gain some sensitivity for those other works that one must name *God's works*—for example, *true love*. That we share in these works of God to a really amazing degree is doubtless the most surprising and in the long run the most satisfying thing a person can experience in this world. Hence Jesus preferred examples out of daily life, and not simply because he was unfamiliar with anything else.

What Bultmann calls the contingent, *the "concrete situation," is now to be brought back into its fitting context of language, namely, that of daily life*. Then there will emerge in us a sensitivity not only for the terrifying and awful, but even more for the wonderful and pleasing. And *then we understand the New Testament again* and ignore the constructions that are used only to lead us past the subject matter itself. It is not as if the "facts" should be despised! But they should be returned to that language to which they belong, when we think of our concrete life between morning and evening. And if we draw back in fear, then it is only because we notice that we have lost our language. But here the New Testament intervenes again. It helps us to find our language again. *The New Testament is itself a textbook in hermeneutic*. It teaches the hermeneutic of faith—in brief, the language of faith—and it encourages us to try out this language ourselves, so that we may become familiar with—God.

Each science orients itself to its subject matter. In this case the subject matter is you yourself, dear reader. And now check and see whether the sorrows you have do not perhaps have something to do with an existence with—God. Then you would indeed already have come in contact with faith. For the faith of the New Testament says that God saves, since love, like the moon, has two halves and is yet a whole.

And systematic theology? Is it not also in upheaval? We are exegetes. Hence we justify our work only hermeneutically, in that we entrust our phenomena to the language that our texts teach us. But does not all this lead to a path between the text and—the sermon? So it does. *The norm of our interpretation is preaching. The text is interpreted when God is proclaimed!* So we should attempt to let ourselves be addressed by the text and to go with the text to the place it wishes to take us. But this is daily life. *In the interaction of the text with daily life we experience the truth of the New Testament.* And the remarkable thing is this, that this book shines brighter and brighter the more difficult daily life becomes. *God intends to remain God. Perhaps this is the fundamental hermeneutical statement precisely for our time.*

But someone will direct a question to my claim that faith is a postulate, the postulate of love—that is, my claim that love essentially places a *demand* upon us, upon us who so often do not live up to love and who in turn are no longer satisfied with love. The question runs: Does not this claim of mine about love's demand assume of my readers or hearers a horrible *sacrificium intellectus?* Especially when I still say faith believes in a life after death? This criticism brings me back to the question of how one comes to faith. To this is to be said: Let no one pride himself on having faith! Let no one persuade himself he believes even though faith makes no sense to him! So long as faith does not make sense to us we cannot believe. And just this long we should not believe! What then should we do? To this one must answer: First you should live! And in your life you should pay attention to the experiences that you have with love. And if this is not applicable, since no one seems to love you, then pay attention to the experiences that your neighbors have with love. Only one thing is to be carefully observed in the process: One is to pay attention not to the bad experiences, not to those in novels, but to the good experiences. It is not human failure that is to be observed, but, put briefly, the history of love itself—yet always in that context of language which is bound up with this history of love in daily life.

Now what motivates people, say, in contacts with small children? Is there not a language expressing itself there quite of its own accord, one that does not so readily find a continuation in our adult life? But—is there no continuation at all? Of course there is a continuation. And if it is not immediately visible, am I not then challenged by love? *Does not love challenge me to believe in the continuation of the history of love?* Surely I believe in this continuation as long as the child is small! I do that as a matter of course. But what if love also calls upon me to take a stand on love in and of itself? What if love demands of me that for the sake of love I believe that it *always* has a history? To this there is but one objection: I can say mankind does not deserve love. Really? And even if that may be true often enough in individual cases, is the question itself thereby answered? No, it is not answered, so long as there is love, indeed so long as there are small children. This long there will also be loving parents, in spite of all evil. Now if man is not in a position to guarantee love, who then does guarantee love? Does not love itself do that? *That is it; love does guarantee itself. He who has this experience believes.* For that is the postulate of faith, to believe that love guarantees itself. Then I will accept no objection to love, not even the objection that man dies. To the contrary, even *death* can serve love. And it is not even rare that that happens. But the crucial point is that *life* even more must serve love. *Now let one replace the word "love" with the word "God."* Then one has understood that *faith in God is the most natural thing that there can be.* And it readily makes sense to our practical reason. On the other hand, it does not make sense that death should dictate to us what we are to think.

To what extent then is there still a "hermeneutical problem" at all? To the extent that *it is not dependent on our good pleasure to know the truth, insofar as the truth has us ourselves as its object.* Either I shade myself out, in which case I can know adequately what has nothing to do with me; or I take myself into consideration—but then it is a question as to whether I am not too prejudiced to know anything about myself. This is why in all human matters, insofar as they are of public interest, society attempts to set up some kind of judiciary institutions, whose verdicts are to keep people from being unable to continue living together. Judicial verdicts and administrative decisions do not necessarily have the status of truth. They prescribe only what is to be done or avoided in the future. So the question remains: *Is there something that is able to bring our life into the light of a truth that also really fits us? This something is to be found only within the sphere of language*. For language is able to lay hold of us even during the night when no one sees us. All it needs is for us to hear. And it doesn't operate by our fantasy having to replace what the eye does not see. Instead, language presses in upon us before or behind objects, in everything that affirms or rejects us. Hence *it is precisely language that belongs to our human nature*. And since only man has the capacity to be himself by giving himself to another, *the language of man belongs in the sphere of love*. Language expresses the experiences of love in such a way that in these experiences a Yes or a No to ourselves "enters our language," i.e., is directly or indirectly spoken. Or should I go so far as to say that really *language never says No but rather says only Yes?* But how must language present itself if it is to lead us to a Yes that is valid for our life? Will we not have to be brought back into our concrete everyday life? Can one do that on paper? In classroom lectures? Is there such a thing as "indirect exhortation" (Bultmann)? Now, after all, why not? If it is true that not everything is our business, and if it is true that some things are very much our business; if it is further true that for our own sake much may not be decided by ourselves, and if it is true that language nonetheless makes decisions which bring us to life, then in our thinking we will have to adapt ourselves to finding out to what extent others must say the truth to us, and to what extent we can find out the truth only for ourselves. For in both cases *our own hearing is required. That is the hermeneutical problem in our daily life*. Why should this problem be any different at the writing desk of the theologian? And just for this reason it is an act of grace if we make any progress. For hearing is something one cannot produce on one's own. One can just be alert not to miss the hour for hearing. And yet this hour is always there! So we must find out to what extent *our mental activity, our seeing, is bound to a hearing. That is the hermeneutical problem*. It is posed for us every day anew. This is the point of departure for the New Testament.

The New Testament speaks the language of hearing. It wishes to lead us into truth, so that we may learn to distinguish correctly between hearing and seeing. A nonlinguistic reality would have relativized the distinction between life and death. Hence a science oriented *ultimately* to the experiment cancels itself out, as we today know. Christian faith, on the other hand, holds fast to the distinction between life and death. Hence it has something to say to everyone.

PART II. American Discussion

4. On Broadening the New Hermeneutic

JOHN DILLENBERGER

San Francisco Theological Seminary

In contemporary theology the problems of meaningful interpretation and of method are dependent on the realities experienced and known. On this point Barth, Tillich, Bultmann, Fuchs,
and Ebeling agree. This formal agreement characterizes the consensus resulting from the basic shift in theology since World War
I. The actual understandings within this consensus present the
major theological options of our time. The new hermeneutic is
a theological program designed to overcome the theological difficulties of what it sees as the major alternatives within this frame
of reference. Tillich is not directly considered since theologies as   *Tillich*
heavily dependent as his upon classical theological and philosoph-
ical categories are not acceptable to the new hermeneutic. The
major theological figures in relationship to whom the new hermeneutic is developed are Barth and Bultmann. From its point
of view the sophisticated, carefully grounded use of objective-sub-
jective categories by Barth still does not sufficiently abandon the   *Barth*
traditional patterns of theological discourse and still wrongly
objectifies the word. While Bultmann's work moves in the right   *Bultmann*
direction, his hermeneutical understanding is too closely identified
with the illumination of a text, and his categories of existentialist
understanding are too closely allied with Heidegger as viewed
from his early period. Clearly it is the intention of Ebeling and

147

Fuchs, and the new hermeneutic generally, to advance beyond
Barth and their precursor, Bultmann.

I

The projected advance is itself a theological position, perhaps
best characterized as a particular understanding of the word of
God functioning in a hermeneutical sense. From the standpoint
of Biblical material, the word of God is the bringing of the text
that was once proclamation into fresh proclamation, that is, into
the situation where it again becomes faith. The accent falls upon
the reality communicated in existential understanding. The word
of God functioning hermeneutically, both as removing obstacles
to faith and engendering faith, is identical with the true intention
of the Biblical text. Theological hermeneutic is therefore identical
with the word event, the happening of faith.

The meaning of this central point of departure is best illumined
by the corollaries that accompany it. The total theological enterprise is the clarification of faith, that is, of true existence. It is not
that faith informs theological reflection, but that theology is the
articulate understanding and coming to understanding of faith.
This means that the various theological disciplines cannot really
be distinguished, though certain sharing of labors can take place.
Ebeling's work, for instance, cuts through the Biblical, historical,
and systematic disciplines. Indeed, since theological work is the
business of bringing to be and of clarifying faith, the divisions
between disciplines can be drawn only in the light of the common
concern for proclamation and faith.[1] Hence, exegesis is completed
in proclamation. Historical disciplines, such as church history, disclose the history of the interpretation of texts for the sake of dis-
closing past mistakes, true intentionality and meaning, and pre-
venting the unintended and unreflective repetition of the past.
Hence the task of church history is in no sense to reconstruct the

---

[1] See, e.g., Gerhard Ebeling, "Discussion Theses for a Course of Introductory Lectures on the Study of Theology," *Wort und Glaube* (Tübingen:
J. C. B. Mohr, 1960; 2nd ed., 1962), pp. 447–457. English translation by
James W. Leitch, in *Word and Faith* (Philadelphia: Fortress Press, 1963),
pp. 424–433.

past even in the light of faith, but directly to serve the word event, the advent of faith.[2] All disciplines are thus theologically-existentially grounded. The difficulties, as will be delineated later, lie in the particular theological stance.

This is already evident in another corollary point. The significant theological concepts are interchangeable, but they all speak directly of faith. Indeed faith is the central overarching category. Ebeling contends that the Reformers never carried through their basic insight, so crucial at one level, as a hermeneutical principle affecting the total theological discipline. Certainly the development of Protestant orthodoxy and its demise testify to the truth of this statement.

But the issue is how one carries it through. Is faith a category which informs all formulation, or is faith itself that which is formulated? For Ebeling, it appears, all concepts are directly concepts about faith. For example, the Christological formulations in the classical sense are entirely abandoned. But could one not say that while they are abstract statements, they were informed by that which faith needed to protect in one period of the history of the church? Insofar as they are now uncritically held to, or perhaps subscribed to at all, they are open to challenge. But for Ebeling they were originally misdirected. They can rightly, it seems to me, be criticized as inadequate for their own period, but only insofar as faith itself was inadequately expressed for the problems of that period. But Ebeling has a diametrically opposite conception of the Christological enterprise. He insists that Christological statements can refer only to the human person of Jesus as the man of faith. The essential and only Christological statement is "I believe in Jesus" in which "I believe" and "Jesus" and "faith" are identical statements. This is because Jesus is the instance of faith, the "author and perfector of faith." Indeed when this point is pressed, it is clear that faith, word, Jesus, God, true existential reality, are interchangeable terms meaning the same reality.[3] But

[handwritten margin note: Christology consists in the statement, "I believe in Jesus".]

[2] Ebeling's delineation of this complex of issues is elaborated in *Die Geschichtlichkeit der Kirche und ihrer Verkündigung als theologisches Problem* (Tübingen: J. C. B. Mohr, 1954).

[3] These aspects are discussed particularly in "Jesus and Faith" and "The Question of the Historical Jesus and the Problem of Christology," in *Wort*

in point of fact they are seen as identical only because they are all understood from the vantage point of a particular conception of the word and of faith.

For Ebeling the starting point is a known word. There is not a word to be made known. The reality of the word includes its being known. It is not appropriate, therefore, to speak of the word to be known or of the appropriation of the word, but of the word being known, coming to language, being the word event. In the word being known, words do not hide or point but express. There is no dialectical delineation of hiding or revealing, or of content to be received; there is only word coming to issue, which is faith.

This view has underlying philosophical assumptions. Ebeling does believe there are affinities between the Greek view of the *logos* nature of reality and the word. The word is the authentic reality in actualization in Jesus and in faith. In analogy with the later Heidegger it is being coming to expression. Faith, therefore, rightly knows and sees. Ignorance and veiling have been lifted and reality is present.

Hence demythologizing follows. Precisely the word-faith complex makes mythological categories impossible. If mythical concepts are taken literally, they function as objective pictures. And, as in existentialism generally, objective picture language, whether mythical or not mythical, is inauthentic. And if mythical language functions poetically or imaginatively, it has the difficulties of all pointing language or concepts. In existentialist theology generally word and language express faith directly. Language conveys no more nor less than it says. It is therefore identical with reality, for it expresses reality directly.

Perhaps that is why the core of existentialist theology has such a circumscribed scope, why the problems and contours seem so reduced. One deals with the nature and essence of faith, just as in the liberal Protestant heritage. The historical linkage is, of course, readily acknowledged by Bultmann, Ebeling, and Fuchs. In all instances the intent is to delineate the nature and contours

---

und Glaube, pp. 203–254, 300–318 [*Word and Faith,* pp. 201–245, 288–304]; and in Chs. III and IV of *Theologie und Verkündigung* (Tübingen: J. C. B. Mohr, 1962).

of faith. And in that delineation differences as vast as any in theology do appear. There is a vast difference between Jesus as the
moral personality, who in that sense is the expression of a life to
be followed, and the kerygma-Christology in Bultmann's theology.
Furthermore, in Ebeling's formulation of the new quest Jesus re-
turns as the instance and, therefore, the basis of faith, providing a
Christological foundation for the kerygma. Such differences are
significant, and in other respects, too, the shift from Bultmann to
Ebeling is illuminating at crucial theological points. Ebeling overcomes the equation of theology with anthropology by utilizing the
philosophical contours of the later Heidegger and by an unambiguous accent on the gift nature of faith, lifted out of the de-   *The*
cisional-obedience setting which beclouds the interpretation of   *character*
Bultmann. Everything testifies that faith is an event, an occur-   *of faith*
rence, an acknowledged gift. It is grace and a new life, a life freed
from the world and the past as burdens. It is freedom for this
world and for the present.

This is the character of faith and what faith does. But is that
all there is to the contours of faith and to the understanding that   *Existential*
accompanies it? It is perhaps all that can be unambiguously and   *ist theol-*
directly expressed in the equations of reality and language in exis-   *ogies guilty*
tentialist theology and in the new hermeneutic. But precisely here   *of blind*
a serious question arises. Have not the existentialist theologies, of   *optimism*
whatever variety, taken language too much at face value, as if it   *regarding*
could express reality directly? Having overcome the objective lan-   *the ability*
guage of world and world picture, have not the existentialist the-   *of language*
ologians developed a kind of objective and objectifying language   *of language*
of the self, a language equally abstract? They have not only rede-   *to express*
fined the nature of language; they have reduced its avenues of   *the truth*
direct applicability to the human. As a result, the contours of   *directly.*
faith have little color and pulse.

II

Contemporary theology is the fruitful product of the existentialist protest against the objectifying word-picture language of past
theology. But existentialist theologies have abandoned many of the

problems expressed in theology in the light of their own concerns and on the assumption that such issues were not legitimate. In his own theological work, and in his analysis of the word, Ebeling has given hints that conceivably could have led to different conclusions. But these different conclusions are probably visible only from the perspective of a different understanding of language and of a somewhat different theological position. In the ensuing discussion the attempt will be made to delineate a diverging—and that word is deliberately used to indicate affinity and difference—hermeneutical understanding.

Let us say that the task of hermeneutic is to help bring to understanding. The language event serves precisely this function, for through it reality and life are conjoined. But it is precisely here that the problem of language arises. Ebeling and Fuchs apparently assume that there is no problem of language, if language is properly understood. And understood, one might add, in a way which combines adequate philosophical analysis and everyday language. For this reason the alleged hermeneutical advance could be made by first penetrating to the intention of a text, a task that may involve a pre-understanding, and then proceeding to win understanding through the text. Indeed, there are understanding and interpretation through a text, and the text fulfills its function only as it brings to understanding. However, if one does not take seriously the problem of understanding the language forms and expressions of the past in their own right, and if one merely affirms that these no longer speak directly to us, one is left with the impression that there is one correct language and way of understanding. But that there is one way of understanding and expressing existence is exactly the position that needs to be challenged. Precisely because the word of God comes to language, the nature of language—language in all its concreteness—needs attention. There is no language *for* all time; it rather functions *in* all time. Precisely because language is expressive, it represents the variety and range of man's experience in diverse cultural periods. In this context documents, texts, and spoken words are not to be distinguished, since when they bring to understanding, they have

---

Marginalia (handwritten):

Existentialist theology simply rules out of court many of the basic problems of theology, claiming that these issues are not relevant.

The methodology of the new hermeneutic

played their role. Proclamation has been too tightly identified with the spoken and audible word.

The broader hermeneutical problem emerges in the encounter with texts and documents of the past. In this encounter hermeneutic is the attempt to penetrate to the intentionality of a document or concept, not in the hope that its essence might be presented in some form freed of overt cultural categories, but rather in the hope that its intentionality might be expressed anew, in and through and despite the cultural media of our own time. The radical consequence of a serious approach from this direction is evident when it is recognized that the intentionality of a theological statement in subsequent ages may have to be delineated through expressions that outwardly contradict the original formulation. For example, the trinitarian formulation originally defended monotheism against the polytheism of the Greco-Roman world, in which creation and redemption were split between two gods and the redeemer god was known by gnosis rather than by revelation. In one expression—and in spite of all the concrete debates—the trinitarian formula affirmed that God was at once creator and redeemer and known as both by the power of his own activity. At a later juncture in history the same monotheistic intentionality—and this expression is deliberately used since monotheism is not a numerical problem—was affirmed through the unitarian protests against trinitarian polytheisms. That point is usually overlooked because the unitarian impulse so rapidly developed an unacceptable rationalistic outlook.

This approach is not to be identified with relativity. The God whose truth is absolute is known by us only in earthen vessels, which disclose truth, but disclose it in relative forms. Therefore, final theological statements are excluded. Proper hermeneutical understanding excludes either a simple acceptance or a simple rejection. Hence, just as theological statements of a period cannot be claimed with absolute validity for their own time or for subsequent periods, so also the outright rejection of theological formulations of a past period because they can no longer be accepted in one's own setting shows one's lack of awareness of one's own

[margin, handwritten: Hermaneutik is the attempt to penetrate through to the intentionality of a document and to release that intentionality into the living context of our time.

Sachkritik]

cultural conditioning. One is known by what one rejects as well as by what one accepts. For example, twentieth-century individuals, Christians and non-Christians, who simply reject the notion of predestination reveal that they are reacting to the predestinarian views of their grandfathers, views that essentially were formulated in the seventeenth century. The acceptance of theological statements as absolute truth and the rejection of theological statements as allegedly irrelevant and untrue reveal an identical mentality. The task of theological hermeneutic is to penetrate to the theological intention in all theological statements, whether the statements are affirmed or rejected. The issue is wider than acceptance or rejection or even than truth or untruth; the issue is one of adequacy to express what is known in and through the word.

The intentionality of a theological formulation cannot simply be captured in and of itself and then translated into another form or universe of discourse. The intentionality of any theological statement can be discerned only in terms of the statement or formulation itself. The problem of interpretation is that of analogically translating from one universe of discourse or configuration to another. But there is never simply an "in between" stage; nor is there the possibility of peeling off layers until the essence has been laid bare. Intentionality and essence are not identical. The problem of the interpretation of theological documents, as of the New Testament, is not that of the kernel and the husks. The program of demythologizing and of the new hermeneutic, whether applied to Scriptural or theological documents, belongs to the liberal Protestant attempt to lay bare a center. But a center never exists by itself, for in that respect it would indeed not be a center at all, but a new statement demanding hermeneutical attention.

The problem of theological hermeneutic as a part of the problem of translation from one form of discourse to another further involves us in the issue of trying to comprehend theological documents in their own right. The problem of intentionality demands distinguishing between intentionality and cultural form, but it does not imply that the two can be separated. However, the distinction between intentionality and cultural form is important,

[margin note: The "intentio-nality" of a statement is not so easily laid bare.]

for without it misunderstanding arises. For example, although Luther and Calvin believed that the Bible was true from cover to cover, it would never have occurred to them to defend the authority of Scripture in the light of its literal accuracy. This temptation occurred only in the Protestant orthodox development, and then for understandable historical reasons. It is a wrong hermeneutical procedure when the Reformers and all periods prior to them are viewed as regrettably believing in the literal accuracy of the Bible. While they accepted a literal accuracy for Scripture, it was not a theological axiom. Indeed, there were no fundamentalists before the seventeenth century, fundamentalism being defined as the defense of Scripture on the basis of literal truth. Fundamentalism therefore is a modern phenomenon, and insofar as it claims the old-time religion, it is neither old enough nor historical enough to be aware of its own conditioning.

III

In modern theology the general hermeneutical problem is particularly complicated by the radical reorientation of ways of thinking in what we call the modern world. The intention here is not to describe or to assess this phenomenon but rather to note its salient features and to differentiate them from the usual descriptions of modernity. It is not that the modern world has become secular, for this, as everyone who reads Bonhoeffer knows, can be interpreted in a thoroughly positive way. It is not simply that the vertical and depth dimensions in culture have disappeared, for on many levels they have been recovered with new insight and meaning. It is not that the culture has become materialistic, for the increasing boredom with a materialistic culture is also a sign of hope.

The problem for theology is rather that its basic formulations were expressed in a universe of discourse that was drastically challenged and destroyed through a process of thought that arose in the seventeenth century, became articulate in the eighteenth, and reached its culmination in the nineteenth. The preceding eighteen centuries of development, whether Aristotelian, Platonic, or neo-

The great transition to modern thought.

Platonic, are shifts within a common framework. The transition to the modern world is the most drastic intellectual fact of Western history. That transformation can be characterized as the transition from the notion that truth has been delivered in the past and is to be uncovered and recovered in every age to the view that truth is fundamentally to be discovered or that it lies in the future. The seventeenth-century "battle of the books" is the first symptom of this transformation of thought, a battle in which the initial thrust was against the automatic acceptance of the authority of Aristotle. Until well into the eighteenth century, the citation of authority was standard practice. Prooftexting was the order of the day and consisted of lining up an acceptable list of authorities from the past on one side and of making a list of unacceptable authors on the other. Part of the thrust of the theological opposition to the new science lay in the latter's allegedly bringing to its support authorities that had been discredited already in antiquity. In a very real sense truth was proportionate to its certification by the right people in antiquity. Theologically this meant Moses, and philosophically, Plato or Aristotle. It is instructive to recall that Isaiah was not particularly significant in interpreting the Messianic expectations, for compared to Moses, he was an upstart. Until the eighteenth century the argument from antiquity was a very powerful motif for the certification and validation of truth. The motto of the Enlightenment—dare to know, have the courage to know—was still directed against the automatic authority of the ancients.

There are many levels at which the notion that truth had been delivered in the past operated in the formulation of theological doctrine. This is illustrated by the idea of prophecy, which existentialist theology and the new hermeneutic have abandoned. The claim that the Messiah had arrived was defended on the basis that he had been predicted. Moses already knew of Jesus Christ, not proleptically nor hiddenly, but actually. Writers in the seventeenth century were still contending for the credibility of prediction on the basis that the extent of time between a prediction and its fulfillment argued all the more for its validity. When we read along in a New Testament text and incessantly stumble upon quotations from the Old that interrupt the flow of the text, and when we conclude that they are not really relevant to make a point, it is important to recall that in the ancient way of thinking their predictive value was significant. If the notion of prediction is accepted, successful documentation is possible; if it is not accepted, documentation is itself the most dubious of all the enterprises of substantiation. One need only recall that the ancients similarly made the attempt to interpret Homer as predicting future political events. Compared to that enterprise and its lack of correlation with actual historical events, the alleged Biblical conception of prediction was indeed comparatively reliable and trustworthy. While it is theologically correct to state that prophecy does not mean prediction, it must be recognized that there was historic justification for once understanding it in that sense. At the same time there was undoubtedly less certitude concerning its validity in the early church than there was in the Protestant orthodox theology of the seventeenth century, just as in the case of the attitude toward miracles. Because on independent grounds men in the early church already believed in the Messiah, the predictive role could serve its function. It was a quite different enterprise when seventeenth-century dogmaticians centered on the predictive as the sole basis of evidence.

IV

Cultural ways of understanding and unique experiences make it inevitable that we can speak only analogically concerning God and man. Ways of thinking do determine what we think of God or faith, but it is not necessary to draw a negative conclusion at this point. Xenophanes said that if oxen could paint, their gods would be like oxen. Yet some of the Greeks depicted their gods in animal form to make certain that their difference from man was unmistakably clear. Not only is an analogy not to be mistaken for identity, it is to be recognized that the analogy depends upon the situation of revelation itself, that God's possibility of becoming known is always in the concrete situations of man's life, including elements of understanding and misunderstanding. The price to be paid for the knowledge of God is an analogical concreteness which is always the truth but never the whole truth. The truth that is given in an historical juncture will inevitably have its own form, though hopefully also the transformation of that form by the genuine encounter with the living God. This is especially evident in the theological exposition of the attributes of God, a problem that existentialist theology sidesteps.

Concepts of omniscience and omnipotence of God are projections of the desires of sinful man.

It is widely and correctly affirmed, largely because of the work of Karl Barth, that the older theologians defined the attributes too abstractly through the use of general philosophical conceptions of omnipotence and omniscience. Barth is further correct in trying to analyze the attributes in terms of the proper correlation of God's love and freedom, as his love in freedom and his freedom in love. In short, Karl Barth wishes to bring the attributes under the criterion of revelation. In this he is correct; but from a hermeneutical standpoint more needs to be said than that the traditional attributes have continued too long under the aegis of general philosophical notions. We must see the full scope of the distortion in the traditional views. The general notions of the omnipotence and omniscience of God define power and knowing in ways that are actually analogous to what sinful man would like to be able to do and know were he himself God. Sinful man would like to have all power to eliminate the problems that frustrate him and the world, and to know all things—past, present, and future. But it may be that God's omnipotence is the love by which he does not need to have such an arrogating power and that God's knowing of man is such that he can be open to the frustrating and joyful dynamics of the future. If this analysis is correct, the true meaning of Rom. 1:18 ff., rather than being a natural theology, is what a full reading of the passage means, that the truth of God has become a lie, the projection of ourselves. The traditional conceptions of omnipotence and omniscience are among the clearest illustrations of the way in which man has made God in his own image, in the image of his sinful self. Here the theological understanding of openness to the future must be taken seriously. One should not hesitate to say that even God does not know what we or others will do next week. He may know better than we ourselves know, for he knows us better than we know ourselves; but on another level he does not know or need to know. His redemptive presence can be forming and transforming the present and thus also determining and changing the future. In this sense God too is involved in time and in history. Eternity is not the way in which all times are compressed but the way in which God is present to time and to history.

God's revealing presence must be known in the categories of our own world, even if that way of delineation stands against former categories. This does not mean that our categories are more true; but it does mean that they are more true for us, for the old way of putting things is no longer feasible or possible. It is no longer possible because older formulations in their original sense pointed to their ground and basis, and never to themselves. But outworn formulations became formulations of which we became conscious and self-conscious. As long as deterministic frames of reference were naturally held by men, God's activity was paramount and never in question. When determinism was no longer self-evident, the determining activity of God became a conscious problem in which the theological point had already become a matter of form and expression. A proper hermeneutic means that formulations must be abandoned the moment in which theological attention shifts from their intentionality to the formulations themselves.

The hermeneutical problem in all the forms we have encountered it is illustrated in the problem of creation, also of little concern to the existentialists. It may be necessary to speak of the risk God took in creation. For God to create man in his own image, to create a man who reflects himself, is to create a man who could act as if he were God. The risk in creation, therefore, is that man may live unto himself, that he may attempt to be as God, instead of entering into or maintaining his reflected relations to his maker. Here too it is necessary to state that God himself did not know the outcome of such a creation. To say that God knew but did not determine the result is the wish to be omnipotent about one's own knowing, but that is hardly an adequate understanding of God. But it may be added that the risk of creation was covered in the heart of God himself. It is in this sense that we can meaningfully talk about the Christological foundation of creation, the notion that all the possibilities are covered in the ground of creation itself. In this sense the supralapsarian instinct is correct, even though the traditional formulation is unacceptable. Its instinct is more certain than the dubious adaptation of the infralapsarian spirit. If this line of approach is feasible, then it is possible to say that man, who in principle could have lived unto God instead of unto self, nevertheless finds himself on the latter path. This is God's risk, which should not be ontologically explicated or explained in terms of the dizziness of unactualized freedom as in Tillich. Man as the image of God cannot live unto himself without disrupting his very being, for as an image he must image forth his ground and source. It is only God who is not image and in this sense the full actuality who could live unto himself, but who, quite unlike man, has chosen not to live unto himself but to live in relation to a creation which mirrors him.

Man as the image of God. [margin note]

In this way of thinking, openness to the future rather than determination by the past is pervasive and dominant, ranging all the way from man's cultural life to the foundations of creation itself. It should be recalled that even when the ancient world lived under the powers of fate and fortune, the Christian movement thought of history in terms of purpose and a teleological direction, that is, as directed toward the future. But that was not identical with openness to the future as we understand it today. Nor should the fact that the nineteenth-century conception of progress-distorted openness to the future keep us from seeing the legitimate transformation of thought categories which has formed the modern world. It is in the light of such developments that one can speak, along with the existentialists, of the past meeting us out of the future. This is a way of saying that the truth of the past meets us in terms of the possibilities of the present, that is, in terms of the forming and transformation of present possibilities. This means that the truth of the past is always our truth. Hence the sheer reconstruction of the past is neither possible nor interesting. Our pre-understanding does determine what we see, though what we may see must also engage us in such a way that our pre-understandings are reshaped. It is the submerging of the latter element that makes existentialism so unexistential when it pretends that it has at last illumined those categories of existence given with existence itself. But a hermeneutic of life means that the givenness of existence in every age is composed of distinctive factors that form human existence, so that there is no such thing as a final analysis of existence itself. Existence is as fluid as the cultural forms that give us life, and that is why all the configurations of history must continually confront and reshape us.

Cultural forms give shape to existence.

Nowhere is this more apparent than in the traditional theories of the atonement, which far beyond the contours of existentialist theology have been widely ignored. On first thought it appears strange that there should be so many theories of atonement, when the atonement is widely assumed to be the central point in Christian thought. But it is precisely because this is the case that there are, and ought to be, so many theories. It is because men experience redemption in terms of the concrete forms of their own need for redemption, that the theories are so diverse. The notion of redemption from cosmic powers and forces of evil expressed the ancient world's way of understanding redemption as the direct, personal release from such powers; the theory of satisfaction had to do with social structures in which relations of lords and serfs in large part played their role; the so-called moral influence theory of the atonement was developed in a social context in which to be incorporated into the actuality of love made manifest seemed a realizable teleological direction. It is not by accident that in our own day we experience redemption as deliverance from meaninglessness, anxiety, despair, loneliness, frustration, etc. If the truth of God meets us concretely, how could it be otherwise? There is therefore no point in looking for a final or classical theory of the atonement. The truth of God encounters us in the concreteness of our historic situation. But the hermeneutic of this situation demands that we see the intentionality in all formulations. This means that the forms and configurations of the past must challenge us insofar as they may have something to say to us about ways in which we no longer (though perhaps we should) encoun-

Theories of the atonement.

Note cultural forms giving shape to the various doctrines of the atonement.

For this reason, the theological thought of bygone generations cannot be for that reason authoritative.

ter the need for redemption; and on the other side, they say to us that we must always be open to new forms of apprehending God's deliverance.

If the preceding analysis is correct, certain conclusions can be drawn for the theological enterprise. The categories and questions of various cultural periods dare not become final for theological work; nevertheless, there is no way around them. They can be appreciated only as the question of their intentionality continues to confront us. There is, however, no way in which an intentionality can be delineated as if it were an essence. There is only the possibility of raising the question of the truth expressed in cultural forms as their configurations are juxtaposed and contrasted to cultural forms of other periods. This does not mean that the truth of one period is as good as another; nor does it mean the relativity of all truth; but it does mean that the absolute truth of God is always known to us concretely and appropriately in the forms of the world in which we live.

Aside from the fact that this situation is inescapable, it is at once an asset and a liability. Unless theologians take it seriously, they will be tempted to believe that at long last they have reached the possibility of theological expression freed of the problems of the past, or they will decide that they have created a new theological method that avoids the pitfalls of the past. There is, moreover, no simple way to return to the New Testament message without going through the intellectual currents and history of the West. There is therefore no way around but only a way through. This means in conclusion that we must take two things seriously. In the first place, the relativity of all cultural forms does express the truth of God. This may mean that the same truth may have to be expressed in forms which appear diametrically opposite in differing periods, as in the case of the trinitarian and unitarian expressions of monotheism. In the second place, it must be clear that the fundamental thought forms since the eighteenth century are different from those of the previous centuries in Western theological history. Moreover, it was in the previous centuries that most of the classical theological problems were formed.

We must, therefore, seriously attempt to penetrate to the center of their formulations, or we shall be caught in the dilemma of having either simply to accept them or simply to reject them. The problem of theological hermeneutic is to engage in an enterprise in which the latter alternatives are laid aside for the sake of the greater and more adequate appropriation by each generation of the truth of God for our concrete particular existence. This is the task of theological hermeneutic. It is a program, not a method, an unceasing, endless enterprise in which imagination, thought, and the courage to make mistakes will play their role. Indeed, it is to be carefully distinguished from theological method. Many have abandoned the older notion of resting in theological answers; many have even abandoned the notion of proper theological questions. But in their place they have vested a confidence in theological method. This is the last deceptive certitude. Hermeneutic is the program by which total configurations, in which truth is enshrined, endlessly confront each other in the totality and concreteness of their central claims.

5. The Hermeneutical Problem and Historical Criticism

ROBERT W. FUNK

Drew University

By intention this essay turns on the axis of the hermeneutical problem as it has been developed by Rudolf Bultmann, Ernst Fuchs, and Gerhard Ebeling. In this respect the writer wishes to include himself among those who have learned much from Bultmann. Fuchs and Ebeling, too, have made distinctive contributions to the discussion, but in which follows it is the concern of Ebeling, set out in his programmatic essay of 1950 and articulated elsewhere, which is to be developed.[1]

It is taken for granted in this circle that a theological hermeneutic must be appropriate both to faith *and* to the categories of understanding which belong to man as man.[2] If this be allowed, it is not immediately apparent how historical criticism[3] can be of service in aiding the occurrence of the word of God, i.e., the proc-

---

[1] "Die Bedeutung der historisch-kritischen Methode für die protestantische Theologie und Kirche," *ZThK,* XLVII (1950), 1–46, now in *Wort und Glaube* (Tübingen: J. C. B. Mohr, 1960), pp. 1–49, English translation by James W. Leitch, *Word and Faith* (Philadelphia: Fortress Press, 1963), pp. 17–61; *Die Geschichtlichkeit der Kirche und ihrer Verkündigung als theologisches Problem* (Tübingen: J. C. B. Mohr, 1954); "The Meaning of 'Biblical Theology,'" *JThS,* VI (1955), 210–225, also appearing in *On the Authority of the Bible. Some Recent Studies by L. Hodgson, C. F. Evans, J. Burnaby, G. Ebeling and D. E. Nineham* (London: S. P. C. K., 1960), pp. 49–67, and in German as "Was heisst 'Biblische Theologie,'" *Wort und Glaube,* pp. 69–89 [*Word and Faith,* pp. 79–97]; etc.

[2] E.g., Ebeling, above, pp. 84 f. This involves opting for Bultmann over against Barth.

[3] Historical criticism is used throughout in a comprehensive sense as it has been developed in relation to Biblical studies, i.e., it embraces both "lower" and "higher" criticism as well as the broader fields normally designated as historical criticism.

lamation. For is not historical criticism fundamentally inimical to the concept of the word of God, as well as to the concept of the Holy Spirit, operating as it does with scientific criteria? On the other hand, is it not dangerous to isolate the word of God from the exegesis of the text, if the word bears any significant relation to the text?[4] In short, how does historical criticism function with respect to the text of faith through which faith believes that its life and its norm are mediated?

This question has been polarized at the less sophisticated level into two antithetical questions: Is historical criticism the arbitrator, from an autonomous and objective locus, in the theological interpretation of Scripture, deciding what is and what is not allowable? Or, is historical criticism in the service of, and subservient to, theological exegesis which ultimately decides what meaning can be assigned to a text? This polarization obscures the hermeneutical problem which lies at the base of both questions. We should ask rather, can historical criticism be taken up into the theological task in such a way that it does not lose its independent critical powers but nevertheless functions positively in the service of theology? The hermeneutical problem, as it relates to this formulation, can be posed as the question of how the word that has come to expression can come to expression anew.

Bultmann, Fuchs, and Ebeling have clung steadfastly to their liberal heritage in insisting that historical criticism has an integral role to play in the movement from text to proclamation. Bultmann in particular has developed the notion of the hermeneutical circle that decisively involves historical criticism with respect to the text. While I affirm this position, I see two aspects of the problem as requiring further elucidation. What precisely is the function of historical criticism[5] in relation to an *interpretation* of the text? This aspect is opened up in Section II. Further, is not the *interpreter* himself involved in a historical circle to which historical criticism is also relevant? The treatment of the second aspect in Section III betrays unmistakable affinities with Ebeling's concerns.

---

[4] Cf. Ebeling, above, pp. 88 f., for a formulation of the problem.
[5] Historical criticism here is used as the equivalent of Bultmann's historical circle as defined by Dinkler. See below, pp. 192–193, n. 83.

[Handwritten marginal note:] What is the role of historical criticism in determining the meaning of the text?

The American situation in this respect presents marked contrast to the situation on the Continent. Although Ebeling has set out good reasons for concern about the critical nerve of historical criticism in German language theology,[6] Biblical studies on this side of the Atlantic have never been theologically shaken to the same extent and so are in danger of continuing on their independent way, critical but increasingly irrelevant. Biblical criticism on the Continent has sustained a closer relation to theology, particularly since Barth, than it has in this country, with the result that the problem may be said to be relevant to both situations for opposite reasons. In Europe historical criticism has tended to become subservient to theological interests, thereby losing its critical powers; on the American side historical criticism has retained its nontheological orientation. Since that orientation received its decisive bent in the theological wars of the preceding era, the nontheological bias of historical criticism tends to take on theological import in the face of a new situation. Neither in Europe nor in America has historical criticism been able to break through to the hermeneutical issue that underlies both situations, i.e., the problem of the conditions under which understanding is possible at all.[7] This essay, however, is aimed primarily at the peculiarities of the American development.

The hermeneutic of Fuchs and Ebeling, depending as it does on a doctrine of the word,[8] both requires historical criticism and yet relativizes it. Why this is so can best be seen by attending to the place that justification by faith occupies in their theological programs. In the present essay the correlation between a doctrine of the word and the function of historical criticism, which is the overarching concern, is implicit in the juxtaposition of exegetical and methodological sections. In the exegetical section (I) an attempt is made to reflect upon the hermeneutical problem in the face of the text, i.e., to ask how the word is heard, how it comes to understanding, and what is concomitant therewith, what the word is. In the methodological sections (II, III) the function of

---

[6] *Wort und Glaube,* pp. 2 ff. [*Word and Faith,* pp. 18 ff.]
[7] Cf. Ebeling, above p. 94.
[8] Cf. Ebeling, *ibid.,* p. 99.

historical criticism, with respect to both text and interpreter, is defined in relation to *that* understanding of the word. The substantive affinities of this approach with that of Fuchs and Ebeling are apparent.

The choice of 2 Corinthians as text requires some special justification. The Corinthian correspondence has recently been brought back into the discussion in connection with the heresy-orthodoxy problem,[9] and it is because this problem can be conceived hermeneutically that the Corinthian letters take on special importance. That is to say, Paul's effort to grapple with the Corinthian heresy can be interpreted as an example of his hermeneutic at work.[10] The exposition of 2 Corinthians lays the basis, therefore, for the methodological discussion which follows.

I. SECOND CORINTHIANS AS HERMENEUTIC

In 2 Cor. 2:14–7:4 (omitting 6:14–7:1) and 10:1–13:13 Paul is giving expression to the word of reconciliation (5:19) as it determines his work as apostle.[11] This theme is renewed from a

[9] James M. Robinson, "Basic Shifts in German Theology," *Interpretation,* XVI (1962), 79 ff., 86 f.

[10] One could even say that the Corinthian correspondence provides the battleground for the current theological debate. It is worth noting that H. Schlier identifies the pneumatic theology of heretical Corinthians with modern existentialist theology (Robinson, *ibid.,* p. 87). This leads to the observation that Paul may have been trapped by his predilection to criticize from within rather than from without, and further that the orthodox way out was to reject not only false implications but also the whole context and language of a theological position (*ibid.,* p. 86). The debate thus has potentially far-reaching implications for theology as a whole. Thus far, however, the discussion does not seem to have come to grips with the central issue, which is whether Paul could meet the Corinthians on their ground and still remain true to the kerygma, or, as I would prefer to put it, whether he could remain true to the kerygma and *not* meet them on their own ground.

[11] I am especially indebted to Ernst Käsemann, "Die Legitimität des Apostels. Eine Untersuchung zu II Korinther 10–13," *ZNW,* XLI (1942), 33–71 (now published as a *Sonderausgabe* by the Wissenschaftliche Buchgesellschaft, Darmstadt, 1956), and Rudolf Bultmann, *Exegetische Probleme des zweiten Korintherbriefes (Symbolae Biblicae Upsalienses, Supplementhäften till Svensk Exegetisk Årsbok 9,* 1947), in the following analysis. Also relevant are: W. Schmithals, *Die Gnosis in Korinth. Eine Untersuchung zu den Korintherbriefen* (Göttingen: Vandenhoeck und Ruprecht, 1956); U. Wilckens, *Weisheit und Torheit. Eine exegetisch-religionsgeschichtliche Untersuchung zu I Kor. 1 und 2* (Tübingen: J. C. B. Mohr, 1959); G. Bornkamm, *Die*

different perspective in 1:1–2:13; 7:5–16.[12] His sentences are set
in the context of a serious challenge to his legitimacy as an apostle, which Paul rightly views as a challenge also to his status as a
Christian.[13] His line of defense is evident from the development of
the argument in both 2:14–7:4 and 10:1–13:13. If the Corinthians understood what it means to be reconciled to God in
Christ, to be a new creation in him (5:16 ff.), they would also
understand the form of the Apostles' ministry, for its form is con-
trolled by the norm of Christ (5:14). Thus, while working out
from his own status as apostle, Paul ends by calling the Corinthians back to faith, i.e., he renews the word as proclamation (e.g.,
5:20 ff.; cf. 12:19 f.; 13:5 ff.).

Paul's articulation of his defense is actually a fresh exposition
of the gospel set in the context of the charges raised against him.
In order to confront the Corinthians with *the* norm against which
all Christian endeavor is to be measured, and not with a comparison of himself and his opponents based on their norms, he is
led to the present-ing of the revelatory event within the horizon
of their mutual status before the Lord. Consequently, he is required to set out the basis of his apostleship in relation to the
kerygma. In so doing, the Apostle exposes the claims of his opponents for what they really are: idle claims based on self-commendation (10:18 and often). Unlike his opponents, who have
no real measure for their boasting, Paul must keep to the measure
that God has allotted him (10:13).[14]

Paul's exposition of the gospel, therefore, is a re-presentation of
the kerygma in language that speaks to the controversy in which
he is engaged. While pre-Pauline kerygmatic formulae have not
been identified in 2 Corinthians,[15] it is clear that Paul is "listen-

---

Vorgeschichte des sogenannten Zweiten Korintherbriefes (Heidelberg: Carl
Winter, 1961).

[12] For the divisions of the letter cf. Bultmann, *op. cit.*, p. 14, n. 16;
Schmithals, *op. cit.*, pp. 18–22; and now Bornkamm, *op. cit.*, pp. 16–23.

[13] 10:7. Käsemann, *op. cit.*, p. 36; Bultmann, *op. cit.*, p. 16; also cf.
Bultmann, *ibid.*, pp. 3 f. on the fluidity of the "we" (apostolic—general
Christian) in 3:12–5:11.

[14] Following Bultmann, *ibid.*, p. 21.

[15] One has to allow for the possibility that pre-Pauline formulae lie back of
such passages as 1:3 ff. and 2:14 ff.

ing" to the kerygma, but in such a way that the terms of the kerygma are heard in relation to the concrete realities of his own life and work (e.g., 1:3–10; 4:7–12; 6:3–10).[16] Especially instructive is his characterization of the Christ event in 13:4a: "True, he died on the cross in weakness, but he lives by the power of God" (NEB), a characterization that is immediately applied to the apostolic office (13:4b). Outside of the Corinthian correspondence *asthenēs* and its cognates are nowhere used to characterize the humiliation side of the kerygma,[17] but they are employed here because *asthenēs* is a catchword of Paul's opponents (10:10; 11:21, 29 ff.).[18] Moreover, the four terms of 4:8 f. (afflicted, perplexed, persecuted, struck down), which arise out of the Apostle's immediate experience,[19] are set in a kerygmatic context (4:10 f.) and show that the power of God is operative only in and through weakness (4:7 and 12:9 provide the norm).[20] A similar observation can be made with reference to 1:3–11, where a comparison of 1:5 f. with 1:8 f. makes clear the intimate relationship between Paul's situation and the way in which the ke-

---

[16] James M. Robinson, *Kerygma und historischer Jesus* (Zürich and Stuttgart: Zwingli Verlag, 1960), pp. 179 ff.

[17] But note Heb. 4:14–5:10 (5:2) and cf. Stählin, *ThWNT*, I (Stuttgart: W. Kohlhammer, 1932), 498 f., Schweitzer, *Lordship and Discipleship* (London: SCM Press, 1960), pp. 71 ff. (*Erniedrigung und Erhöhung bei Jesus und seinen Nachfolgern* [Zürich und Stuttgart: Zwingli Verlag, 1955], pp. 67 f.).

[18] Käsemann, *op. cit.*, pp. 34 ff.; Bultmann, *op. cit.*, p. 20; cf. Wilckens, *op. cit.*, pp. 37 f., 212.

[19] *thlibomenoi:* cf. 2:4 (occasioned by the Corinthians themselves); 1:8 (experienced in Asia); 7:5 (experienced in Macedonia); 6:4; 8:2 (also the lot of the Macedonian churches).

aporoumenoi: cf. 1:8.

diōkomenoi: cf. 11:23 ff.; 12:10; 1 Cor. 4:12.

kataballomenoi (only here in Paul): whether this term means that the Apostle was struck down with a weapon (6:5; 11:23–25), thrown into prison (6:5; 11:23), or simply abused (6:4 ff.; 11:26 f.), it is descriptive of his history. The verbal parallels are significant, of course, only as 4:8 f. is read with 1:8 ff.; 6:2 f., and 11:23 ff. in view. Sentences such as 12:10 provide the basis for the Apostle's repeated reference to his personal history and bear out the contention that the language is evoked by his situation. In 4:8 ff. the first term of each pair expresses his "weakness," the second gives negative expression to his "power," i.e., his weakness does not and cannot lead to total defeat.

[20] Cf. Käsemann, *op. cit.*, p. 53.

rygma comes to expression.[21] Other passages, such as 2:14 ff., 6:3 ff., and 8:9 likewise support this view.

Thus while the Apostle's thinking is informed by the kerygma throughout, the kerygma is coming to expression here in a new context, which requires that the language of the kerygma be shaped to that context. How else can the word occur? If the observation that Paul is here present-ing the kerygma within the horizon of his and the Corinthians' mutual status before the Lord is correct, it follows that the word of reconciliation is coming to expression *anew* because it is being *heard* anew.[22] That is to say, it is being encountered in a context in which the categories, say of Romans or even 1 Corinthians, do not immediately speak, without translation, to the new situation. In such a context the articulation of the kerygma may, therefore, have little or no verbal continuity with the tradition, or with the Apostle's own artic-ulation of it elsewhere.[23] It may, therefore, be set out as a guiding principle that the discontinuity in the language of the kerygma is directly proportional to the discontinuity in the language char-acter of the situation into which it is received. It is necessary, however, to go on and inquire whether the kerygma only *allows* for such discontinuity, or whether in fact it *demands* it. The an-swer is self-evident: if the kerygma is the norm that probes Chris-tian life before God in the world, then it follows that the kerygma must come to expression in language that is bound up with that life.

It has to be reaffirmed, nevertheless, that it is the kerygma as

[21] James M. Robinson, "The Historicality of Biblical Language," *The Old Testament and the Christian Faith,* ed. by Bernhard W. Anderson (New York: Harper & Row, 1963), pp. 145, 149.

[22] The connection between the word coming to expression anew and being heard anew is evident in a passage like 2 Cor. 3:4 ff. Perhaps the methodo-logical text for Paul is 1 Cor. 4:6.

[23] Fuchs, *Zum hermeneutischen Problem in der Theologie. Die existentiale Interpretation* (Tübingen: J. C. B. Mohr, 1959), p. 291, has warned against attempting to refer Paul's choice of antitheses and theological concepts only to actual occasions. It is a warning that is well taken. Nevertheless, Born-kamm, *op. cit.,* p. 14, notes that since Paul's opponents in Corinthians are not the Judaizers of Galatians, the doctrine of justification by faith plays no role in 2 Corinthians. The point to be made here is that it is precisely the doctrine of justification by faith that is coming to expression in 2 Corinthians in different language.

tradition which is informing Paul's thinking throughout. This implies, among other things, that the word that comes to expression is one—if it is the true word. On the assumption that Paul was converted via the kerygmatic Christ, i.e., the Christ known to him in the kerygma,[24] it must be said that the kerygma functions for Paul as text, for it is back upon the text (= tradition) that he must ultimately fall for the *norm* of his gospel, as seen particularly in 1 Cor. 15:1 ff. (note especially 15:11 and Gal. 2:2[25]). The kerygma as he knew it from the tradition (learned probably before his conversion) serves him as text as he unfolds the gospel. What is the relation between this text and the proclamation that arises out of it? It has already been affirmed that the text cannot merely be repeated but must be heard anew, and this means that it comes to expression in language indigenous to the context of hearing, if it is to function as probing word. It thus appears that the tradition-Scripture problem is implicit already within the New Testament, and with it the hermeneutical problem.[26]

The constellation to which the dialectic of hearing/speaking belongs consists, therefore, of the kerygma understood as protocreedal affirmation (in this instance, pre-Pauline), the kerygma understood as God's word to man, i.e., the incarnation, and the articulation of the kerygma as proclamation, e.g., in 2 Corinthians.[27] Since discontinuity within the protocreedal kerygma

---

[24] Bultmann, *Theology of the New Testament,* I (New York: Charles Scribner's Sons, 1951), pp. 187 f.

[25] Paul's apprehension, expressed in the phrase "lest somehow I should be running or had run in vain," is related to the presentation of his gospel to the leaders of the Jerusalem community. Similar uses of *kenos* and *eikē,* elsewhere give expression to the potential failure of his work as apostle (*kenos:* 1 Cor. 15:10, 14, 58; 2 Cor. 6:1; Phil. 2:16; *eikē:* Gal. 3:4, 4:11; 1 Cor. 15:2). In spite of the protest in Gal. 1:11 ff.—which is often misunderstood —Paul is not denying his dependence on the apostolic kerygma, but is insisting that his appropriation of it was the result of revelation (note especially his use of the phrase, "the *truth* of the gospel," in Gal. 2:5, 14).

[26] Cf. Ebeling, *Theologie und Verkündigung. Hermeneutische Untersuchungen zur Theologie* 1 (Tübingen: J. C. B. Mohr, 1962), p. 42.

[27] Ebeling's criticisms of the ambiguity of the term kerygma when used in this manifold way are not to be overlooked. See *Theologie und Verkündigung,* pp. 26–51, esp. 32 ff., 39, 41 f., 49 f. While I am in agreement with the thrust of his remarks, I take it that one has the option of dropping the term altogether or using it with greater care.

itself, and between the protocreedal kerygma and its articulation, presents itself already behind and in the New Testament, the problem of continuity becomes acute. From the foregoing it is clear that this problem cannot be solved *verbatim ac litteratim*, yet it is equally clear that it is a problem of language. If the language of the kerygma in all its forms is wholly historical, i.e., contingent, then it follows that the continuity must lie in that to which one is ultimately attending, if by this is meant that which one is hearing in and through language.

But that to which one is ultimately attending, i.e., God's word to man, never draws near except as word event (Ebeling), so that there is no escape from the linguistic character of the kerygma. The incarnation is itself word event. *What* one is hearing in and through language and the *hearing* are inextricably bound up together.

Historically speaking, the question with respect to Paul may be delimited as the relation between protocreedal affirmation and kerygmatic articulation in a new language context, since Paul's access to Jesus as the Christ is primarily through the protocreedal kerygma. The problem may, of course, be pushed back one step and turned into the question of Paul and the protocreedal kerygma in relation to Jesus as the Christ, but the hermeneutical problem is not thereby avoided, as has already been indicated. Inasmuch as Paul is here under scrutiny, the problem may be posed as it presents itself to him.

Thus for Paul the proclamation arises out of hearing, but it is true word only insofar as it evokes faith, i.e., is a word that cannot fail. It must therefore be *heard* as the word of grace and received by faith. In this sense Paul's hermeneutic requires that the saving event be understood as word and word only,[28] as the word

---

The ambiguity is aggravated by the fact, noted by K. Stendahl (*ThLZ*, LXXVII [1952], 719), that the kerygma in its formal sense (= protocreedal affirmation) is not necessarily kerygmatic. There is therefore the non-kerygmatic kerygma and the kerygmatic non-kerygma, as well as the potentially kerygmatic kerygma and the non-kerygmatic non-kerygma. But this observation points to the problem, already articulated, of the dialectic between speaking/hearing.

[28] Cf. Ebeling, *Wort und Glaube*, p. 22 [*Word and Faith*, p. 36].

spoken by God in Christ (cf. 5:19). This hermeneutical principle may be explicated in relation to Paul's word to the Corinthians.

The apostolic ministry is characterized as the ministry entrusted with the word of reconciliation (5:19 which is equal to the word of the cross 1 Cor. 1:18). The apostolic ministry is that which spreads the fragrance of Christ. To those perishing it is the fragrance of death, but to those being saved the fragrance of life (2:14–16; this theme dominates the whole of 2:14–7:4 and 10:1–13:13). The sufficiency (*hikanos*, 2:16, is another catchword[29]) of the apostle for such a ministry does not rest on self-commendation (3:1–3, 5; 5:12; 6:4; 10:17 f.; cf. 12:11), but on the sufficiency which is of God (2:16b; 3:5f.; 4:1, 5, 7; 5:21, etc.). Out of such God-based sufficiency there flows, according to 2:14–4:6, the *pepoithēsis* and/or *parrēsia* of the apostle (3:4, 12; 4:1, 13 f., 16; 5:6, 11 ff. [the last without specific restatement of the theme]).

But the fragrance of Christ, the *zōē*, the *doxa,* which is the fruit of this ministry, appears to the world as a fragrance of death and as weakness (2:14 ff.; 4:7–12; 11:30; 12:9 f.). Since, however, this ministry is in reality vested with the power of God, its form in the world is rife with ambiguity (6:4–10; cf. 12:11 f.; 13:3 ff.). But this is all for the sake of the basis of the ministry, which can be only the power of God (1:9; 4:7 ff.; 12:9; etc.), and hence for the sake of the power of its message.

For this reason the word of reconciliation itself is the unveiling of the glory of the Lord (3:18; with which cf. 4:2 ff.), which produces a new basis for life in Christ (5:17). The divine power is made perfect in weakness so that faith may be faith. The Corinthians, at the instigation of Paul's opponents, were asking that the Apostle legitimize himself to them, i.e., provide some extrinsic signs of his apostleship. To this demand Paul can only reply: to provide such authenticating signs of status *apart from the word that calls faith into being,* would itself be faith's corruption. So the word, too, is characterized as death (2:16), as that which is veiled (4:3), and as weakness (10:10; cf. 1 Cor. 1:18 ff.; 2:1 ff.; etc.). With the hearing of faith, however, all this is reversed. The

---

[29] Käsemann, *op. cit.,* p. 35.

word cannot, therefore, be understood as pointing to something
else, something extrinsic, which can been joined as the basis of faith
—whether it be Jesus of Nazareth,[30] or the resurrection, or the faith
of the early church itself! The word of reconciliation points only
to itself. It is valid only as occurring word, as the word that evokes
faith and concurrently arises as confession, as the word which is
itself the saving event.

It is necessary to observe, however, that the present-ing of the
kerygma, its exposition, takes place as the expositing of him who
hears and is, therefore, self- and community-probing.[31] It should
not be understood that it is thereby a negative process. The authority that Paul exercises as apostle is for building up and not
tearing down (10:8; 13:10), so that when he speaks in Christ he
does so for their upbuilding (12:19b; cf. 13:9; 7:8 ff.; 1:24;
etc.). The word which he speaks is first of all a healing, saving
word, the word of grace.[32] But because it is that, it is also a testing,
probing word (13:5-7). What it destroys when heard in faith is

---

[30] This injunction is used in the customary Bultmannian sense, i.e., that
one cannot go *behind* the kerygma (which does not here mean traditional
formulations: Ebeling, *Theologie und Verkündigung,* p. 41) in order to val-
idate it extrinsically. Cf., e.g., Bultmann, *Glauben und Verstehen,* III (Tübingen: J. C. B. Mohr, 1960; 2nd ed., 1962), 22 f., translated by S. M. Ogden
in *Existence and Faith: Shorter Writings of Rudolf Bultmann* (New York:
Meridian Books, 1960), p. 79. Ebeling has proposed to understand Jesus as
the basis of faith in another sense: "Certainly not a support which relieves
us in part of the need for faith. Rather, the basis of faith is that which lets
faith be faith, which keeps it being faith, on which faith, that is to say,
ultimately relies." *Das Wesen des Christlichen Glaubens* (Tübingen: J. C. B.
Mohr, 1959), pp. 83 f. English translation by R. G. Smith, *The Nature of
Faith* (London: Collins, 1961), pp. 70 f. Cf. "Jesus und Glaube," in *Wort
und Glaube,* pp. 205–254 [*Word and Faith,* pp. 201–246], and *Theologie und
Verkündigung,* pp. 19–82. The matter may be formulated thus: Jesus *as the
word* is the basis of the proclamation and therefore of faith. With this the
injunction above does not stand in opposition.

[31] Fuchs, *Zur Frage nach dem historischen Jesus* (Tübingen: J. C. B.
Mohr, 1960), pp. 389 ff., 400; Ebeling, *Wort und Glaube,* p. 451, proposi-
tion 7 [*Word and Faith,* p. 428]; Wilckens, *op. cit.,* pp. 214 f. Cf. Ebeling,
"Hauptprobleme der protestantischen Theologie in der Gegenwart," *ZThK,*
LVIII (1961), 125 f.

[32] Cf. 2:2 ff.; 5:20; 7:8 ff. Cf. Fuchs's understanding of the word as
permission in *Hermeneutik* (Bad Cannstatt: R. Müllerschön Verlag, 1954;
2nd ed., 1958), ¶ 6; *Zum Hermeneutischen Problem in der Theologie,* pp.
282 f.; *Zur Frage nach dem historischen Jesus,* p. 427; Bultmann, *Glauben
und Verstehen,* II (Tübingen: J. C. B. Mohr, 1952; 3rd ed., 1961), 10,
English translation by C. G. Grieg, *Essays Philosophical and Theological*

"all that rears its proud head against the knowledge of God" (10:5, NEB). As the word of reconciliation, the proclamation requires the participation of him who hears in the reality which is communicated, and therefore in faith.

It follows that the exposition of the text, in this case the kerygma that Paul knew from the tradition, fulfills its vocation only as proclamation, and that means precisely as the probing word that brings life. Exposition that does not lead to proclamation is sterile, just as proclamation that is not exposition tends to be uncritical.

It remains to inquire what the exposition of the kerygma in 2 Corinthians exposes. We may begin with the Apostle himself. It is clear that the body of the letter exposes the basis of the apostolic ministry and thus exhibits the inner connection between the nature of the word that is proclaimed and the basis of the ministry that proclaims it. In the section 2:14–4:15 (from thanksgiving to thanksgiving), Paul sets out the form of his ministry which gives the appearance, on the one hand, of weakness, self-commendation, deceitfulness and guile, but, on the other hand, manifests sufficiency, confidence, and open appeal to the truth. His sufficiency, which is of God (3:5; etc.), is accessible only as he embraces the "weakness" of Christ (4:7–12; cf. 12:9). But it is for this very reason that he is confident and bold (introduced in 3:4 and reiterated often). In 3:12–18 *kalymma* is developed as the contrasting term to *parrēsia*, i.e., uncovering the face is boldness. He is thereby reversing the charge made against him: he is said to have acted deviously, clandestinely, with cunning and guile, to have adulterated the word of God (4:2; cf. 2:17), all of which are practices characterized by *kalyptō!* The opposite, he affirms, is in fact the case: he speaks in the sight of God, i.e., submits himself to the judgment of the word (2:17), and so can commend himself only by the open statement of the truth (4:2; cf. 3:2, 18).

Nevertheless, his question "Are we beginning to commend our-

(New York: The Macmillan Company, 1955), pp. 11 f., had already expressed a similar notion.

selves again?" suggests that he is never free from the temptation to boast a little on his own behalf. One expects the Apostle to refute the charges leveled against him by invoking his own powers as a pneumatic, by reference to his own achievements. In fact, in 10:7 ff., 11:1 ff., and 12:1 ff., he appears to launch into just this type of defense. But at every crucial point he subtly shifts the burden of his argument, and ends by turning it upside down. The passage 11:21–30 is characteristic: he begins by noting that he speaks as a fool, a madman (11:21b, 23), and ends by reversing the thrust of his list of "achievements" so that all he can legitimately offer to support his claims are the things that show his weakness (11:29 f.).

It is not without significance that the Apostle makes his defense in the form of a renewal of the proclamation, but in such a way, of course, that it is directly related to the problem at hand. The polemical cast of 2:14–7:5, though much milder to be sure than that of 10:1–13:13, is evident throughout, reaching its peak in the concluding section 5:11–6:10. Following the initial polemic,[33] which Paul grounds once again in a kerygmatic formulation (5:14 f.), he proceeds to the ultimate basis of his confidence and boldness as apostle, which has dominated the argument since 2:14. With Christ the old way of knowing has passed away and the new has taken its place (5:16), with the result that the Corinthians can no more know Paul *kata sarka* than they can the Christ. The appeal for reconciliation that Paul directs to them (5:20) is then renewed in 6:1 as the appeal not to accept the grace of God in vain (cf. Gal. 3:1–5 following on 2:20 f.), both of which are bound up with the final polemical note in 6:3. Correctly understood, 6:3–10 is a peroration that sums up the character of his ministry as determined by the norm in 5:14 f.[34] As

----

[33] The phrase "we persuade men" (5:11) is here as in Gal. 1:10 a slogan of his opponents (cf. Bultmann, *Exegetische Probleme des zweiten Korintherbriefes,* p. 13); "what we are is known to God" is probably directed against the charge of furtiveness and insincerity (cf. 4:2); 5:12 refers to the charge of self-commendation (cf. 3:1; 4:2) which Paul now turns around in order to give the Corinthians a "handle" to use if they wish, in their defense of him (cf. 12:11); 5:13 is concerned with his failure to accredit himself as an ecstatic (cf. Käsemann, *op. cit.,* pp. 67 f.; Bultmann, *op. cit.,* p. 14).

[34] Cf. Bultmann, *ibid.,* pp. 18–20.

such, it calls for the Corinthians to view him as they must view Christ, and thus to adjust their seeing (or knowing) to their hearing.[35]

This integral relationship between defense or apology and proclamation, both of which are referred to the text, is specified here and there throughout the epistle. The new situation[36] at Corinth which appears to have provoked 2 Corinthians, especially 10–13, is the appearance of itinerant "superlative" apostles (11:5; 12:11), who preach another Jesus than Paul preached and who, consequently, cause the Corinthians to receive a different spirit and submit to a different gospel (11:4). If Paul is forced to defend his ministry, it is because he sees that the gospel itself is being called into question. The intruders in Corinth have seduced the congregation into believing that Paul lacked all the marks of a legitimate apostle (12:12; 13:3) and that his ministry was therefore to be characterized as weakness.[37] He is accused of being *tapeinos kata prosōpon*, i.e., of being pliant, subservient, abject (Bauer) when in the presence of opposition, but of being arrogant when away (10:1, 10). This goes together with his lack of facility in extempore speaking (10:10; 11:6), which was regarded as the mark of a true pneumatic.[38] He had apparently made little of his own visions and ecstasies (12:1–6; cf. 5:13), but this, too, was taken as a sign of weakness. Signs and wonders, which were also understood to be the mark of a true apostle, were apparently performed by Paul among the Corinthians, but they had not recognized them as such (12:12).[39] Since Paul had not given suffi-

---

[35] Bultmann sets "seeing" over against "hearing" in the sense of a doctrine of God and the world as opposed to hearing as obedience (*Hören als Gehorchen*), e.g., *Glauben und Verstehen*, I, 271, 272 f., 324. The former goes with *Weltanschauungen*, with "theory" (*theōria*), with a spectator's and hence a detached knowing. There is, however, a "seeing" of faith, e.g., in the Gospel of John (*ibid.*, p. 293). To put the matter succinctly, "seeing" as theology has always to be probed and corrected by "hearing" of the word.

[36] Bornkamm, *op. cit.*, pp. 15 f.

[37] According to Käsemann, *op. cit.*, p. 34, the leading theme of the objections *and* response.

[38] Käsemann, *ibid.*, p. 35.

[39] It is significant that Paul qualifies his claim to signs and wonders in 12:12 with the phrase *en pasē hypomonē*. This means that he places such deeds within the horizon of sufferings patiently endured for Christ, e.g., 1:6;

cient evidence of spirit possession, his authority (*exousia*) is to be questioned (10:8; 13:10), and therefore his power (*dynamis*) (10:2 ff., 21; 12:9; 13:2 ff.). Lacking the requisite authority and power, he could not make a claim on the Corinthians for support (11:7 ff.), nor could he offer letters of certification such as the intruders were able to present (3:1).[40]

It has already been noted that Paul specifies as the norm of his ministry the weakness of Christ, through which alone he has access to genuine power (12:9 and 13:3 f.). His weakness signalizes his participation in the sufferings of Christ through which he is able to minister salvation and comfort (1:5 f.).[41] It is precisely that which the Corinthians—prompted by the intruders—now find objectionable in Paul that the Apostle must offer as his only legitimate claim, although he can, to be sure, play the game of comparison on their terms (10:7 f.; 11:17, 21 f.; 12:1 ff., 11). Nevertheless, if he is to boast, he can boast only of his weakness (11:30; 12:9 f.), only of that which shows that his sufficiency is of God (3:5 f.; 4:7; 6:4 ff.), only of the Lord (11:17 f.). Thus it is through his exposition of the kerygmatic text as the basis of his apostleship that he confronts the Corinthians once again with the word of reconciliation, in such a way that their seeing of the Christ, the Apostle, themselves, is probed by a fresh hearing of the word. If Paul now appears *tapeinos* to them (10:1), it is not because he is without authority or power, nor because he cannot stand up to powerful opposition (13:2 ff., 10),[42] but because his

---

6:4 ff.; 11:23 ff. Käsemann, *ibid.*, pp. 62 f. These elements—*sēmeia, terata, dynameis*—singly or in combination, are regarded as legitimizing (e.g., Gal. 3:5; Rom. 15:19; Acts 2:22; Heb. 2:4), although they may be quite deceptive (e.g., 2 Thess. 2:9). The question is, what are the legitimate signs, wonders, and mighty deeds? Paul had already dealt with this question in 1 Cor. 12–14, and Gal. 3:5 makes it equally clear that such wonders can arise, i.e., be "seen," only out of faith.

[40] Bornkamm, *op. cit.*, p. 12.

[41] 1:3 ff. is not to be psychologized, as the reference to *sōtēria* in 1:6 shows. 1:3–11 as a whole has a soteriological reference.

[42] It may well be that the "vacillation" which appears to be the subject of 1:15 ff. (the explanation for which continues through 1:23–2:13; 7:5–16!) arises out of his threat to visit them a third time and exercise his power (13:1 ff.; cf. 10:2). In which case his decision not to come in order to spare them would be open to further misinterpretation as weakness.

weakness should lead to their strength (13:9).[43] This manner of speaking can be understood, of course, only in relation to the Apostle's power vis-à-vis his churches: he does not and cannot lord it over their faith (1:24), since if he did, faith would not depend solely on their hearing. For the same reason it is of no consequence that he is poor in extempore discourse, or that he refuses to boast of his visions and ecstasies, or that he offers signs and wonders of dubious character. His opponents demand what he cannot deliver: legitimizing evidence *ex ergōn nomou* (Gal. 3:5). Such visions, ecstatic experiences, and the like as he has had do not concern the Corinthians at all, they concern only his relation with God. What does concern the Corinthians is his conscious day-to-day conduct of his ministry (5:13).[44] He must refrain from boasting of private experiences so that no one may think more of him than what he sees in him or hears from him (12:6b). Moreover, he is not inferior in knowledge (*gnōsis*) (11:6), which, however, will appear as foolishness apart from faith.[45]

Paul's refusal to accept support from the Corinthians is grounded in 11:7 in an interesting kerygmatic formulation: he abased himself in order that they might be exalted (*tapeinoō/ hypsoō*), i.e., he accepted support from other churches to serve them. One is reminded of the language of the Christ hymn in Phil. 2:6–11.[46] It has often been noted that a similar formulation, utilizing a different pair of terms (*ptōcheia/plousios*), is employed in 8:9 as the basis for the Apostle's appeal for the relief offering. The latter is connected, on the one hand, with the "proof" (*endeixis*) of their love (8:24), and the "test" (*dokimē*) of their service (*diakonia*), which attests their obedience in confessing

---

[43] In 10:1 his entreaty is by the meekness and gentleness of Christ; cf. 4:11 f.

[44] Bultmann, *Exegetische Probleme des zweiten Korintherbriefes*, p. 14.

[45] Note the catchword *aphrosynē* (and cognates) in 11:1–12:11 and cf. 1 Cor. 1:18 ff., esp. 2:6 ff.

[46] And of the Synoptic sayings found in Luke 14:11 and elsewhere. The fact that it is attested in the Rabbinic literature (J. Jeremias, *The Parables of Jesus* [New York: Charles Scribner's Sons, 1955], pp. 82 f.) does not alter the case that it is used by Paul with a christological reference. Cf. the kerygmatic use of *hypsoō* in John (3:14; 8:28; 12:32, 34).

(*homologia*) the gospel of Christ (9:13), and, on the other hand, with Paul's characterization of his own ministry (6:10). We have, then, a clear case of the kerygma coming to expression as the norm of Paul's financial relation to the Corinthians and of their financial relation to the Jerusalem church. In both instances its language is adapted to the specific terms of the situation.

And finally, Paul cannot offer letters of recommendation because the Corinthians themselves are all the recommendation he requires: they are a letter from Christ ministered[47] by Paul and his co-laborers (3:1–3). He may boast of them only as God has allotted them to his ministry, and hence he cannot, like the intruders, boast in another man's labors (10:13 ff.). But insofar as God has used him as an ambassador of Christ, they are his boast just as he ought to be theirs (1:14). In the last analysis, the proof of his legitimacy as apostle is dependent upon whether or not he has communicated to them the word of reconciliation so that it evokes faith. Aside from this, the question is idle.

Just as the Corinthians, under the provocation of wandering apostles, have put Paul to the test (13:13), having missed the signs of a true apostle (12:12), so Paul must put them to the test (13:5) by a fresh exposition of the kerygma. He must, in this instance, achieve the latter by submitting himself to the test. If the Corinthians fail to find Christ in themselves (13:5), Paul himself will have failed (13:6), even though it matters little whether he *appears* to meet the test if the Corinthians do what is right (13:7). His *apparent* failure may in fact serve for their improvement (13:9). Thus it appears that Paul's case must ultimately rest on a fresh hearing of the word of reconciliation, a hearing in which both he who speaks and they who listen participate, thereby giving rise to common understanding. The word must be heard within the spectrum of Corinthian individual and community, and if it is heard in the language of their own existence, then they themselves have vindicated Paul—and the hermeneutical function of the word has achieved its fulfillment.

---

47 Play on *diakoneō*.

II. The Word as Self- and Community-probing and Historical Criticism

Two factors in the theological development since the Reformation can be said to have converged to raise the hermeneutical problem to the center of the discussion. Heiko Oberman has summed them up with these words: "It [the ongoing effort to translate the Scriptures] unfolds under the abiding tension of a dual freedom: the freedom obediently to conform to the apostolic witness, and the freedom creatively to translate that witness for the experiences and thought patterns of successive generations. This is a task of freedom because it is the Holy Spirit who leads the Church into new responses to the unique historic revelation in Christ."[48] Broadly speaking, these two factors can be referred respectively to orthodoxy, which insists on obedient conformity, and to liberalism, which seeks above all to make the gospel relevant. With the theological renaissance in this century the question of what transpires when these two meet became a burning issue.

If it can be said that Barth won back the legitimate demand of the word of God for obedient conformity, it may also be said that this victory brought with it a potential if not real threat to the critical historical method with which the so-called liberal theology had fought with so much success against old orthodoxy. The danger that presented itself had consequences for both sides of the hermeneutical problem: The text cannot speak for itself if it is not painstakingly exegeted in its own context, and it cannot be interpreted if it cannot be brought into intimate relation with contemporary modes of thought and experience. As a defense against this threat Ebeling has set out a series of propositions concerning the function of the Bible in theological work. We may quote a portion of proposition 7: "Criticism is an integral element in the effort to understand the text. It is directed *to* that which

---

[48] *Christianity Divided. Protestant and Roman Catholic Theological Issues,* edited by D. J. Callahan, Heiko Oberman, and D. J. O'Hanlon (New York: Sheed and Ward, 1961), pp. 76.

the Biblical text wants to bring to understanding and *against* anything and everything that stands as a hindrance in the way of
the hermeneutical function of the text."[49] As set out here, the two
sides of criticism, which are really one, correspond to the dual
freedom of faith (Oberman): The possibility of obedience depends on access to what the text intends to bring to understanding,
and creative translation depends on the effective removal of impediments to the hermeneutical function of the text. It is clear
that these two sides are interdependent and form a circle.[50]

The affirmation that historical (Biblical) criticism is an integral
element in the effort to understand the text does not, however,
answer the question of *how* it functions. The *how* remains a
crucial problem because the so-called scientific study of the Bible,
especially on this side of the Atlantic, has developed a splendid
isolation from the theological task. Its isolation is due in no small
measure to the effective disappearance of the thing against which
it fought in an earlier period.[51] It stands in need, therefore, of a
basic reorientation to the current theological situation.

Before proceeding to this question, however, it is necessary to
recognize a basic premise without which the historical method is
simply irrelevant. That premise is the radical historicity of the
word of God.[52] The rise of historical criticism brought with it the
acknowledgment of the contingency of the word, and therefore of
the relativity of every expression of the word. It is this proposition
which must be affirmed over against theologies of transcendence
which emphasize the givenness of the word.[53] Only if the word is

[49] "Diskussionsthesen für eine Vorlesung zur Einführung in das Studium
der Theologie," *Wort und Glaube,* p. 451 [*Word and Faith,* p. 428]. (Italics
mine.)

[50] This is to say that when one side is lost, both are lost. Herein lies the
irony of the denouement of both orthodoxy and liberalism. Cf. Ebeling, *Wort
und Glaube,* p. 451, proposition 6 [*Word and Faith,* p. 428].

[51] One certainly has to take note of local differences in this respect. Nevertheless, even in those places which regard themselves as bastions of conservatism, liberalism has had a silent, if empty, victory.

[52] Cf. Ebeling, above, pp. 101 f.

[53] This is a way of saying that the labor of putting the New Testament
in its context has not been wasted. On the other hand, it needs to be recognized that to reduce the New Testament to its context is to *deny* the full
historicity of the word, since every historical phenomenon is also absolute,
i.e., not repeatable, unique. This refers, for example, to the language of the

regarded as a fully human and therefore historically conditioned word can historical criticism be of service.

Historical criticism is not inappropriately named. It is criticism in the generic sense developed out of and against historical perspectives. Its circular movement is thus a constitutive element in its program. So understood, how can it function effectively with respect to the text? We may set out our answer in a series of propositions accompanied by brief expositions.

1. Historical criticism is the means of gaining authentic access to the intention of the text. Authentic access is achieved by removing obstacles that impede the hermeneutical function of the text. To this removal of obstacles we now turn.

2. Historical criticism is designed to preserve the distance between text and interpreter.[54] As commonly understood this means reading the text in its own context, with regard for its full historicity. It goes without saying that the recognized tools of the historical method are entirely appropriate and indispensable to this purpose. Historical criticism strives to understand the historical as the particular, which means, in the case of the New Testament, as something that is strange and alien, given the distance of the twentieth from the first century. But it is not always recognized that this distancing function serves also to thwart the tyranny of the question, i.e., it pushes the past away as that which cannot, without further consideration, be brought into relation to the present. The history of historical criticism itself provides the clue to this understanding of its task.[55] As the antidote to the tyranny of dogmatic theology, historical criticism held up the dog-

New Testament; although New Testament Greek has been referred to its position in the history of the language and within Koine, an achievement that is not to be gainsaid, there is nevertheless justification for treating New Testament Greek, as the language of the community of faith, as a special phenomenon. Cf. F. Blass and A. Debrunner, *A Greek Grammar of the New Testament and other Early Christian Literature,* translated and revised by Robert W. Funk (Chicago: University of Chicago Press, 1961), Paragraph 1. This observation does not call for a revival of the question in what way the New Testament is unique, i.e., on the basis of invidious comparison, but demands a regard for every historical phenomenon as something to be encountered in its own right, a demand to "let the thing be."

[54] Ebeling, *Wort und Glaube,* pp. 33 f., 36 [*Word and Faith,* pp. 46 f., 49].

[55] Cf. Ebeling, "The meaning of 'Biblical Theology,' " *JThS,* VI (1955), 210-225, also in *Wort und Glaube,* pp. 69-89 [*Word and Faith,* pp. 79-97].

matic appropriation of the text against the integrity of the text and found the former to be wanting. As a result, dogmatics was denied the right, at least in principle, to base its claims on the text. Therewith was decreed the divorce between dogmatic theology and Biblical studies that has had its disastrous effects down to the present time.[56] Viewed as a means of thwarting the tyranny of the question, historical criticism does not function merely as the opposition party; on the contrary, preserving the distance between text and interpreter is another way of saying that the sole means of legitimate access to the text is the understanding of the historical event in its particularity, and if in its particularity, in those modes of thought and experience which come to expression therein. As it attempts to illuminate such modes, it clears away the obstacles that hinder the hermeneutical function of the text.

3. Historical criticism, moreover, attempts to establish chronology. This does not refer primarily to the determination of absolute dates (although these may be helpful, even indispensable), but to the ordering of events. Such ordering at its most profound level has to do with observing the vicissitudes of tradition, i.e., with the mutation of the appropriation of past events. It is concerned, therefore, with the way the past is taken up into the present, and thus not only with the immanental causative factors that are operative in a given epoch or locale, but also with the fresh appropriation of the past for which the past itself provides the stimulus. In this regard, too, historical criticism is endeavoring to conserve the particularity of the historical at those points where proximity in time and/or space invites the reductionist fallacy. Reductionism in this sense is called harmonizing when applied to the Old or New Testament. It can be seen that the effort to preserve the distance between the text and its interpreter is directed toward a more flagrant form of the same error that is being resisted here.

As applied to historical theology, the ordering function of criticism will seek to read New Testament theology as the history of the theological appropriation of the Christ event in the New

---

[56] This point currently applies more generally to Anglo-American theology than to Continental theology.

Testament period, and church history/history of dogma as the history of the theological appropriation of the text.[57] This view of historical theology as the history of hermeneutic is based on the assumption that the way the Christian community appropriates a particular segment of its past, i.e., the originating events, is determinative for its life as the body of Christ. This is not to say, however, that historical theology will confine itself to the history of the interpretation of specific texts; it will also interrogate the community concerning the way in which the word that comes to expression in the New Testament comes to expression in various periods in the community.

To the preceding must now be added a fourth: 4. Historical criticism exposes the word of God as a fully human word by exposing the human situation into which it is received as radically human. This procedure may be termed "unmasking." Unmasking is used here in the sense suggested by Peter Berger[58] and involves calling in question all human claims to access to the divine. It is important to grasp the connection of this formulation with Bultmann's repeated emphasis on history as a closed causal continuum as the presupposition of the historical method,[59] an emphasis shared by Fuchs.[60] The historian cannot presuppose supernatural intervention in the causal nexus as the basis for his work any more than the interpreter of the Biblical text can presuppose the Holy Spirit as the basis for his. This assertion, however, is not forced upon theology from the outside, but is connected internally with the basis of faith. *Sola fide* means the rejection "of all secret revelational docetism by means of which the historicity of revelation is sidestepped and which turns revelation into a history *sui generis.*"[61] Authentic faith is therefore compelled to accept the full historicity of the word since it denies to itself any extrinsic basis.

---

[57] Ebeling, *Die Geschichtlichkeit der Kirche und ihrer Verkündigung als theologisches Problem,* pp. 78 f., 81 ff.

[58] *The Precarious Vision* (Garden City, N.Y: Doubleday & Company, 1961), esp. 152 ff.

[59] E.g., *Glauben und Verstehen,* III, 144 f. [*Existence and Faith,* pp. 291 f.].

[60] *Zur Frage nach dem historischen Jesus,* pp. 227 ff., 230.

[61] Ebeling, *Wort und Glaube,* p. 45 [*Word and Faith,* p. 56].

For this reason "faith is at the mercy of the complete question-ableness and ambiguity of the historical."[62]

If the historian or exegete is engaged in the ruthless exposure of the text as a human word, he is opening the way for a fresh appropriation of the intention of the text because he is helping to let faith be what it is by exposing human pretension in all forms, and also because he is directing his criticism against the text from a locus occupied by himself. Apart from such exposure a genuinely historical appropriation of the past is rendered impossible with the result that the past degenerates into a kind of fate[63] which dominates the present to the degree that social and personal fictions are left unexposed.[64] The Bible no less than other documents is subject to such distortion. If it is understood that the church must renew its life at its source, historical criticism in this sense is not an option but a necessity.

5. Under the aegis of its presupposition that history is a closed unity and prompted by its methodological aim not to presuppose its results, historical criticism is *blind*.[65] It is blind in that it strives for objectivity; it attempts to posit the past as something discrete from the present and thus release it from every relative appropriation. It can explain every historical event by reducing it to cause and effect on the immanent level. It debunks all human achievement by exposing it as enmeshed in the skein of natural, social, and psychological causes. It recognizes no sacred precincts. This blindness is characterized also by disinterestedness, which means that the question of the existential meaning of an event or document for the present is not the *first* order of business. Even though the subject-object schema, on the analogy of the natural sciences, is not valid for historical investigation, historical criticism

---

62 *Ibid.,* p. 45 [p. 56].

63 I have borrowed this formulation from my colleague, Gordon Harland, whose perceptive analysis "The American Protestant Heritage and the Theological Task," in *Drew Gateway,* Winter 1962, pp. 71–93, as well as many conversations, has helped shape this essay.

64 One thinks, e.g., of various forms of nationalism which tend to idealize the past and hence lose their self-transcending and thus their self-correcting power. The result is invariably disastrous.

65 Cf. the remark of Georges Rouault: "Subjective artists are one-eyed, but objective artists are blind." (Quoted in *Rouault,* Pocket Library of Great Art, 1954, under the caption "Rouault on His Art" in an appendix.)

presupposes that a free decision with respect to the past is itself subject to historical causality.[66] Its blindness, therefore, stands in conscious opposition to the historicity of the historian, and makes it possible for the critic to take his historical work seriously. That these are methodological aims and not achievements goes without saying. Nevertheless, the virtue in this blindness is not to be overlooked. If the historicity of the interpreter makes historical criticism necessary, the blindness of the historian makes it possible. For—and with this we return to proposition (1)—authentic access to the text arises out of the blind exposure of the full historicity of the text in conjunction with the exposure of the historicity of the interpreter. By means of historical criticism, then, an opening occurs for a new hearing of the text, a hearing in which the text gives rise to the future as its own, i.e., the intention of the text is executed. Such an opening occurs only at the point where the function of historical criticism, understood as letting the text be by pushing it away, ordering it and exposing it as human, is related to the hearing. It is this dialectic of letting be/hearing which brings historical criticism to its fulfillment, since it is here that the world as self- and community-probing becomes effective.

The problem that now arises, however, is that because historical criticism is blind it tends to become irrelevant. And if irrelevant, then it suffers reduction to techniques preoccupied with bits of knowledge. When it thus loses its effectiveness, the temptation to make the a-historical leap from text to Biblical theology arises and is put down only with difficulty.[67] It may be concluded, therefore, that if historical criticism continues relentlessly on its independent course, it stands in danger of sacrificing its relationship to theological work altogether, and its position in theological faculties becomes an anomaly.[68] Its critical power vis-à-vis the theological appropriation of the text consequently depends on its capacity to

[66] Bultmann, *Glauben und Verstehen*, III, 144 [*Existence and Faith*, pp. 291 f.].

[67] Cf. Ebeling, *Wort und Glaube*, esp. pp. 28 f., 36, 46 ff. [*Word and Faith*, esp. pp. 42 f., 48 f., 57 ff.]. The whole essay is concerned with this problem.

[68] This is not to say that Biblical criticism cannot be carried on outside the theological faculty, either with or without reference to the theological situation.

readjust itself to the unfolding situation. This problem will be the concern of the following section.

III. Proclamation as Hearing Anew and Exegesis of the Text

Proclamation may be defined as the occurring word of God, i.e., word of God as word event.[69] As such it is dependent upon a fresh *hearing* of the word. The relation between text and interpreter needs now to be opened up from the side of the interpreter, i.e., from the side of the hearing through which the text comes to expression as proclamation.

Bultmann has mediated to the contemporary discussion the view that one can interrogate history meaningfully only with "some specific way of raising questions, some specific perspective."[70] Posing relevant questions to a text depends, according to Bultmann, on a prior life relationship to the subject under consideration.[71] This notion is embodied in his concept of pre-understanding. Although Bultmann has illustrated this concept in relation to subject matter suggested by various types of texts, e.g., those whose subject matter is music, mathematics, philosophy, religion, etc.,[72] his entire program has been worked out in relation to the existentialist analysis of Heidegger, which he accepts as a viable basis from which to raise relevant questions.[73] He is careful to make the distinction between existential and existentialist,[74] and

---

[69] Ebeling, above, pp. 85–89, 104 f.; Fuchs, e.g., *Zum hermeneutischen Problem in der Theologie,* pp. 281–305; *Zur Frage nach dem historischen Jesus,* pp. 424–430.

[70] *Glauben und Verstehen,* III, 146 [*Existence and Faith,* p. 292]; cf. Ebeling, above, p. 92, n. 21, for further references.

[71] E.g., *Glauben und Verstehen,* II, 216 ff. [*Essays Philosophical and Theological,* pp. 239 ff.]; *Glauben und Verstehen,* III, 146 f., 149 [*Existence and Faith,* pp. 293 f., 296].

[72] E.g., in his essay on hermeneutic, *Glauben und Verstehen,* II, 217 ff. [*Essays Philosophical and Theological,* pp. 241 ff.]. Cf. *Glauben und Verstehen,* III, 146 [*Existence and Faith,* p. 293].

[73] E.g., *Jesus Christ and Mythology* (New York: Charles Scribner's Sons, 1958), pp. 54 f., 66 f., 74; cf. 45–59; *Existence and Faith,* pp. 92–110; S. M. Ogden, *Christ without Myth* (New York and Evanston: Harper & Row, 1961), pp. 45 ff., 56 f.

[74] E.g., *Jesus Christ and Mythology,* p. 74.

points out that the latter, as a philosophical analysis of existence from which he proceeds, is a formal analysis that has to do with the structure of existence as such.[75]

It will be observed that Bultmann proceeds from an analysis of the human situation as such.[76] But the structural analysis of the human situation, while it aids in understanding the subject matter given expression in historical documents, is deficient in mediating an interpretation of those documents in that it produces an interpretation that is universally applicable. An interpretation that is universally applicable cannot, without further consideration, be brought into relation to the specific existence of a given period or individual. That is to say, the human situation must be *interpreted* in terms of the concrete existence of a particular community or person.[77]

It follows that the questions that arise out of the pre-understanding must themselves have historical body if they are to bear fruit in the interrogation of the text. This is required in order that the text can be *heard* in relation to the realities of present historical existence. What is at issue is the dialectic between the human situation (*existentialist*) and the historical situation (*existential*).[78] If the human situation is the situation of man *qua* man

[75] E.g., *Kerygma und Mythos,* II (Hamburg-Volksdorf: Herbert Reich, 1952), 192, English translation by R. H. Fuller in *Kerygma and Myth* (New York & Evanston: Harper & Row, 1957), p. 195; *Jesus Christ and Mythology,* p. 74; *Existence and Faith,* pp. 93 ff.

[76] Emil L. Fackenheim, *Metaphysics and Historicity* (Milwaukee: Marquette University Press, 1961), distinguishes the human from the natural and historical situations: "This concept is additional to those of natural and historical situation. But the human situation is not a source of additional limitations. Rather, it is the ontological ground of both the natural and the historical situation, and is in turn individuated only in these. Correspondingly, the recognition of the human situation cannot be divorced from that of the natural and the historical situation; it is achieved when the natural and the historical situation are understood radically, as specific manifestations of a universal condition. It is the radicalization of the natural and of the historical situation which discloses the human situation." (P. 76.)

[77] Cf. Section I, above.

[78] Fackenheim, *op. cit.,* pp. 48 ff., provides a discussion of the concept "historical situation." Man is historically situated 1) by his own past acting and 2) by the acting of other men (pp. 50 f.). "The historical situation both limits and augments what it situates; and it is the togetherness of both which alone can constitute a situation as historical" (p. 53).

and the historical situation is the situation of man *qua* historically individuated, the two must stand in dialectical relationship to each other; man never wholly transcends the context of his historical situation, yet he cannot be reduced without residue to his historical situation without losing his character as man.[79] The point to be made here is that the human situation is always individuated in the historical situation, though, of course, it remains in dialectical relation to it. And if such individuation is characteristic of the human situation, the historical situation must enter into the constitution of the pre-understanding as well as serve as the matrix of interpretation.

The circularity of pre-understanding and understanding, which Bultmann correctly urges, is still deficient in that it proceeds *from* the human situation *to* the human situation without entering seriously into dialectic with the historical situation on the side of the interpreter. To put it succinctly, the circle on the interpreter's side is lacking in fullness—a fullness that is taken as axiomatic on the side of the text. What is objectionable in the existentialist analysis is that its framing of the questions tends to be undertaken in isolation from the pre-history of the situation. In other words, existentialist analysis is likely to be a snapshot which arrests man in his history, cuts across it, and exposes the skeleton. Bultmann's "now," the moment of decision, is thus open to the danger of becoming an empty abstraction.[80] There is the disposition in this type of analysis, moreover, to ignore the social character of existence. Although it is doubtless correct to saddle the individual with the decision that goes with faith, such decisions are never made in a vacuum, as Bultmann himself repeatedly emphasizes. Furthermore, while theology cannot dictate the specific *existential* content of faith in a given instance, neither can it fulfill its vocation without raising such content into a theological key and thereby probing it. In

[79] Cf. Fackenheim, *op. cit.*, pp. 76 ff.

[80] It should be made clear that Bultmann's intention is not being called into question: "Indeed, the questioning itself grows out of the historical situation, out of the claim of the now, out of the problem that is given in the now." *Glauben und Verstehen*, III, 148 [*Existence and Faith*, pp. 294 f.]. Nor is his insistence that theology cannot proceed apart from the help of philosophical analysis being contested.

short, the existentialist analysis converts the particular into an abstraction, thereby cutting it out of its historical nexus. Such analyses, while indispensable, are inadequate for the same reason that sociology that is confined to one generation is myopic, and psychological analysis that is not based on the history of the individual and/or culture is a distorted fragment.

It can be allowed, however, that Bultmann's way of posing the question, i.e., his own pre-understanding, has more historical body than the above criticism suggests. His own theological work is often explicitly informed by an analysis of the pre-history of the present situation,[81] and his participation in the theological upheaval of the twenties indicates that he is acutely aware of the historical dimensions of his work. Furthermore, his dependence upon Heidegger can be justified in this connection by understanding the latter's work as historical in distinction from metaphysical. The existentialist analytic may be interpreted as belonging specifically to our own period.[82] The estimate of Bultmann's work in this respect will depend in part on whether one thinks he has correctly read the way in which the present is determined by the past,

[81] Note the appendix to Vol. II of his *Theology of the New Testament,* pp. 241–251, and his essays in *Glauben und Verstehen,* I, 1–25, 114–133. Cf. also his remarks on pneuma in *Glauben und Verstehen,* III, 144 [*Existence and Faith,* p. 291], and his treatment of the problem of revelation in "The Concept of Revelation in the New Testament," *Glauben und Verstehen,* III, 1–14 [*Existence and Faith,* pp. 58–71]. One thinks also of his concept of demythologizing in relation to the man to whom the gospel is to be preached; cf. Kendrick Grobel, "Bultmann's Problem of New Testament 'Mythology,'" *JBL,* LXX (1951), 99–103; "The Practice of Demythologizing," *JBR,* XXVII (1959), 28–31.

[82] M. Heidegger, *Sein und Zeit* (Tübingen: Max Niemeyer Verlag, 9th ed., 1960), pp. 20 f. English translation by J. Macquarrie and E. Robinson, *Being and Time* (London: SCM Press, 1962), p. 42: "The ownmost meaning of Being which belongs to the inquiry into Being as an historical inquiry, gives us the assignment [*Anweisung*] of inquiring into the history of that inquiry itself, that is, of becoming historiological. In working out the question of Being, we must heed this assignment, so that by positively making the past our own, we may bring ourselves into full possession of the ownmost possibilities of such inquiry." Cf. Fackenheim, *op. cit.,* pp. 77 ff., n. 44; 80, n. 45; Thomas Langan, *The Meaning of Heidegger* (New York: Columbia University Press, 1959), pp. 143–151. I do not propose, either here or elsewhere in this essay, to engage the question of whether philosophical inquiry is to be subsumed wholly under the historical question or not. That Heidegger's work may be so understood is one way of justifying Bultmann's dependence on his analysis vis-à-vis the historical situation.

and in part on whether he speaks to the present situation. The two, of course, are interrelated.

It is nevertheless the case that special histories, personal and collective, operate in us too, and these must be exposed before the word can be heard anew. The problem, then, is the unexamined past as fate involved in the pre-understanding in relation to the formulation of questions.

A pair of propositions pertain to Biblical criticism, both of which are double-edged: 1) historical criticism in the preceding period was shaped by that with reference to which it was critical; and 2) historical criticism was channeled into the service of its own presuppositions.

The characteristics of Biblical criticism to which these two propositions point can be regarded either as its vitality and relevance or as its undoing. They may be regarded as the former if the object against which criticism is directed remains a viable option (better: *the* option), and if the presuppositions which underlie its positive work are conceived historically and can be recalled and critically re-examined at crucial points in the development. They are to be taken as debilitating if the object of criticism is retained only as a straw man, and the presuppositions lost to view so that they operate as a fate. The two sides in each case go inevitably together.

Now, of course, a judgment with respect to the stage of the development in a given period is itself a historical judgment. There is no escape from the circularity of the problem. Nor can there be if historical criticism is to function critically, for to function critically means also to function historically. The hermeneutical circle, consequently, applies to the interpreter and his past as well as to the interpreter and the text.[83]

---

[83] The hermeneutical circle as defined by Dinkler, *Journal of Religion,* XXXII (1952), 87–96, and *Journal of Religious Thought,* XIII (1955–1956), 20–30, refers to the relationship between interpreter and text: the interpreter brings a question to the text, listens to what the text has to say, corrects his question, and begins again. To this circle is added the historical circle, i.e., setting the text in its historical nexus. While acknowledged in principle by Bultmann and Dinkler, the correction that is being urged here appears to be a widespread deficiency in existentialist hermeneutic in that

In carrying this analysis forward, there is the initial handicap, which needs sorely to be remedied, that Biblical criticism has not been sufficiently interrogated with respect to its wider historical and epochal nexus, and further that it has not developed sufficient transcendence to be able to read its own internal development historically for the period just ended.[84] This deficiency notwithstanding, it is necessary to probe that development tentatively as a means of elucidating the point.

Biblical theology[85] began by having to challenge the very basis on which it rested, viz., the orthodox doctrine of verbal inspiration.[86] The challenge was necessitated by the desire to break the effective control of dogmatics over the interpretation of Scripture and thus to establish Biblical theology as a historical discipline. Having abandoned its fundamental connection to dogmatics, it could now pursue its own course independently as Biblical criti-

---

it merely assumes the relevance and body of the question arising from the existentialist analysis.

[84] Bultmann's appendix to his *New Testament Theology;* Ebeling's programmatic essay in *ZThK,* XLVII (1950), 1–46, reprinted in *Wort und Glaube,* pp. 1–49 [*Word and Faith,* pp. 17–61], his essay on Biblical theology in *JThS,* VI (1955), 210–225, reprinted in *Wort und Glaube* [*Word and Faith,* pp. 79–97], pp. 69–89, and the article "Hermeneutik," in *RGG*[3], III (Tübingen: J. C. B. Mohr, 1959), 242–262, provide broad internal assessments. Cf. Emil Kraeling, *The Old Testament Since the Reformation* (New York and Evanston: Harper & Row, 1955). The American development has received very little attention. Amos N. Wilder has opened up the question of the difference in Continental and American traditions for the development of Biblical theology in a pair of essays: "New Testament Theology in Transition," in *The Study of Bible Today and Tomorrow,* edited by H. R. Willoughby (Chicago: University of Chicago Press, 1947), pp. 419–436; "Biblical Hermeneutic and American Scholarship," in *Neutestamentliche Studien für Rudolf Bultmann* (Berlin: A. Töpelmann, 1954), pp. 24–32. Cf. C. T. Craig, "Biblical Theology and the Rise of Historicism," *JBL,* LXXII (1953), 281–294. J. Coert Rylaarsdam has written a provocative essay, "The Problem of Faith and History in Biblical Interpretation," *JBL,* LXXVII (1958), 26–32, in which he raises the question of the destiny of Biblical criticism. Of particular interest is the suggestion that certain historical disciplines were developed in the service of orthodoxy, while others appear to have been the outcome of certain liberal perspectives. He identifies the vitality of Biblical scholarship as its ability to transcend theological systems (p. 31).

[85] It is not necessary here to distinguish between Biblical theology as a historical discipline and historical criticism.

[86] Ebeling, "The meaning of 'Biblical Theology,'" *JThS,* VI (1955), 219, reprinted in *Wort und Glaube,* p. 81 [*Word and Faith,* p. 89].

cism. Nevertheless, that course was determined in no small measure by its repeated need to justify itself by producing new and more devastating criticisms of the orthodox view.[87] In America at the turn of the century this need was still operative, for example, in the program of the Chicago School.[88] The writings of S. J. Case illustrate very well the tenacity with which Biblical criticism has remained true to its initial thrust.[89] In the course of the de-

[87] Ebeling, *ibid.*, p. 218, reprinted in *Wort und Glaube*, pp. 79 f. [*Word and Faith*, pp. 88 f.].

[88] It may be conceded that there was good reason to revitalize the attack in reaction against fundamentalism.

[89] In *The Historicity of Jesus* (Chicago: University of Chicago Press, 1912; 2nd ed., 1928), Case makes the observation that liberal theology believes that religious knowledge is no longer supernaturally acquired, which means it can no longer rely "upon some record of a supposedly supernatural revelation . . ." (p. 7). Reason and human experience have been made fundamental (pp. 7 ff.). This point is made again, this time on his own authority, in *The Evolution of Early Christianity* (Chicago: University of Chicago Press, 1914), e.g., pp. 4 f., and then expanded in *The Social Origins of Christianity* (Chicago: University of Chicago Press, 1923) in a chapter entitled "The 'New' New Testament Study," pp. 1–37. The upshot of liberal criticism is that "the quest for a normative result was gradually abandoned, and the past was allowed to go its own way independently of present-day needs and interest" (pp. 35 f.). The Programmatic essay which introduced the new *Journal of Religion*, "The Historical Study of Religion," *JR*, I (1921), 1–17, strikes the note that "Belief in the normative function of history rests ultimately upon that pessimistic philosophy of life which interprets the present as a deterioration of humanity, a condition to be remedied only by the restoration of an idealized past. . . . But when history is viewed scientifically, as an evolutionary process in human living, the past inevitably loses its authoritative character" (p. 14). The same note has grown stronger by 1943 in *The Christian Philosophy of History* (Chicago: University of Chicago Press, 1943) partially in reaction to dialectical theology which Case believes is not primarily interested in history (p. 94). It is of interest to compare Case's 1921 essay in *JR* with essays by F. C. Porter, "The Historical and the Spiritual Understanding of the Bible," and B. W. Bacon, "New Testament Science as a Historical Discipline," in the Yale memorial volume, *Education for Christian Service* (New Haven: Yale University Press, 1922). Bacon, for example, affirms that "the development of criticism has been quite as truly under divine direction as the fixation of the canon" (p. 95), and "the New Testament . . . is a book which *enforces* criticism" (p. 99), yet he is concerned to show, as the title of his chair indicates (New Testament Criticism and Interpretation), that historical criticism may be utilized to bring men "into vital contact with the eternal Word" (p. 107). E. F. Scott, too, is concerned to expose the limitations of the historical method in "The Limitations of the Historical Method," in *Studies in Early Christianity*, edited by S. J. Case (New York and London: The Century Co., 1928), pp. 3–18, but he implies that it may well be invoked against false notions of revelation

velopment, however, Biblical criticism tended to obscure its critical function vis-à-vis itself and became, as a result, increasingly dogmatic at those points where it thought it was least dogmatic.[90] In the struggle against the doctrine of the verbal inspiration of Scripture the question of the function of Scripture got misplaced and then lost in the equally dogmatic proposition that the past can have no normative function for the present.[91] When this question is reopened, e.g., by Barth and Bultmann, the Biblical criticism that was shaped by the older conflict cannot help but misunderstand the new form of the question, and hence finds itself critically sterile.

To return to the question with which we began, the interpreter must interrogate the text from a particular locus in history, i.e., from his own present as it is informed and shaped by the past. Historical criticism as an integral element in the interpretation of the text is subject to pre-understanding. But the pre-understanding that is brought to the text is itself (both humanly and) historically situated and must itself be submitted to historical criticism. The full circularity of question/text has to be taken

(pp. 3 ff.). There is also the possibility that it may provide a kind of apologetic in reverse (p. 5).

The differences between Chicago and New England are significant in illuminating the shape of the opponent in the struggle of historical criticism for ascendancy. It may be said that Chicago has the better of the debate in carrying through the radical historicity of the text, while the Easterners are concerned not to let the question of revelation get lost. Under the duress of orthodoxy and fundamentalism it was perhaps impossible for the hermeneutical question to emerge.

[90] Ebeling, "The meaning of 'Biblical Theology,' " *JThS*, VI (1955), 218 f., reprinted in *Wort und Glaube,* pp. 79 f. [*Word and Faith,* pp. 88 f.].

[91] Cf. Case, *The Christian Philosophy of History:* "Revelation is thus only what every sincere religious man believes to be divine truth, and it is capable of as much variation as marks the life and thinking of different persons living under different conditions in the various periods of history" (p. 170); ". . . heritages from the past will justify their right to survive only by the measure of their functional value in the experience of the continuing Christian society" (p. 183). What is at stake for Case is the ideality of the past as opposed to the ideality of the future (see pp. 158 ff.). Attention has been called to the strange similarity of "modernism" and fundamentalism in rejecting the historical basis of the Christian faith, the former deliberately, the latter unconsciously. Cf. Dillenberger and Welch, *Protestant Christianity* (New York: Charles Scribner's Sons, 1954), pp. 226 f.

with seriousness and not circumvented by the attempt to derive a pre-understanding from outside of history. In relation to Biblical criticism, it can be said that every critical effort must presuppose the history of its own development.[92] The exposition of its own history is subject to the same principles that apply to the Bibical text. At this juncture the intimate relation between Bibical criticism and the history of theology becomes evident.

Bultmann and Fuchs have rightly insisted that the subject-object schema is invalid for historical knowledge, that the latter is never closed because a historical event is known only by its future.[93] If the meaning of historical events is disclosed ever anew in the future by the way in which they are reappropriated, it becomes all the more apparent that historical criticism has as its primary function the thwarting of the tyranny of the question. But what does this mean in view of the assertion that it is only by means of some question that the interpreter can interrogate history at all? The interrogation of history would be a deceptive mental exercise unless the past is encountered in its own integrity, and this means unless the pre-understanding that is brought to it is subject to criticism from the standpoint of that past. But the past is not something "out there" which can be confronted, say, as a tree or a mountain; it is embodied in historical texts and monuments, in the individual and collective memory both conscious and unconscious, in the way it functions in the present either as a fate or as a creative possibility for the future. Historical criticism must, therefore, function as the *probing* of the *present* in such a way that the past is released from its appropriation by the present in distorted form. For every appropriation of the past, while it may lay hold of truth, effects at the same time the exclusion of other possibilities. The fresh appropriation of the past,

[92] There is regrettable deficiency in this respect in the majority of modern works. Even where such histories are provided, as often in older studies, they are descriptive rather than analytical, and far too narrowly conceived. There are, of course, instances where the assessment of the development is obvious though not set out explicitly.

[93] Bultmann, *History and Eschatology* (Edinburgh: Edinburgh University Press, 1957), pp. 120 ff.; *Glauben und Verstehen*, III, 148, 149 f. [*Existence and Faith*, pp. 294, 296]; Fuchs, *Zur Frage nach dem historischen Jesus*, pp. 227 ff., 283 f.

therefore, is a recurring task in the service of which historical criticism must be placed. Historical criticism, then, can function only in relation to a particular appropriation of the past, and it must always function critically in relation to that appropriation if it is to fulfill its vocation. To let history speak for itself means to let it speak critically with reference to the present grasp of history, and thus in a way that is relevant to the present.

6. The Word as Address and the Word as Meaning

AMOS N. WILDER

Harvard Divinity School

I rejoice so far as with others in this discussion I can contribute in any way to wider acquaintance with the vital discussion of hermeneutic now going on and especially with the notable contributions to it of Ernst Fuchs and Gerhard Ebeling. Their work continually focuses upon the substance of the faith and clears away matters that becloud it. The act of faith is purified of adventitious features, either secondhand belief or evidential props and supports which really dissolve it. The revelation is dissociated from inherited and even Scriptural formulations which may once have been wings to the word but today have become drags. God's love in action in the Christ is freed of elements not intrinsic to it, such as the matter of his self-importance or his importance in the eyes of the world.

In Fuchs's presentation it becomes admirably clear that we are not our own, we are in God's hands, we ask no signs even of Easter. We are caught up in that meaningful world of language where the shoutings of death or the bans of law and necessity fall silent, where the love set in motion by God envelops us despite all the hostilities of "the time being," where we do not disturb ourselves about historical finalities. Such apocalyptic matters can be left to God. To understand the New Testament the interpreter takes up his position at the "place" where all such disclosures are relevant.

I am glad to acknowledge my great appreciation of the present paper of Gerhard Ebeling. I am particularly appreciative of his discussion of the relation of the Greek *logos* to the Biblical word, and his refusal to separate these in any final fashion. I appreciate his understanding of the word as word event, and of the text as not only object of interpretation but also as itself already interpretation. I agree that when the text is thus seen in its dynamic character, existentialist interpretation comes into its own as an indispensable method. I particularly value the emphasis on the word as human word and the insistence that there is no true grasp of the word except at that "place" in our human present and our special contemporary situation where our secularity and experience is lighted up, where we ourselves are brought to language, and where we thereby stand forth in our true humanity.[1]

As we stand back from the whole discussion of hermeneutic of the recent period we should take into account a number of factors that condition our special activity. The first of these is the situation in secular philosophy. The statements of Ebeling and Fuchs with which we are concerned are couched in existentialist categories. It is to be recognized that our two authors are not adopting Heidegger's formulation as a whole; indeed, it is recognized that his undertaking has been and is in movement. Fuchs, in the first edition of his *Hermeneutik*, writes that it is a question for him of at least finding himself in a silent conversation with Heidegger,[2] who in any case has "prepared the terminology that we need if we . . . wish to have done with the subject-object schema."[3]

In what follows, my insistence on the word as meaning may seem out of order as not recognizing the ontological premise of Fuchs and Ebeling. I ask for meaning in what may seem a subject-object dimension. However, I am convinced that any fundamental-ontological understanding of being and of language ought

[handwritten margin note: things (4) that need to be taken into account in any discussion of hermeneut...]

---

[1] See also "Hauptprobleme der protestantischen Theologie in der Gegenwart," *ZThK*, LVIII (1961), 131–135.

[2] *Hermeneutik* (Bad Cannstatt: R. Müllerschön Verlag, 1954; 2nd ed., 1958), p. 62.

[3] *Ibid.*, p. 70. See the review of Fuchs's relation to Heidegger in H. Franz, "Das Denken Heideggers und die Theologie," *ZThK, Beiheft* 2 (1961), pp. 86–90. Ebeling summarizes his orientation to Heidegger in the same *Beiheft:* Theology necessarily encounters his thought since a basic exploration of history and language is imperative today for the theologian. Moreover, that which is genuinely Biblical moves in the same direction as Heidegger with respect to the overcoming of metaphysics (p. 123). See further James M. Robinson and John B. Cobb, eds., *The Later Heidegger and Theology* (New York and Evanston: Harper & Row, 1963), pp. 69–76.

to allow for my concern in theology and preaching. Hence my thesis may at least put in question the completeness of the categories now being used.

A second factor of which we need to take account is the continuing movement of historical scholarship in our field. The importance of this is brought home to us in the paper of James M. Robinson, "Basic Shifts in German Theology."[4] Exegesis and interpretation must come to terms with new findings so far as they establish themselves. Robinson's paper makes it evident, for example, that the frontiers of New Testament scholarship together with Old Testament studies may well affect essential features of New Testament theology, particularly eschatology, and thereby may well impose a modification of the kerygmatic norm as employed by Bultmann and Fuchs in their hermeneutic. In brief, it sets the interpreter in the midst of a divine action or word event still moving toward its term, rather than at the point of eschatological decision in response to a word already finally spoken.[5]

Another factor affecting our task is that of the changing views of historiography and historical method in secular quarters. The new hermeneutic as we know it has related itself to this. Yet a basic question remains. If we take the work of H. G. Gadamer, *Wahrheit und Methode,*[6] as indicative, theological hermeneutic in the existentialist tradition meets with questions that are not satisfactorily dealt with in the procedure of Fuchs. Gadamer's understanding of language in its ontological depth and of the historicity of understanding takes issue specifically with Bultmann,[7] and has further features that could prompt Fuchs to greater recognition of the interconnectedness of language with our human reality,

[4] *Interpretation,* XVI (1962), 76–97.

[5] I take this to be the implication of Käsemann's article, "Die Anfänge christlicher Theologie," *ZThK,* LVII (1960), 162–185, when read in the light particularly of W. Pannenberg, R. Rendtorff, T. Rendtorff, U. Wilckens, *Offenbarung als Geschichte, KuD, Beiheft* 1 (1960) and of D. Rössler, *Gesetz und Geschichte. Untersuchungen zur Theologie der jüdischen Apokalyptik und der pharisäischen Orthodoxie* (Neukirchen: Neukirchener Verlag, 1960), despite the replies to Käsemann by Fuchs and Ebeling in *ZThK,* LVIII (1961), 227–267.

[6] *Wahrheit und Methode. Grundzüge einer philosophischen Hermeneutik* (Tübingen: J. C. B. Mohr, 1960).

[7] *Ibid.,* pp. 313 ff.

that is, of the semantic importance of traditional speech. This is confirmed by Heinrich Ott's appeal to the later Heidegger in his *Denken und Sein*.[8] But quite outside the program of existentialist and Heideggerian thought the task of historical interpretation and method has been dealt with in challenging ways, as is illustrated by the book of Richard R. Niebuhr, *Resurrection and Historical Reason*.[9] The method employed here does not require the total rejection of the Western metaphysical tradition, but neither is it open to the charges made against objective historicism. It has the advantage of dealing with a total historical experience without the antitheses of knowing, which dog all forms of the new hermeneutic and reach their most troubling expression in the contrast of historical and historic.

A fourth factor of which our work should take account is contemporary secular literary interpretation and criticism, especially as it bears on the understanding of imaginative and symbolic texts. The New Testament is only one body of literature in which inherited social imagery and mythos are used. The psychological aesthetic and semantic laws that obtain in this kind of discourse, whether poetry or prose, govern the material in our canon as elsewhere. Hermeneutic has much to learn here, especially as a warning against abstracting or reductionist translation of plastic discourse into proposition or other alien modes. This bears again upon what is done with eschatological language.

I. PERSONAL FOREWORD

The present paper by Ernst Fuchs does us the compliment of opening up the question of hermeneutic in its widest scope and fundamental presuppositions. This appears not only in the contents of the article but also in its tenor, particularly in the candid personal statement with which it opens. It is for this reason that I begin my contribution in the same vein as Professor Fuchs, even

[8] *Denken und Sein. Der Weg Martin Heideggers und der Weg der Theologie* (Zürich: EVZ-Verlag, 1959).

[9] *Resurrection and Historical Reason* (New York: Charles Scribner's Sons, 1957).

in an unacademic way, though to the end of better understanding the main issues.

Permit me, then, immediately at this point to set forth the basic hesitations I have with the program of the new hermeneutic and to sketch in some personal background for this disagreement. The crux of the matter is our understanding of revelation and of how and where faith takes hold of it. Both in Fuchs and in Ebeling we rightly have our attention drawn to the "place" (the *Wo* of Fuchs, the *Ort* of Ebeling) of the believer or the interpreter. This means the question of man himself and of his central core of need, of questioning, of freedom. Here also is the issue of the necessary pre-understanding. My criticism, briefly stated, is that we are offered an unsatisfactory anthropology. It is a special question whether the existentialist categories condemn the procedure to this inadequacy. But man as created, and as we actually know him in the Bible and elsewhere, is and seeks more than what is indicated by Bultmann and even by Fuchs.

Now on the other side of this is the question of the word, the revelation, the kerygma, or in Fuchs's richer formulation, the language of the gospel. The word as understood by existentialists seems opaque. It involves mainly obedience or consent rather than understanding; and this view beautifully corresponds to the view of man in question. Existentialist man is mainly conative and the word for him is mainly imperative. So far as the event is seen as grace and "clearing," the opening up of meaning is still a-cultural and has to do with man only in a partial sense.

Man, I would urge, is not only conative; he is not only a focus of freedom; he is not only one who seeks authenticity or love. He is created as a maker, as artisan and symbol-user, endowed with intellect, sentiment, imagination; in short he is a cultural being. The questions he puts to God have to do with his fulfillment in such dimensions. What is he saved to? So far as this ultimate question is that of salvation from nonbeing or lostness, these other aspects are not supplementary but also of the essence. Man is made to share in the works of God and not only in his love. His *archē* and *telos* have structures. It would seem that we can find intimations of this in more recent considerations by Heidegger, even though directed to technical analysis of the truth of being.

Against this background let me then respond in kind to the candid personal preface to Fuchs's paper. I would like to speak of certain factors in my own experience and setting in the American scene which no doubt condition my later observations. This setting and our particular Christian tradition impose a special task on us who would let the gospel speak to American society. The "word of God" neo-Protestantism, unless acclimated to our situation, tends only to confirm Biblicism and dogmatism instead of liberating the word, and in consequence it confirms our dated liberal theology in its defensive position. Theology and apologetics have a special task on this side of the water. American empiricism is a factor that should not be discounted in any area of life, least of all with respect to Christianity. Moreover, what Christian traditions we have are deeply associated with our social and political patterns, despite separation of church and state, and this association is by no means entirely a matter of surrendering the gospel. Our best strategy is to use these links of a Christianized culture and not break with them.

Ernst Fuchs delighted me by citing the play, *Our Town*, by my brother. Let me then invoke Thornton Wilder's sanction for my thesis that American culture is *sui generis*. He has observed that all Americans are autodidacts: they spurn the wisdom of the ages, and like Thoreau and Poe and Whitman they propose to begin the human quest for wisdom all over again. In his Frankfort Peace Prize address of 1956, my brother scolded his German friends by confronting them with the traditional hierarchical feudal aspects of their society even after two World Wars. By contrast, he has spoken to American audiences of the new-world trait of loneliness in our "lack of those 'loved, trusted repetitions in customs, manners and history' which Europeans have."[10]

Now this explains precisely why many American Protestants stand in a much looser relation to the European religious past, confessional and ecclesiastical. From our point of view, much of

[10] *Oberlin Alumni Bulletin*, Vol. 10, No. 3 (1953), p. 2.

Protestant Europe lives almost in a ghetto, so massive is the weight of pre- and post-Reformation habits. I see the work of the Bultmann group as a heroic effort to surmount the rigidities of centuries as well as of first-century mythology. This shows itself even in the radical change of terrain to existentialist categories. This represents an extreme recourse to overcome the dead hand of the past in just this situation. It is a way of salvaging confession as faith without confession as doctrine, the word as address but not as meaning—for meaning has become hopelessly identified with outworn associations.

In short, the new hermeneutic rests on a violent a-cultural and anticultural impulse and sees both the divine word and the human response in a kind of cultural vacuum. From the point of view of language strategy this may be congenial to nihilistic trends. But from the point of view of substance it seems to me inadequate to the New Testament. For myself, faith and theology are most vital and communicable not in dialectical terms but, with all the risks, in cultural terms, that is, exploiting and redeeming the current secular ideas and images that provide meaning for men. In America this means: in terms of a cultural Christianity as we know it in our own theocratic tradition. Our world over here, of course, knows as everywhere the conflict of God and Satan, but our world is not broken as between the revealed word and the common life. Christendom in our social and political life can hear and respond to the gospel proclaimed in culturally relevant terms. I suspect that Continental theology since Barmen has disengaged itself too completely from the deeper social and cultural hungers that were exploited by Nazism. A dialectical theology will never reach them. It is true that Gogarten, Ebeling, and Fuchs make much of the secular as the place in which the word arises and where it meets us. However, they seem not to recognize that our full empirical experience is involved in the coming of the word and in the meaning of the word, that creation or givens, sociological and psychological, set the terms for redemption in every aspect.

Or again, it is a question of our view of man. The "Man" with whom we are concerned, the Adam, the conversation partner with God from the beginning, is not to be reduced to an unmasked formula of existential decision. If we are concerned with man in his givenness (and all the humanisms of East and West are legitimate sources of our estimate), we cannot stop with his historicity in the form in which it is presented to us in existentialism.

II. The "Place" of the Interpreter

Let us consider in more detail this question of the locus of revelation. The new hermeneutic, I maintain, does not include adequate recognition of the human factors in hearing. We get a kind of existentialist skeleton of human nature, a kind of X-ray photograph, and a fleshless mathematics of the divine-human transaction. This cannot all be put down to the inevitable necessities of existentialist statement. In this hermeneutic, man is not man as we know him, but a kind of generalized *anthropos*.

I realize again that I can be charged here with misunderstanding. Fuchs presupposes a radically different approach to reality and to knowing based on Heidegger's revolt against subject-object thinking, his existentialist analysis of *Dasein*, and his special understanding of being and of language as historic in the sense he gives the term. Writing out of this context, Fuchs certainly means to deal with our full human reality seen in this perspective. My questions may, nevertheless, be valid as inviting a more reassuring exposition of the matters queried.

It is true that with regard to revelation and its locus, Ebeling in the present paper clarifies and adds something to Bultmann's view of the word as encounter and as eschatological decision by insisting that it is a real human word in our human experience. It is not a heavenly or supernatural word. The word is not made flesh in the sense of accommodation. As Fuchs would say, there is no fracture of the human reality; rather our earthly existence is lighted up from within by the divine action. This view, happily, makes more place for our participation in revelation. Indeed, both Fuchs and Ebeling boldly restore the category of experience with the word. Fuchs also defines the place of faith and the meaning of the new self in ways less bound to the existentialist categories of Bultmann.

Fuchs notes that the position of W. Herrmann puts a good question to Bultmann.[11] It is only through our actual here-and-now struggle with the *imagines mundi* in *our* situation that the word can enable us to share in the Christ-drama and in his victory of the past and present. What he implies is that Bultmann's kerygma may remain unhistoric for us—à la Kierkegaard—unless it is brought into direct relation with our here-and-now wrestling with idolatry in its modern forms. The renewal of our self-understanding must be related to our present experience and not only to our present decision.

There is another point at which Fuchs enriches our understanding of the act of repentance, faith, and interpretation. Its "place" is not to be identified only with such familiar existentialist categories as insecurity, anxiety, and dread. The "place" is man as a creature defined by his need not only of forgiveness or of right self-understanding but decisively of love. The word rightly seen is then not only a message calling for eschatological decision and obedience but a wordevent in the sense that it has "set love in movement towards its goal," a language which assembles a community of love about it.[12] As Fuchs writes in our present paper, you may come to believe if you "pay attention to the experiences that you have with love."[13] In all this Fuchs is clarifying further how we lay hold on the gospel and is insisting on the concrete human situation. For example, with reference to wrong views of man's contact with God, he writes of both Paul and Jesus: "Paul has exchanged the ecstatic-prophetic sphere into the ordinary down-to-earth sphere of our bodily existence. He was only doing what the historical Jesus himself did, in my view, for Jesus at least in his parables exalted ordinary daily life into the 'stuff' of the revelation event."[14]

Thus I grant that Fuchs and Ebeling have gone far to dedogmatize what is meant by the word and to develop the human side of the act of revelation. But should they not go further if it

---

[11] Fuchs, *Hermeneutik*, pp. 74 f.

[12] Cf. "Was ist existentiale Interpretation? C," III–IV, *Zum hermeneutischen Problem* (Tübingen: J. C. B. Mohr, 1959), pp. 98–104.

[13] See above, p. 142.

[14] "Muss man an Jesus glauben. . . ." *ZThK*, LVIII (1961), 53.

is possible in the existentialist categories in which they are now implicated? Fuchs ordinarily replaces the term word by language and language event and so overcomes much of the arbitrariness usually associated with the former term. Language is always for him the word in a given place and time. "To believe in Jesus means then to relate ourselves in the name of God to our time and our place as the time for faith and the place for faith and to hold fast to this call."[15] In this context Fuchs deals with the way in which faith arises in the resurrection of Christ and discusses the interpretation of 1 Cor. 15:3–8. I agree with him that this rehearsal of the appearances in the context of Old Testament prophecy is not to be read as though it were what Schlier calls a *Kerygma-Dogma*, imposing assent under the weight of evidence. It has rather the character of witness or confession, and what is authoritative (as in our own acknowledgment of the lordship of Christ) is the underlying event as it grips us and not the form in which it is stated. But Fuchs's characterization of the gospel in this connection seems to me to have a high degree of abstraction and at the same time to sound like a truism. I quote: "The Christian message in 1 Cor. 15 as well, consists in the proclamation that for all of us, this time, the time to believe, has now already arrived, and that this call to believe has entered this actual place, namely, the world. It follows then that man is no longer only a doer, but above all a hearer; and all [authentic] being depends on whether or not we can hear. . . . Thus so far as concerns our doing God would often be a hidden God, while in the realm of our hearing he is wholly revealed."[16]

Fuchs here is rightly insisting that the gospel of the resurrection is personal, that faith in it does not depend upon external proofs, and that this faith arises out of a concrete situation, indeed, at a point where the time of salvation encounters my own actuality. But just how concrete is this situation where faith arises? If it is answered that we are here presenting faith in existentialist terms and therefore are not concerned with psychology or sociology or public history, this does not satisfy me. Since salvation takes place

15 *Ibid.*, p. 63.
16 *Ibid.*, p. 63.

in an actual world of human relationships and events and is conditioned by them, existentialism should find some way to take account of these and not resort to a depth that dodges them. Moreover, since the gospel availed itself of very particular current language and symbols as the *sine qua non* of its impact, existentialism should use the category of word or language in such a way as to take account of such stubborn elements of the problem. Instead, it resorts to a phenomenology of communication and meaning which abstracts from the real situation calling for salvation. Why should it at least not be made clear that the particular steps by which particular believers come to faith in different times and places involve all sorts of sociological and psychological and semantic factors, and that these are not accidental and gratuitous and interchangeable accompaniments but essentials in the action of God in time and place?

III. SPEECH AS MEANING

No doubt effective interpretation must "attain a relation to cultural streams of our time which can provide a context in terms of which [the] message can be communicated," or "attain broader cultural relevance for the message."[17] But to grasp the true sense of this demand it is essential that we recognize the way in which the New Testament writers and the earlier oral witnesses used language that was, precisely, culturally relevant. It should be clear that for the early hearers of the New Testament message such terms as "word," "gospel," and "revelation of the righteousness of God," as well as such terms for the action of God as "sent his Son," were current plastic terms with a meaning that, as a matter of course, engaged itself not only with some exclusive theological dimension but with the whole web of their social and cultural existence. The existence to which these terms referred was one or other very specific human state of affairs in the Roman Empire. The concrete situation, similarly, was not a segregated

[17] James M. Robinson, "Basic Shifts in German Theology," *Interpretation*, XVI (1962), 91.

moral-existential situation but a very complex ramifying state of affairs in Hellenistic times.

I realize that Fuchs would not deny the public and worldly aspects of the transaction of faith in the New Testament. He insists that he wants to get behind this to the existential core of the matter from which all public and social relations and factors arise. But this is a dangerous schema and sounds too much like our liberal individualistic illusion: Change a man's heart and his worldly action will take care of itself. Or, contrariwise: The empirical conditions of a man's life do not have anything to do with his religion: this is a matter of the heart.

I have reached here the crux of my objection. It has to do with the content of faith, its belief aspect. Revelation in the legacy of Kierkegaard, in both Barth and Bultmann, is too unrelated to meaning. The content of the kerygma as an object of faith is obscured and the New Testament teaching on belief is slighted. Man is asked to respond as a matter of the will alone; all that we associate with mans' reason and imagination is neglected. The word of God has no structure, and there are no human structures to which it is meaningful. Logos is divorced from truth and belief, and this is connected with the anthropological criterion used. The word is isolated from the divine plenitude; the kerygma is isolated from the Biblical fullness; man hearing is isolated from man seeing, knowing, symbol-making and feeling. Ernst Fuchs's language revelation is indeed located in daily life, but the cognitive, persuasive, semantically meaningful terms of the divine address and self-impartation are sterilized away. If revelation has to speak against culture it has also to speak through it and by it. This is not only a question of obtaining broader cultural relevance for the message. It is a question of the message itself.

There could be two objections to this line of thought. It could be said that Bultmann and his followers have always recognized the interrelation of self-understanding *and* world-understanding *and* history-understanding. But they have not done so in the empirical way that I believe is needed. Otherwise they could not abstract so easily from the actual language, existentialize so easily, demythologize so easily, decosmicize and dehistorize so easily. Their way of putting the question as to man narrows the whole program. The most transparent loss of reality appears in the inadequate grasp of man's social life and the church.

The second objection is more interesting. Granted that there is structure in God and structure in man as a creature, is it not just the feature of the eschatological crisis with which the gospel was identified that cultural structures were dissolved? So Ernst Fuchs can associate myth with a world whose order is fluid; where the law of groundlessness obtains. Nevertheless, I would insist, the mythological speech of Jesus and of the early church, while it may find men in chaos and meaninglessness, invokes order and appeals to them in the name of order and in the memory of order. It is in terms of meaning that the word comes to men even when the structures of culture are undermined and the fashion of this age is passing away.[18]

When revelation or the word of God is spoken of in the New Testament, its aspect as truth or wisdom is presupposed or explicit. The word has a meaningful content. The faith response involves consent of a noetic as well as a voluntary kind. The wisdom or ideological element is, of course, determined by the cultural context. We may take as an example the Epistle to the Hebrews. The whole epistle provides a semantically meaningful understanding of the Christian message, itself identified in the following passage: "For the word of God is living and active, sharper than any two-edged sword, piercing to the division of soul and spirit, of joints and marrow, and discerning the thoughts and intentions

---

[18] In his *Hermeneutik,* ¶ 11, pp. 166–176, Fuchs discusses mythos in relation to rite, logos, and the aesthetic order. In the rise of Christianity we can see a new awakening of mythological language. This mode of language in depth continues to act as a safeguard against new forms of legalism or metaphysics or moralism in the church and against the secularizing of history. Mythos points behind laws and continuities to the boundary of existence where the free play of the forms of life originates. Christianity used it to highlight its historical dimension over against temptations to see revelation in only ethical or metaphysical terms. Now all this is well urged. But the mythos, I would suggest, still has a cognitive, a truth aspect, which need not be confused with world view in the bad sense. I seem here to detect again a hiatus between existentialist reality and the public reality in which man lives in culture.

of the heart. And before him no creature is hidden, but all are open and laid bare to the eyes of him with whom we have to do" (4:12–13).

Here the revelatory role of the word as calling for decision is stated. But the epistle as a whole interprets the word or message in terms of its content and meaning. The word is commended to the hearers or readers in a rich context of cultural wisdom. The whole epistle serves as a characterization of the word, drawing on the symbol-familiarity of its time and place. Käsemann's *Das wandernde Gottesvolk*,[19] for example, suggests the apperception-mass in question of reason, sensibility, and imagination. Appeal is made not to the will alone, but to the will instructed by truth; not to hearing only in the sense of obedience, but to hearing in the sense of discernment or vision; not to the ear only, but to the eye. The appeal is made to man defined not only in terms of his moral-existential freedom but also in terms of his *physis,* his Adamic, creaturely nature and endowment.

Moreover, this nature presupposes a future for the deployment of these endowments. His response is then not only a matter of the removal of sin, and peace with God, but also the exercise of his native faculties in the new creation. All this is suggested in Hebrews by the image of the inheritance, by the concrete mythological language for the future—Mount Zion, the city of the living God, innumerable angels in festal gathering, and the assembly of the first-born (13:22–23), and by the references to the *polis,* the *patris,* the *basileia.* The word makes appeal, again, not only to the man as individual but to social man as suggested by these figures. The appeal, moreover, assumes a cosmic extension and concern and not only an anthropological one, as is evident both in the apocalyptic thought-world drawn upon and in the sophisticated gnostic-haggadic conceptions that lie behind this "word of exhortation."

There are then, it seems to me, presuppositions in Fuchs's method that must necessarily limit its impact. Our author deals with language phenomenologically; at a level where language is

---

[19] Göttingen: Vandenhoeck and Ruprecht, 1957.

elemental gesture, where it is a question of language versus silence, of sheer address and response, where word is act and love. But after all language also involves meaning and we cannot neglect the matter of semantics. The aspect of idea and even of ideology, the noetic element of the word and even of mythos, these must be given their rights. Faith involves consent to truth as well as obedience to an invitation or a call. Now this issue runs through the whole of Fuchs's existentialist presentation.

That Fuchs finds such considerations unnecessary emerges at various points in his writing. There are recurrent disparagements of faith in terms of "conceptions." His recurrent arguments against the futurist dimension in the early Christian message rests on a view of this as secular ideology or speculation. He does not envisage the possibility that such mythos, including the apocalyptic, may have a prerational truth content. His basic motive throughout is a laudable one: to divest faith of the secularization and woodenness of crystallized belief, of less-than-personal encounter with the word as event. Thus, as he rightly urges, the Easter faith itself obscures the central thrust and immediacy of the revelation as initiated by the historical Jesus if the resurrection event and experience are isolated and made a matter of knowing.

In his discussion of the object of faith as Jesus understood it, Fuchs sets aside belief in Jesus, belief in the kingdom, belief in principles. Faith rather is consent and obedience to the fact that God is operating here in ordinary life. The Beatitudes and the parables do not set forth a doctrine; they celebrate this reality, this astounding coincidence of God's work with ours. Fuchs exalts the divine *Novum;* love is set in action in our time and place, and this is of God and is irreversible. We do not inquire as to the human factors in this event, we do not inquire as to secondary causes; we do not inquire as to the cultural-semantic role of God's address to men. Fuchs is interested in the "place" of language, the "place" of such new dialogue, and in the fact that language in this order occurs at all. All comes back finally to love as the source, and love's persuasions.

But is not man a noetic creature, a cognitive and not only a conative creature, an imaginative and symbol-using creature,

and not only a center of freedom? Fuchs is rightly afraid of
"belief," of speculation, of ideology, of metaphysics, of apocalyptic
curiosity, and of gnostic wisdom. But there is no "pure word"[20]
that is not a cultural word. Grace brings truth in the sense of
wisdom and world orientation as well as in the sense of love. It
is strange that Fuchs, with his admirable paragraph on Jesus
as having no office and as meeting men in the actuality of the
language of his parables, does not open up the question as to
the there and then meaningfulness and persuasiveness of his Jewish imagery and vocabulary. Thus with his emphasis on love
apart from meaning and structure, he exposes himself to a charge
of voluntarism.

My chief difficulty throughout, then, is that Fuchs refuses to
define the content of faith. He is afraid of the loss of immediacy
that is associated with world view. He is afraid of the word as
convention or as a means of conveying information. He is afraid
of anything that will remove us from the cross, whether curiosity
or lyricism. This I can understand. He is right that language in
the family as in the gospel is more meaningful in the sense that
it is more affective and affectionate there than outside. But Fuchs
carries this so far that revelation, as it were, reveals nothing!
Thus Jesus himself, his person, has no special character: he be-
haves like any other person; any mighty works he performs are
not signs except with reference to the time. The significance
attaches to the time, not to him. Jesus calls, indeed, for decision,
a decision that places the hearer on the side of God and of the
marvelous divine operation. Now all this is true in the sense that
Jesus appealed to no extrinsic authority of office or miracle. But
surely his words, deeds, presence, person, and message rested
on ideology, if we can use the term in a good sense, upon dogma,
eschatological and theocratic.

Again, with respect to the disciples' faith in connection with
his healings and mission, Fuchs holds that such faith is not in
an article of belief or in a principle, but "quite simply a practi-

---

[20] Ebeling, "Hauptprobleme der protestantischen Theologie in der Gegenwart," *ZThK*, LVIII (1961), 133. Here the author exalts "das reine Wort"
of the gospel over against Christian social activity in a disturbing way.

cal obedience that is willing to be told that now the time has
come in which God comes forward as God."[21] Here again we
agree that faith directed toward Jesus was not belief in a prop-
ositional sense. But surely the consenting faith in this case arose
in a context of cultural meaningfulness. Fuchs goes on: This
concrete revelation of God is meant not "as something still to be
awaited, which is not yet even here at all, instead it is present."[22]
Of course, he observes, God is also, as for the prophets of the Old
Testament, "the almighty creator of heaven and earth, who is
able to make the dead alive. . . . But such thoughts are beside
the point, since they do not do justice to God's presence."[23] Jesus
has made God present by his word. But here again, I say, acceptance of Jesus' message by his hearers had a context of meaning,
of understanding, in the sense of how men orient themselves in
life and in time. We should not disallow the future dimension of
the message in this way.

At this point I call attention to Fuchs's discussion of Käsemann's "Die Anfänge christlicher Theologie."[24] Here too the
future element in the post-Easter Christian prophecy is viewed as
not part of the meaning of the kerygma. This would be ideology
in the bad sense. Faith properly understood does not ask for assur-
ances as to the future. The futurist apocalyptic is seen as external
and extrinsic. But may not such apocalyptic-eschatological imagery be held in faith without harm to faith? May it not be transparent for faith rather than a false objectification? Thus the
future aspect of the kingdom is really part of the content of faith.
In Fuchs's view, for God to speak in Christ must exclude any
future completion since how else could Christianity be different
from Judaism? If a future were still awaited, would we not have
only a pale expectation like that of the *marana tha* of the Did-
ache? Fuchs sees only presence and assurance in the present, but
here he is in as vulnerable a position as that which we associate
with Kierkegaard's "moment." The concluding pages of this ar-

[21] See above, p. 129.
[22] *Ibid.*
[23] *Ibid.*
[24] "Über die Aufgabe einer christlichen Theologie," *ZThK*, LVIII (1961),
245–267.

ticle set forth the existentialist phenomenology of time in such a way as to exhibit disparagement of any time or actuality except that of revelation and its language.[25]

In concluding this section I recur to the question as to whether I do justice to the categories that Fuchs uses. He demurs at my plea for the meaning of the word—that is, meaning in the usual sense of the social significance of language—as a misunderstanding of his position. In the depth in which he discusses language, such meaning is absorbed into a more significant dimension. For him, the great fact is that God calls me, names me, addresses me; here is an unimaginably great meaning for me in my mystery-bounded ephemeral days. I am made at home in the world by his love. Is that not meaning enough?

When I urge recognition of the indispensable cultural meaning of early Christian language, I am not proposing to bind the dynamic word of God in the chains of first-century expression, nor to confuse faith with beliefs. Nor do I intend to ignore the initiative of God in the personal dimension. I am saying only that such initiative could not reach me apart from the already existing creaturely givens of my world including its modalities of apprehension and communication. I am not falling back into that objective worldly order of knowing of which we are all rightly disabused.

IV. Adam and His Arts

Fuchs's understanding of "language" and "language-event," influenced no doubt by Heidegger's discussion,[26] has a close rela-

---

[25] Ebeling in his discussion, "Word of God and Hermeneutic," points out (p. 99) that the word of God rightly understood has itself a hermeneutical character; that is, it unfolds *meaning;* and furthermore "the structure of the understanding peculiar to theology must result from the essential structure of the word of God." It has a structure and a content, and we attend to what it teaches and receive it in terms of the structures of our own understanding. This position of Ebeling seems to me to require more noetic or ideological content in the act of faith than appears in Fuchs's presentation.

[26] *Hölderlin und das Wesen der Dichtung* (Munich: Langen und Müller, 1937), reprinted in *Erläuterungen zu Hölderlin* (Frankfurt a.M.: Vittorio Klostermann, 1944); 2nd enlarged ed., entitled *Erläuterungen zu Hölderlins Dichtung,* 1951, pp. 31–43. English translation by Douglas Scott, *Existence*

tion to the widely familiar views of "primitive" language, mythological mentality, prerational and precategorical speech, and
symbolic discourse as they are held by anthropologists, by students
of early languages and of myth and ritual, and by literary critics.
It seems curious to me that he does not appeal more often to such
"secular" investigations as those of Cassirer, Langer, van der
Leeuw, Eliade, and Pettazzoni. From my point of view the apologetic advantages of such a frank hospitality to social science
would be great. It would mean, however, that the widely recognized cognitive element in speech, gesture, and language would
have to be taken seriously. The birth of language and mythical
speech in their primary context involve social and cosmic orientation and life-meaning. It would mean that the whole discussion
of the word of God and its hearing among men would have to
submit to the relativities of cultural, semantic, and psychological
observation. It is this kind of development which I find missing at
many points in the new hermeneutic. As a result it has too much
the character of an inner-theological pursuit. This issue appears
especially with respect to anthropology.

Thus the view of man that New Testament theology has
worked with of late is restrictive. It tends to be moralistic, as
though the whole problem of salvation were that of the forgiveness of sins. Or it tends to be masochistic-man being defined in
terms of his lack and his weakness rather than also in terms of
his powers. Finally, it tends to be solipsistic. Theology is focused
too exclusively on man rather than upon all beings and the great
theater of all beings and the glory and activity of God in which
they all share in varying degrees. We are too obsessed with man
and with his inwardness, especially his moral inwardness. The
recent American sculptor, John B. Flanagan, devoted himself
throughout his life to the sculpture of animals, and this meant for
him a deliberate repudiation of what he called our narcissistic
obsession with the human figure. "Man should not praise him-

and Being (London: Vision Press, 1949), pp. 291–315; also published as a
Gateway Paperback Edition (Chicago: Henry Regnery Company, 1960), pp.
270–291.

self," he said, "but kneel in adoration before the vastness of the creation."[27]

Now we can support this Biblically and theologically without falling into pride and idolatry. One drawback of the Christomonism of much theology today is that the whole transaction of redemption loses its solid context in creation and becomes unreal together with all the elements in it including man. A corollary of this is the way in which the modern emphasis on the kerygma has often led to a Christological soteriology that hangs in the air. I quote here from Professor W. D. Davies: "The discovery of the kerygma within the complexities of the New Testament was liberating. But the kerygma now came to be isolated. . . . The danger arose of treating the kerygma as if it existed in a vacuum, and cutting it off or isolating it particularly from two things. First, there was its threatened separation from the milieu within which it emerged . . . interest in its rootedness in the world of the first century waned. . . ."[28] Davies goes on to speak of the isolation of the kerygma from the historical Jesus. This problem is being met today.

My concluding concern is that word-of-God theology and hermeneutic do not take sufficient account of the creative word of Genesis especially as concerns man the creature and his endowments and works in the creation. Man as we know him in the Renaissance and in the Romantic Movement, men like Goethe, Wordsworth, and Lincoln, should serve to remind us of what is said in the Old Testament as to the mystery of man, and should therefore help us to define the "place" of the interpreter and the believer in ways more satisfactory than that of the present existentialist perspective.

The New Testament anthropology, I believe, has a view of man and salvation which corroborates my plea. When the Philippian jailer cries out, "What shall I do to be saved?" this must be

[27] Walter Pach, "John B. Flanagan, American Sculptor," *The Kenyon Review*, V (1943), No. 3, p. 383.

[28] "A Quest to be Renewed in New Testament Studies," in *New Directions in Biblical Thought*, edited by Martin E. Marty (New York: Association Press, 1960), p. 50.

read in terms of the craving of Hellenistic man in the widest sense and as suggested in the plastic eschatology used by the author of Luke-Acts in his prologue and in the evangelical humanism that speaks through his entire work. Nor should Rom. 7:24 be read in a narrow sense. What the *genus homo* craves (the "place" to which the gospel speaks) is not in a narrow and exclusive sense the forgiveness of sins. Rather it is best defined by the terms in which Paul at various points in his letters expands upon the groaning and transfiguration of the creation. Professor Fuchs goes far to meet this point when he defines the "place" not only in terms of bondage or guilt but in terms of the need of love. But man's nature is seen in the Old Testament and elsewhere in terms of action, his fulfillment in the New Testament is seen in the glorifying and enjoying of God, which surely means a participation in his activity. If this is our understanding of man, then the "place" we select for the interpreter should be open to this kind of gospel and promise.

PART III. Reappraisal and Response

7. Faith and Culture

JOHN B. COBB, JR.

Southern California School of Theology

The function of this essay is to reflect on the issues raised in the American criticisms of the German contributions. Ideally such reflection should lead to clarification of the less explicit reasons for dissatisfaction on the part of the Americans with the position represented by Ebeling and Fuchs. Little attention will be paid to the wide areas of agreement among all contributors to this volume.

The preceding chapters and the oral discussions at the Drew Consultation have shown the difficulty of formulating objections in such a way that they appear relevant and appropriate to those criticized. Rather than summarize these criticisms, it may prove more helpful to consider more basic assumptions that seem in many cases to underlie them.

For the most part, criticisms by the American contributors are not directed to features of the work of Ebeling and Fuchs peculiar to them. On the contrary, Ebeling and Fuchs are recognized as having gone far toward satisfying some of the objections directed toward their predecessors.[1] Nevertheless, they are seen as sharing in a wider movement of theology the orientation of which imposes certain limitations.[2] For the purposes of this essay this wider move-

[1] See above, Wilder, pp. 206–207, 218; Dillenberger, p. 151.
[2] See above, Wilder, pp. 199–200, 207, 211–212; Dillenberger, pp. 150–151.

ment of theology in which Ebeling and Fuchs continue to participate will be called existentialist theology.[3] What is said about
existentialist theology, then, is held to be generally applicable to
Ebeling and Fuchs, but it may not always be illuminating of their
distinctive contributions.

The point at which all the American essays criticize what we
are now calling existentialist theology is on the question of the
relation of faith and culture or history. All three American contributors see in existentialist theology a tendency to treat existentialist categories themselves unhistorically and thereby to separate
faith too much from its concrete involvement in culture.

This generalized criticism and many of the specific criticisms
formulated by Dillenberger, Funk, and Wilder may appear to
those criticized in one of two ways. They may appear to be valid
and valuable emphases and warnings of which it is the intention
of existentialist theology to take full account. They may appear
to be based on misunderstanding.

The thesis of these reflections over the discussion is that although some of the criticisms can be treated as matters of emphasis and expressions of misunderstanding, a substantive question is
also at issue. This is the question as to the nature of faith especially as this determines our understanding of its relation to culture. This issue can be stated systematically in abstraction from
the arguments given in the five preceding essays. It may then be
possible to throw light upon the tensions expressed in these essays
without attributing to any one writer unequivocal commitment to
any of the views of faith which have been abstractly formulated.

I. FORMAL AND EXISTENTIALIST VIEWS OF FAITH

In *The Nature of Faith* Ebeling contrasts faith as he understands it with an image of faith as "an empty sack whose nature

[3] The attitude of Ebeling and Fuchs toward this classification of their
thought is not clear and they may correctly distinguish their positions from
a narrowly defined existentialism. However, there is in their words also a
strongly positive relation to existentialism, and in the American essays the
association is taken for granted.

it is to serve as a container for specific objects."[4] What he is chiefly rejecting is faith understood as credulity, with that about which one is credulous left undetermined so far as the definition of faith as such is concerned. Few theologians would choose to affirm the image of the empty sack, yet it may prove a useful one in sketching a general systematic possibility for the understanding of faith.

The understanding of faith as an empty sack suggests that faith is a form which can embody more than one kind of matter. Thus it is a vivid, if unattractive, symbol for what we may call the formal view of faith. This view is distinguished by its envisioning a conceptual separability of the form from the matter of faith. It is called formal because in all cases a definite form is definitive of faith as such, whereas the matter need not be determinate. These highly abstract statements can be explained by brief discussion of the two main subtypes of the formal view of faith.

In the first of these two subtypes faith is understood as a human faculty or capacity which can have diverse objects, contents, or matter. In addition to credulity, examples of such stable characteristics of man, sometimes called faith, are trust, commitment, comprehensive vision, and life orientation. It may be held, for example, that all men have some commitment, and that the religious question is what this commitment is directed toward. In a general way the commitment may then be regarded as the form of faith, a form open to a diversity of matter according to the object of commitment.

It is important to note that in this analysis the object to which commitment is given is not identical with the matter of commitment. One may commit himself to a political party, but the party as such or as it appears to a neutral observer is clearly not the matter of the commitment. The matter of the commitment will be determined by the individual's emotional, imaginative, and noetic apprehension of the party.

[4] Gerhard Ebeling, *Das Wesen des Christlichen Glaubens* (Tübingen: J. C. B. Mohr, 1959), p. 15: English translation by Ronald Gregor Smith, *The Nature of Faith* (Philadelphia: Muhlenberg Press, 1961), p. 19.

Formal
Definition
of Faith

Christian faith in these terms would be commitment to God revealed in Jesus Christ. Hence the object as such is always self-identical. However, the matter of the commitment is not God himself nor even God as objectively revealed in Jesus Christ. Rather the matter is the particular individual's total apprehension of that revelation.[5]

In the second of the two subtypes of the formal view of faith the form or defining characteristic is identified as a relation to God rather than as a human capacity that may or may not be oriented toward him. Faith may be defined as the human response to God's grace. This definition is formal like the other since it does not specify what the response will be. Any response that is truly man's response to God's grace will serve as the matter of faith. Conceivably this response may sometimes include beliefs, at other times feelings, at other times acts. The beliefs, feelings, and acts may alter from time to time. If any restriction is to be placed on the matter of faith, it must be based on the conviction that in fact God's grace in all circumstances calls for one kind of response rather than another, for example, love and openness, and that we can therefore test the authenticity of faith by its fruits.

The distinction between these subtypes of the formal view of faith may be summarized as follows. In the first type the form or defining characteristic of faith is a universal possibility of man; in the second, it is a relation to an object for which the object is responsible. In the first type the indeterminate matter is a function of the way in which some object is perceived; in the second, it is the response of the believer to the act of the object.

The second subtype sketched above offers a natural transition to what may be contrasted to the formal view as the existentialist view. If the response to the encounter with God, despite the diversity of contexts, always and necessarily involves a given element, structure, or dimension of existence, this element may be seen as that which alone is properly designated as faith. If so,

[5] Tillich defines faith as ultimate concern rather than commitment, but otherwise his position could be formulated in parallel terms. See, e.g., Paul Tillich, *Dynamics of Faith* (New York and Evanston: Harper & Row, 1958), pp. 1–12.

one cannot distinguish the defining form of faith from its matter. One can only describe the structures of faith, its origin, and its relations with other structures. Faith is either present and effective or it is not. One cannot speak of different kinds of faith.

II. The Involvement of Culture in Faith

In the formal view of faith, the form by which it is defined as faith is self-identical through all historical changes, but the matter of faith is composed of noetic and imaginative elements which are laden with cultural significance. Since form never exists apart from the matter of which it is the form, every occurrence of faith is an occurrence of the form-matter totality. Hence in every occurrence of faith cultural meaning is ingredient.

The situation is very similar when viewed from the perspective of the existentialist view of faith. Here too faith as such is self-identical in all of its occurrences. But faith never occurs except in a total situation. This total situation is laden with cultural significance. Hence in every occurrence of faith cultural meaning is ingredient.

Despite the identity of the conclusions of the two preceding paragraphs, a subtle difference exists in the systematic implications of the two views of faith for the understanding of the relation of faith and culture. The two views agree that in the total occurrence in which faith occurs culture is ingredient, but they differ in their views of the ingredience of culture in faith itself. This difference is concealed so long as we identify faith with the form of faith in the formal view. Culture is not ingredient in this form any more than it is ingredient in the structure that is faith in the existentialist view. But the relation of form to matter is different from the relation of a structure to the total existence in which it occurs. The relation of faith to culture in the two views differs accordingly.

In the formal view of faith an individual man's faith is the form-matter totality. It is his belief in, vision of, or response to (according to the particular definition of faith) this or that object. Hence cultural meaning is ingredient in his actual faith.

Only by abstracting the form of faith from the actuality of faith can a supracultural essence be designated.

In the existentialist view an individual's faith is a structure that occurs in a total situation. Its occurrence qualifies the entire situation as an occurrence of faith. Cultural meaning is ingredient in this situation. But the cultural meaning is not ingredient in the structure that constitutes the situation as an occurrence of faith.

The systematic difference may be more clearly indicated by analyzing the total situation in which faith occurs in the two views. In the formal view we have first, the total situation, second, the concrete totality of faith as an element in that situation, and third, the form of faith, its defining essence. In the existentialist view we have first, the total situation, and second, the faith that occurs in it, a faith that cannot be further analyzed into an unchanging form and a changing content. In these terms, if we compare the second factor in the two only, we can state the difference between the implications for the relation of culture to faith as follows: For the formal view of faith, culture is ingredient in faith. For the existentialist view, culture is not ingredient in faith.

The contrast may be stated more precisely in terms of the distinction between internal and external relations. Since these terms too are subject to misunderstanding, further explanation may be appropriate. The relation of one entity (A) to another (B) is internal to B if changes in the state of A affect the state of B. If the internal state of B is not affected by changes in A, then the relation is external to B. For example, at present I see before me a book. Since I see the book, the particular state of the book (e.g., its leaning against another book) affects the total state of my experience. My visual relation to the book is internal to my total experience. If the book slides, my experience will be altered. However, so far as we know, my visual relation to the book has negligible effects on the state of being of the book. Hence this relationship is external to the book.

Since every example has its limitations and disputable assumptions, and since this one may be regarded by existentialists as assuming the abhorred subject-object schema, I shall offer a second. In the present moment my experience is related to my previous experiences. What occurred in those previous experiences conditions, modifies, or affects my present experience. The relation of memory between my present experience and certain past experiences is internal to my present experience. However, those past experiences are not modified or affected by being remembered. Hence this relationship is external to them.

My thesis is that for the formal view of faith, the relation of culture to faith is internal to faith understood as the form-matter totality. For the existentialist view, the relation of culture to faith is external to faith. Both views are open to affirming that the relation is internal to culture, but this important question must be set aside here.

The two views of faith may be considered briefly in terms of their systematic relation to the problem of historical relativism. This problem briefly stated is that all noetic and imaginative elements of culture appear to be affected by the changing historic situation, whereas those who hold a particular belief or image generally view it as having a truth objective to or independent of the conditioned situation in which it arises. In view of the apparent fact that changing conditions lead to mutually incompatible beliefs and images, the acceptance of their objectivity or independence is increasingly difficult. Hence appropriateness and inappropriateness in a given historical situation or culture supersedes truth and falsity as the mode of evaluating beliefs and images. The extreme diversity of cultures suggests that no one belief or image is likely to have universal appropriateness.

If we view the situation in this way, we must ask critically how faith is related to this relativity. The existentialist view of faith affords us a powerful answer. The cultural situation is externally related to faith. Hence its changes do not change faith. The beliefs and images appropriate or inappropriate to one culture or another are not internal to faith as such. Faith expresses itself through them but without any commitment to them. The loss of power or appropriateness of certain beliefs and images requires the reformulation of faith in terms of new beliefs and images, but

[margin handwritten notes:]

Formal view of Faith: Relation of culture to faith is internal to faith

Existentialist view of Faith: Relation of culture to faith is external to faith.

The existentialist considers only that aspect of faith to be important which is culturally unaffected. He can scrap the form at will and keep the content

The formal-ist, however, considers that which is culturally conditioned to be an essential part of faith.

it is the same faith which seeks expression. Hence faith as such escapes the relativity of history even though every occurrence of faith is an occurrence in this history and every expression of faith is involved in the relativity of history.

The problem is much more difficult from the perspective of the formal view of faith. Here culture is seen as internally related to faith, and hence culturally conditioned beliefs and images are part of faith, even in its purest actuality—not only of its self-understanding, expression, and communication. What can be viewed as superior to the relativity of history is only the empty form of faith which as such seems devoid of power or value. However, several answers to the challenge of relativism are possible even from the formal view of faith, and these may be conveniently treated in terms of the two subtypes of this view outlined above.

Through the years, he is stuck with an outmoded form which tends to invalidate the content.

Those who identify faith in terms of a general human possibility may seek in the form itself a norm for determining the suitability of the contents. For example, trust is properly directed toward what is ultimately trustworthy. Hence the historically determined flux of objects of trust may always be judged by a suprahistorical norm, namely, ultimate trustworthiness. Other adherents of this view may simply acknowledge the flux of matter which is informed by faith and see the unity of Christian faith through history as a matter of continuity of influence rather than identity of object or content.

This is the great dis-advantage of the formalist position.

Adherents of the view of faith that sees the defining form in the object that meets man rather than in the mode of man's response can accept the total relativity of the response. That to which it is the response may be perceived differently in each historical situation. But it is believed that ultimately it is the same reality that is met and that this reality transcends the historical flux.

The foregoing discussion of the relation of the existentialist and formal views of faith to historical relativism shows the profound advantages of the existentialist view. Indeed, its historical origin is to be understood in part as a response to a theological crisis engendered by the inability of formal views of faith to deal with historical relativism. The response to this relativism on the part of those who hold the formal view is still chiefly a matter of unfinished business. Careful analysis would show that both responses sketched above constitute an exceedingly precarious escape from total relativization of Christian faith.

Despite the danger of total relativism, adherents of the formal view may be reluctant to accept the existentialist view. Insofar as the existentialist view systematically escapes relativism, it does so by excluding noetic elements from faith as such. The only exception to this is that faith may be allowed some knowledge of itself without introducing thoroughgoing cultural relativism into faith. This exception has been ably exploited by existentialists. But unless faith's knowledge is strictly limited to knowledge of itself, hence avoids interpreting itself in terms of something other than itself or using itself as evidence for something beyond itself, the escape from relativism is rendered questionable. This means that God, Jesus Christ, Holy Spirit, and other such key elements in the Christian scheme of things ought systematically to be treated as dimensions or structures of faith and not as transcendent of faith. The question is whether this may not prove too high a price to pay.

III. RELEVANCE OF THE TYPOLOGY

Thus far this paper has been devoted to a discussion of ideal types of theological positions. The value of such a treatment lies in its explication of the systematic interconnectedness of certain sets of ideas, doctrines, and problems. The limitation of the approach is that the positions identified as types rarely coincide with those actually adopted by men of flesh and blood. For example, although I can identify myself as an adherent of the formal view of faith, I cannot identify myself unqualifiedly with either of the two subtypes described. It would be surprising if others found their actual views readily identifiable in this typology.

Nevertheless, I do believe that the criticisms directed by Dillenberger and Wilder against Ebeling and Fuchs are illuminated by the typological analysis. Ebeling and Fuchs may deny that for them "faith, word, Jesus, God, true existential reality, are inter-

[margin note: The existentialist position, however, has a hard time escaping complete relativism.]

changeable terms,"[6] but Dillenberger is surely not wrong in sensing that the noetic element in faith tends to be limited to faith's
knowledge of itself. Likewise they may deny that they seek an
unchanging center of a changing whole[7] since they may agree that
every formulation also of the center is relative to time and place,
but Dillenberger is surely right in sensing a tendency to regard
the faith to which the changing formulations witness as self-identical through time and to regard all formulations as subject to
judgment in terms of their appropriateness to the faith and their
effectiveness in its communication.

Similarly, Ebeling and Fuchs may deny that they deal in their
theology with a skeletal man.[8] They know about man's creativity,
his beliefs, his imagination, his aspirations, his total cultural involvement. Yet Wilder is surely right in calling attention to a
tendency to relate faith most closely with those aspects of life
least affected by the vicissitudes of cultural change and to min-
imize faith's involvement with beliefs and images of one culture
or another.[9] Even if Ebeling and Fuchs agreed to devote more
attention to those sides of human experience they have tended to
neglect, the fundamental difference would be likely to remain.
They could probably discuss these matters as aspects of the context in which faith occurs or of the relation of faith to this context
but not as aspects of faith itself, whereas Wilder sees them as the
very matter or substance of faith in a given epoch.

At all these points the distinction between the formal and existentialist views of faith may be illuminating. However loosely
Dillenberger and Wilder may sit to the schematism by which the
formal view has been characterized, their criticisms do conform
to those dictated by the presupposition of this view. However
loosely Ebeling and Fuchs may sit to what has been called here
the existentialist view of faith, they are being criticized for those
aspects of their thought which appear to express it or to conform
to it. For these reasons I believe that the distinction between for-

6 See above, Dillenberger, p. 149.
7 *Ibid.*, p. 154.
8 See above, Wilder, p. 205.
9 *Ibid.*, pp. 204, 209.

mal and existentialist views of faith and the concomitant views of the relation of culture to faith as internal and external to faith do provide a clue to understanding the criticisms directed against Ebeling and Fuchs by Dillenberger and Wilder. Since these issues are not themselves directly treated but rather lie at the level of presuppositions on both sides, decisions about them can be only indirectly facilitated by the discussion. For the present we may hope that theological and exegetical work will continue to be guided by both sets of presuppositions with increasing mutual understanding and fructification.

The distinction between formal and existentialist views of faith does not seem to be helpful for understanding Funk's criticism. This criticism is a plea for greater attention to the historical situation in which theological work, specifically hermeneutic, takes place.[10] Such attention will reduce the danger that the categories employed in historical research will be themselves treated unhistorically, an error which Funk does regard as infecting some existentialist hermeneutic. This warning is compatible with either the formal or the existentialist view of faith and should be heeded by adherents of both.

Thus far in this reappraisal the word hermeneutic has hardly occurred. This tardiness in introducing explicit discussion of the theme of the volume parallels that of Fuchs who found it best to survey his general stance before taking up his distinctive views on hermeneutic. The justification in the present instance lies in the fact that the disagreements expressed in the foregoing essays do not focus on the special characteristics of the new hermeneutic but rather on the relation of faith and culture. This suggests that the new hermeneutic in its more controversial aspects is a consistent consequence of the view of faith that it presupposes.

Little attention has been paid by the critics in this volume to the interesting point that in the new hermeneutic what is interpreted is ultimately and decisively the existence of the hearer of the proclamation.[11] The text, rather than being the object of in-

10 See above, Funk, pp. 181–188.
11 See above, Fuchs, p. 141.

terpretation, as with Bultmann,[12] becomes an aid in the interpretation of present existence. In order that it may serve as such,
historical research employing all the tools of that difficult trade
must be vigorously pursued. As in Bultmann this research understands itself as subserving the final task of proclamation. Fruitful
attention is given to the interaction of the pre-understanding with
which the text is approached and the autonomy of its own intentionality and challenge to the pre-understanding. Funk's warning
against an insufficiently historical view of the pre-understanding
in question may well be accepted as an important contribution to
the internal development of the new hermeneutic, and his analysis
of 2 Corinthians as itself an example of Paul's hermeneutic will
surely stand as a model illustration of the application of the new
hermeneutic. Whether or not Dillenberger and Wilder fully adopt
the new hermeneutic as their own, they do not seem to take issue
with the principles identified in this paragraph.

Yet it is a short step from these principles to those applications
against which Dillenberger and Wilder do protest. A single example must suffice.

Wilder calls attention to Fuchs's consistent depreciation of the
apocalyptic element in the New Testament.[13] From Fuchs's point
of view this element is not a real part of the New Testament message. This rejection may be in part a matter of objective, historiographical research, but the new hermeneutic does not require
that historiographical research be decisive. Objective, historiographical research is not a completely autonomous activity on the
basis of which a set of conclusions is achieved—conclusions that
are then for the first time subject to theological appropriation.
The research is from first to last governed by a pre-understanding
and by the goal of proclamation, i.e., the interpretation of the
existence of the hearer. The exclusion of the apocalyptic element
from the New Testament message appears to be fully justified by

---

[12] Bultmann, "The Problem of Hermeneutics," *Essays Philosophical and
Theological,* translated by James C. G. Grieg (London: SCM Press, 1955),
pp. 234–261.

[13] See above, Wilder, p. 214.

these concerns—justified, that is, given the decisive pre-understanding of faith.

If the apocalyptic element is to receive the serious theological attention Wilder believes it deserves, its objective prominence in the New Testament must be established. But in addition, one must challenge either the relativization of objective historical research or the particular pre-understanding of faith. Wilder's argument hinges more on the latter point.

If faith is viewed as a structure of existence that either occurs or does not occur, then the witness appropriate to faith cannot be essentially a proclamation about a temporally future event. It must be a witness to the occurrence of just that structure of existence. If it is indeed faith to which the New Testament witnesses, the futuristic apocalyptic element cannot be essential to its intention. Hence this apocalyptic element should not be given serious theological attention.

If, on the other hand, faith is viewed formally as a total vision of reality or a total way of responding to God's gracious act in Jesus Christ, then the witness to faith may well be a description of reality as viewed through newly opened eyes. In this case visionary apocalyptic imagery and even confident belief in a chronologically imminent end of the age may be recognized as fundamental aspects of the matter of primitive Christian faith.

Thus in this instance we can see how different views of faith—the existentialist and the formal—lead to different practice of hermeneutic even when extensive agreement is possible on the principles of the new hermeneutic. This may suggest that there is a range of theological problems decisive for the actual work of hermeneutic but not soluble within the context of the hermeneutical circle.

8. *Response to the American Discussion*

ERNST FUCHS
University of Marburg

June 20, 1963

Dear Mr. Robinson,

You would like a response to our so invigorating meeting at Drew University in 1962. Only to a limited extent can I undertake this task. I choose the form of a letter so as to permit myself a certain freedom of expression, which is initially designed as an echo of the conversation that we have recently been continuing in our friendly way here in Marburg.

At Drew too the theme was the hermeneutical problem. Two essays in the series recording our meeting at Drew go into detail with regard to me: your careful, and in my opinion successful, presentation of what I have published thus far and the paper by Amos Wilder, who enters into discussion with me. I can only express to you and Amos Wilder my very sincere thanks.

Robert Funk and John Dillenberger develop the hermeneutical problem with which our conference was concerned in terms of their own areas of specialization, New Testament exegesis (Funk) and church history or the history of Christian theology (Dillenberger). Obviously both have an eye to the tensions and questions within the American discussion, a trait that is doubtless at least suggested in all the American contributions.

John Cobb summarizes the discussion. His was doubtless the most difficult task. Much like Gerhard Ebeling, he had to be fair without betraying his own opinion. The best approach for Cobb to have taken would have been to advocate a viewpoint that was not only superior but also right. To the extent that his view could help toward an American consensus of his partners, Cobb's summary does indeed give the impression that work with the "new" hermeneutic could now rest a while. For we have expressed ourselves on it. Yet the American consensus needed for such an inference does not really seem to have been achieved. Hence I should like to call attention to a few unresolved questions, in the way in which they also directly concern Ebeling and me.

Apparently in America many theologians are primarily concerned to investigate and take into consideration both historically and theoretically the "cultural" conditionedness of all our statements in the past and present, including our statements of faith. We are not to surrender "culture"! For this reason Amos Wilder distinguishes between two aspects of language, on the one hand the "language event" (as I put it; Ebeling prefers to say "word event") and on the other, "speech as meaning." His question, indeed his criticism, is that my emphasizing the language event (which he understands contrary to me as narrowed all too much to interpersonal encounter, as event which merely underlines the nature of encounter as encounter) neglects "speech as meaning," so that I would do better to speak of an "event of speaking," as Rudolf Bultmann also objects—but then I would have ruined everything! Wilder censures this supposed neglect of cultural reality as a characteristic of "existentialist" theology (and thus makes Bultmann share the blame for my mistakes).

The same criticism is taken up by John Cobb in his way. For this purpose Cobb distinguishes between faith in general, i.e., the concept of faith in the widest sense of the term, in which faith is religious but not necessarily Christian, and on the other hand faith in a special sense (faith in the word of God), which Ebeling and I have in mind and which is the only thing we are willing to call "faith" (since it is only the event of the word of God that defines faith as what it is).

John Dillenberger for his part introduces the category of analogy in view of the evident dialectic between movements and countermovements in the history of one and the same formulation (e.g., the term God). This category makes it historically possible, when we have to do with the reactions of different generations or epochs as they succeed each other, almost to identify theses and antitheses, for the same formulations often take on opposing meaning, e.g., the formula *Extra nos*. An instance is the modern (Cartesian) protest against the concept of authority in antiquity and the Middle Ages, especially as formulated by Protestant orthodoxy, and against the principle that the oldest statement has more weight than any that follows it—incidentally, a hermeneutical principle that the Apostle Paul himself also made use of on occasion, when he used an exegesis of Gen. 15:6 to oppose circumcision. One could summarize John Dillenberger's view by saying that history operates full of slyness for the sake of the truth.

Now all these considerations and observations are valid in their place, since they are evident here and there. No one of us denies the validity of historical analysis. In our intellectual situation it is without doubt a duty, a command. And I do not deny at all, as Wilder knows and acknowledges, that all human efforts at thinking are culturally conditioned, no matter how much in individual instances that may be due to direct opposition to cultural habits or conventions. And with regard to "speech as meaning," this formula does correspond to the noetic character of every expression, irrespective of how the ontic may have been grasped and formulated. Indeed the ontic itself helps decide this, since to be sure everything a person says or thinks is intentional in character. Hence the phenomenological motto "to the subject matter itself" has become common property. Historical analysis should see to it especially that the "object"—including the "intention" of the statement or of the author—may remain what it is: object. Hence Robert Funk rightly bases his presentation upon a brilliant exegesis of 2 Corinthians, which does honor to Rudolf Bultmann's work. Thus he spares us having to use examples drawn from Luther's theology, which due to special conditions is not so well loved in America. In brief, the possibility of exegetical discussion among specialists was and is given. It is not the case that we cannot reach agreement on anything because of cultural differences. In this way reflections and statements that are scientifically responsible, i.e., arrived at by scientific means, bear intercontinental fruit in theology too.

And yet our discussion, insofar as it is a real conversation, is still at its beginning. The conversation has not really gotten into motion. There are various reasons for this. As I said, one reason may reside in the situation of the inner-American discussion, where, as a historian of the modern kind, one must guard against certain naïvetés which all too easily establish themselves as a result of an undisturbed development. That is a problem within a scientific tradition. Precisely where historical research is undisturbed, there easily emerges a trait inconsistent with the openness of historical research: a result that is attractive, perhaps "culturally" pleasing, is dogmatized. That was after all the scientific fate of liberalism, which in its way became a model of scientific intolerance, all the more because it could know it was in the right over against a stupidly orthodox system.

It is at this point that John Dillenberger lays hold of the problem. Doubtless he is reticent with regard to our point, and yet he was our most important discussion partner. For this very reason we must ask Dillenberger himself whether he too is really consistent enough. Has he adequately reflected that the Cartesian shift leading to the "science" of the modern mind is indeed the legitimate outcome of the tradition preceding it (in reaction against authoritarian thinking)? Has he considered, on the other hand, that the same shift obscures not only older protests, but also profound insights of a theology not infrequently guided by the New Testament—a theology that one should not dress and undress in all too sociologically tailored robes, even if one surely also has a historical right to do so?

Has it been taken into consideration, e.g., that Luther once advocated the *externa claritas* of Scripture in a *Christological* sense? Why, in the period of the Enlightenment after Luther, did this insight into the clarity of Scripture, as the text of preaching carried out in the body of Christ, take on such a completely different character? Why did the text of Scripture witnessing to Christ become in the Enlightenment the text of research, the historical "source" for the reconstruction of period portraits of the past, in which Christology was relativized? Was this simply the fault of Christology? Or was it the fault of the reaction against

Protestant orthodoxy? From now on the "text" was no longer primarily the text of proclamation, but rather at most its vehicle, even though in the practice of the church one did not like to admit it, owing to the fact that one had previously misused the text for creating doctrines. In any case Amos Wilder and John Cobb almost deliberately overlook the fact that Ebeling's and my own effort at hermeneutical reflection, materially speaking, is concerned with how the text, seen as a merely historical source, can again become the text of preaching—without our denying that the text is also a historical source, e.g., for the question as to the historical Jesus, a question that in view of Christology is not irrelevant. Preaching is certainly not simply retelling stories, as was clear already to the evangelists. Why, I ask, has the text, as the text of preaching, been so decisively lost for the historical method that Dillenberger cannot get along without the category of analogy (in the traditional sense of this term), and is almost obliged to erase the term God in order to be able honorably to use it? Why do students so often not know how they should move from historical exegesis to proclamation (the problem worrying Barth, as you show)? How does Amos Wilder protect these students from presenting, instead of the preaching of the gospel, the perhaps constantly modified "culture" to which they happen to belong and for which they are rightly thankful? Is it true that as a Christian one must say yes to just *everything?* Do we want to mold the world like modeling clay? Or is it only poets who do that? In any case, God does not do it. This is true. One should be able to learn from historical analysis how easily men, even Christian men, can play at being God. Dillenberger emphasizes this quite rightly.

We know today that the modern man can, by a turn of his hand, reach agreement with people like himself, at least on scientific terms. And to prove that I do not want to have anything to do with abstractions let me add: In modern politics this process of reaching an understanding operates with somewhat greater difficulty. Yet it can succeed, since scientifically trained men in this field, too, are today forced to calculate more than previously. And yet, it almost seems that modern theology, for which historical analysis has all but become common knowledge, still has the greatest difficulties in reaching understanding. Why is that? Is it because theology enters in upon the most intimate sphere of human life? I do not accept such an explanation. Literature and a part of scientific writing today reach an understanding with everyone everywhere about the most intimate processes of our life, without protest being raised seriously against it. What we soak up in movies and television is still there in us and between us as we continue our living. But where in all that intimate life is the power of a gospel that has not merely become a cliché? Where is the text of a Bible that is not projected on the screen, a Bible without Hollywood? If I were to say that Rembrandt is the painter normative forever, Beethoven, the musician normative forever, or Goethe, the poet normative forever, I would be a barbarian who indeed had not grasped the essence of culture. But what is false in the field of culture must be risked in the field of theology: that there is only one gospel. Has not Robert Funk made precisely this intention of Paul evident? What would result from this for our discussion if we tried for once not to contradict each other with the naïvely used antithesis between abstract and concrete?

Now one can, like Dillenberger, ask radically what sense there is in talking about God. Bultmann has done that, and he is still doing it. Will not our efforts have to be directed toward asking why terms such as "God" or "resurrection of the dead" are still used at all? Of course historical analysis can provide a lexicon for this purpose, which of course will constantly have need of new editions. Our own insights, too, will doubtless be relativized sooner or later. But should we for that reason avoid maintaining them? For we do not need to lose sleep over the possibility that one day space travel may change considerably man's biological nature, when we are in a position to lodge men on other bodies in space. Perhaps we will get longer necks there? What is that to us now? We would do better to stick with the relevant question as to why our preaching (yes, our ecclesiastical preaching) is and can be *bound* to a text. Or to put it otherwise, we must ask whether the proclamation of the gospel today, at this pinnacle of historical analysis, still provides the center around which theological work revolves; whether theological work becomes theological work by reflecting centrally upon the proclamation of the gospel and even consciously prolongs the struggle of the confessions and denominations for the sake of this cause—which does not mean that one burns down the house of the person who holds another view.

The hermeneutical problem got its real acuteness first in this situation. We see that the historical question was always at work behind the old efforts at hermeneutical rules! One always wanted to respect fully the distance of the interpreter from the text, but for the same reason one wanted also to overcome it. This is true, e.g., for the whole Alexandrian theology, Athanasius not excluded. Precisely its conscious allegory was aware of the historical question. The fact that the historical question, rather than seventeenth-century Protestant orthodoxy, became *the* theme in the Enlightenment signifies, as far as the occasion goes, only the protest against a *one-sided* hermeneutical answer to the historical question, e.g., against the sudden reversal of allegory into the doctrine of verbal inspiration, that is to say, against procedures of a Scriptural interpretation that continued to claim *historical* truth for itself. It was necessary and desirable to move on into helping the historical question to gain a verifiable right, so that theological philology need not have any guide lines laid down for it other than those that lie in the historical question itself. In this way one restored the honor of the *universitas litterarum,* the university. That was the situation in the seventeenth and eighteenth centuries. The scientific successes of historical research in the nineteenth century attained a peak of performance that can be expanded today only by means of the discovery of new material.

But in the time of this victorious march of historical research, preaching itself—the church's preaching—failed in ever-growing dimensions—a process partly revealed, partly hidden and altered, by pietism. Pietism met modern times with Biblicism. It first called for the scientific exposition of the Bible, only to hinder it later all the more. However, the hermeneutical circle between the interpreter and his object, to which Wilhelm Dilthey again drew our attention, is also a consequence of pietism's freedom and love for the text. And yet, all that was attained on this path was that now the modern historian, too, could feel himself to be a proclaimer. Rather than returning the text to proclamation, this hermeneutical deepening had as its consequence around 1900 that one could exchange the text for a religiously conditioned, more or less secular culture, as was the case with Ernst Troeltsch.

It seems to me that the situation in the inner-American discussion today is largely an expression of this dilemma. We can call this dilemma the dilemma of positivistic analysis, which, except for artistic additions and the individual vitality of the interpreter, loses its material relation to the object. There has emerged at this point, since Troeltsch, a new element that is clearer to us today since World War I—an element coming into your field of vision in America as well? We all see that our modern culture as the culture of the world is not only built upon a higher standard of living but also endangers the continued existence of the world without anyone being able to undo this development, this trend toward the whole. One can say that since the emergence of historical analysis—this has become a test case of scientific thinking as a whole—man must take responsibility for a whole, namely, the world, by risking himself for it. As Friedrich Gogarten rightly emphasizes, this is a fact that was introduced by Christian culture and hence works back upon it and puts that culture itself in question, or at least tests it without respite. This fact demands a radical self-examination especially by theology and forces *the hermeneutical problem* upon us anew in its whole depth. Retouching will not help any more, as if it were merely a matter of modifications of historical portrayals, or of an *a priori* that included a religious *a priori* after all. Today it is no longer a matter of religions, nor is it a matter of religion, but of what everyone means when he says existence.

But why "new" hermeneutic? Answer: Precisely for the sake of the ancient hermeneutical problem as to how it is that preaching should use specifically the Bible as its text. Within dogmatics the question appears as follows: Why does Christian faith rest upon proclamation? Seen from a hermeneutical point of view dogmatics then becomes quite consciously a doctrine of the word of God. The dogmatic question now applies centrally to the relation between God's word and faith. This you all know—and our partners in debate criticize precisely at this point. But let us proceed! Now of course God, word, faith belong on the same side. But that does not mean these words or expressions should be used promiscuously. One can raise the critical query as to whether faith does not belong emphatically on the other side and word between the two sides, the side of God and that of man. But that would be a misunderstanding. God, word, and faith in this context are not at all concepts and most of all not metaphors. Rather they are the expression of an event, they are "language event" and are thought about, or at least are to be thought about, as such.

Such clarifications seem so absurd to some in Europe too that they can offer resistance by describing us with a cliché that is indeed absurd and hence to be rejected: that we carry on existentialist theology or, as they prefer to say in such a case, existentialism. They understand such a theology as a subjectivism that has given up and is basically pessimistic, and which in the long run is not only thankless but also dangerous, since it turns the fate of the world over to an individualism like that which in the Germany of 1933 turned into the terror of despair. And so one or the other critic may have the feeling that by refusing the risks of our theology he is warding off the mortal danger in which the world finds itself today. But this feeling is a sweet dream, an illusion. Of course one can reject our theology without further ado. Yet one should know before one does so that our theology has directly in view the atheism that grew up over us all with scientific thinking since Descartes. Our hermeneutic thinks with Friedrich Gogarten that it knows this whole development to be a late but nonetheless strict consequence of Christian faith. Hence, the question can be posed as follows: Is it permissible to exchange or supplement the Biblical text with other contents simply because one has noted that the radicality of the preaching of faith has at the same time bred its enemy atheism? Or—and this is the question of the "new" hermeneutic—does the necessity that faith can be the *decisive* answer only to a proclamation calling for decision rescue for preaching those texts regarded by historical analysis only as sources of a part of our tradition?

It is *this* question that we, Ebeling and I, have methodically answered. In my *Hermeneutik* of 1954 the first sentence speaks of faith's "doctrine of language."[1] This is of course not meant in the sense of linguistics. What is meant is the fact that a word can have the characteristic—which is what first makes it "word"—that, in contrast to nothing, being happens for us. When we are met with love, then love, as being, comes in the word and into language, and it remains there, too. If love goes, the word goes. And when in the language event I give priority to love—to which Amos Wilder takes exception—then I maintain that love has the widest radius that being can have and, hence, that love is at stake in all "culture." Love is not simply sex. The essence of language is its movement toward love, derived from love. Is God love, as the New Testament says (1 John 4:16)? That is decided by the word, whether at the right time and place the word of love, its Yes, is possible or is denied. All our work and indeed our whole human existence has this trait, the pull to where one does indeed have grounds and an occasion to speak again of "good" works in faith. Of course we live from a language in which we find ourselves. This language can be misused. But its trend toward love still cannot be killed off. For this reason there is a "language gain," as I say in my *Hermeneutik*.[2] And this language gain—in our view it

---

[1] [Cf. above, p. 55, n. 156, Tr.]

[2] [The 2nd ed. of the *Hermeneutik* in 1958 adds the sentence "Language *is* language gain" at the end of the following discussion: A self-understanding is possible only because there is that which is commonly understood as a matter of course. Thus self-understanding, in distinction from self-consciousness, is supplied by one's heritage. The basic function of self-understanding is to work with language, in sharing in the linguistic administration of the common understanding transmitted in the heritage. Only when the common understanding is put in question does the self-understanding become consciously a problem. This problem is a problem of language, in that one is no longer in common agreement as to the "world" in terms of which one lives. "The individual alone cannot master this situation, since he is and remains dependent on language, i.e., on others, i.e., on common understanding with others. So what results as self-understanding in this situation is never dependent on the individual alone. For this reason this self-understanding cannot be communicated directly, but can be 'understood' only belatedly, in the language produced *anew* in a *contested* or *newly occurring* common understanding. This new language will have to distinguish itself from the old, and at the same time still make clear the call involved in understanding, in which we are to respond 'with ourselves.' Then we say to each person, or, better, we give him to understand, what is to be expected of him, for him to be

flows from Jesus' preaching in spite of the other (kerygmatic) terms that emerged after Jesus—is what makes our "text" possible as the text of a proclamation. In the world one must *believe* in love. And one can do that only when the word *to* love—as proclaimed word *of* love—puts us in decision as to what we think of our present.

In my *Hermeneutik* I did not draw out the implications rigorously, whereas Gerhard Ebeling, guided by his knowledge, went to work in his characteristic way. But in the first volume of my collected essays I have nonetheless drawn attention to the fact that our existence as men is constituted more by "linguisticality" than by "questionability."[3] With this step I have moved beyond the position of Heidegger's existentialist analysis in *Being and Time*. I do not claim that my path has been made wide enough yet. But it is there.

The cliché about a theology of "existentialism" as some critics use it is not identical with what we say. But I have a further question to put to our American discussion partners. Measured by the inner-American discussion, our location of the hermeneutical problem means that you will not advance if you do not give up all dialectic artifices. I address this especially to the respectable contributions of John Dillenberger and John Cobb. They should ask what happened when the New Testament arose, i.e., what makes the New Testament the New Testament. And the fact that this question can be posed to you is in my opinion proven by Robert Funk's interpretation of Paul. For this does not fall outside the historically comprehensible discussion with the past, but on the contrary shows that historical analysis can find precisely the language intent of its text, if it only proceeds in a sufficiently reliable way. Does not historical analysis come into its own precisely when it does *not* permit itself to exchange its concrete object, the text, for its metaphysical premise? It is a difference

---

able to live in common agreement with us—in case we do not withdraw ourselves from him completely." It is this role of language in stating and sharing a new self-understanding that the 2nd ed. regards as the basic characteristic of language as "language gain." Tr.]

[3] *Zum Hermeneutischen Problem in der Theologie, Gesammelte Aufsätze I* (Tübingen: J. C. B. Mohr), p. 115. [Cf. above, p. 55, Tr.]

residing in the *subject matter,* whether the object of analysis brings one into dealings with the language event or not. This is decided by the text. It is precisely the metaphysical premise of historical analysis, namely, the category "object," that drives us positively even to the discovery of the full function of the word as a language event in the texts, and can and should serve to win from our tradition exactly that which can—and is intended to— unite us with people of long ago, overcoming the distance of time. And it becomes apparent—and this should be said to those inquiring about "culture"—that our distance to the "neighbor" can be greater than to the Apostle Paul, although not a few come to help the neighbor as soon as he needs us in body or soul.

But I do not hesitate to add that the American culture perhaps senses the language event less as a problem than do we because your culture stands nearer to love, as was shown when America helped the Germans to an existence shared with America and saved us out of destruction (although not all our brothers could take part directly in this help). I ask you to regard the fact that we stand by these experiences even over against the inner-American theological discussion as an expression of our thanks to you all.

Your

(signed)
ERNST FUCHS